# DEVELOPMENT ECONOMICS: A POLICY ANALYSIS APPROACH

# Innovative Economics Textbooks

The purpose of this series is to provide economics textbooks for specialist, optional or advanced courses. Published in hardback at paperback prices and written by acknowledged experts, *Innovative Economics Textbooks* are comprehensive and reliable. Each includes a range of learning aids to assist both lecturer and student.

# Development Economics:
# A Policy Analysis Approach

ECKHARD SIGGEL
*Concordia University, Canada*

ASHGATE

Published by
Ashgate Publishing Limited
Gower House
Croft Road
Aldershot
Hants GU11 3HR
England

Ashgate Publishing Company
Suite 420
101 Cherry Street
Burlington, VT 05401-4405
USA

Ashgate website: http://www.ashgate.com

**British Library Cataloguing in Publication Data**
Siggel, Eckhard, 1938-
    Development economics : a policy analysis approach. -
    (Innovative economics testbooks)
    1.Economic policy - Evaluation 2.Developing countries -
    Economic policy 3.Developing countries - Economic
    conditions
    I.Title
    338.9'0091724

**Library of Congress Cataloging-in-Publication Data**
Siggel, Eckhard, 1938-
    Development economics : a policy analysis approach / by Eckhard Siggel.
        p.   cm. -- (Innovative economics textbooks)
    Includes index.
    ISBN 0-7546-4293-3
    1. Economic development. 2. Economic development--Case studies. 3. Developing
countries--Economic policy. 4. Developing countries--Economic policy--Case studies.
5. Development economics. I. Title. II. Series.

    HD82S54 2005
    338.9--dc22

                                                                    2004028574

ISBN 0 7546 4293 3

Printed and Bound in Great Britain by TJ International Ltd, Padstow, Cornwall

# Contents

# List of Figures

# List of Tables

# Preface

This book has grown out of my experience of teaching economics courses for over 25 years. During these years it became obvious to me that in economics we tend to teach students a lot of theory, but we do not show them sufficiently how to use the theory for economic analysis of real-world problems. It is true that students taking econometrics courses usually get to work with such data, mainly for testing hypotheses. But economic analysis does not begin with the econometric estimation of parameters and the test of hypotheses. It also includes non-quantitative methods of analysis, inferences based on non-stochastic methods, simple manipulation of data and the computation of indicators.

The objective of this textbook is to introduce students to the practice of economic policy analysis in the context of developing countries. Policy analysis differs from the general economic analysis in that it requires an examination of economic states over time. First, it must be established what are the theoretical consequences of a policy or policy change. This leads to a prediction of the expected outcome of a policy. Second, the economy subjected to the new policy must be analyzed before and after the policy change. In other words, the time dimension is a crucial factor in this approach. Most of traditional economic theory is of static nature, but it is used in the analysis of change by comparing the conditions before and after the policy changes.

A further question arising from the title is: What makes the analysis of policies for economic development different from the analysis that applies to high-income countries. In principle, I believe that economic analysis does not differ, whether it is applied in rich or in poor countries; but there is a difference in emphasis and the nature of the problems to be analyzed. The present text concentrates on problems that are typical for the poor countries, for instance how to accelerate economic growth and development, how to diminish income disparities and poverty within countries, how domestic saving and investment can be increased, how foreign savings can be used to accelerate the pace of development, how foreign trade can contribute to faster growth, and how economic policies can be applied successfully to stabilize inflationary and debt-ridden economies.

The specific contribution of this textbook is to combine the presentation of theory and institutional facts with real-world case studies. In the case studies, students are briefly introduced to the geographic and historic context of the policy situation, and provided with data to be used in the analysis. In order to answer the assigned questions of the case studies, students will use the data for computations and/or statistical analysis, interpret the results, consult the assigned readings and compare the findings with those of other studies. The case studies permit students to apply the analysis in a hands-on fashion.

The country case study, I believe, is the best framework for policy analysis. Case studies are increasingly found in textbooks, but rarely in the form of assigned problems. In that sense the book combines the lectures and a workbook of case studies into one. In nine out of 17 case studies the solutions are provided, following the assigned questions. They are the odd-numbered ones, with two exceptions: Case Study 12 is also solved, due to its central importance, and Case Study 15 is not solved because it involves only reading of two recommended articles and no computational analysis. The even-numbered case studies from 2 to 10, 14, 15 and 16 are not solved in this volume, but their solutions are available to instructors, who may adopt the text for their classes by contacting me by email.[1]

In some of the case studies, the data used are not the most recent ones. I have decided to keep the case studies concerned, nevertheless, in this volume for two reasons. Either the data are unique and not available for more recent time periods, or the data relate to specific policy changes that are of particular interest.

The audience addressed by this textbook consists mainly of advanced undergraduate students, but graduate students at the beginning of master's level may also find it useful. Its prerequisites are intermediate micro and macroeconomic theory, as well as a complete statistics course including the basic regression model. Prior knowledge of development economics is an asset, but is not required, since the basic concepts of development economics are explained in the volume. The text lends itself for a single-term course of development economics in the last year of undergraduate economics programs. It can also be used in programs of political science, provided that the participating students have taken a sufficient amount of economics courses.

---

[1] Eckhard Siggel (siggel@vax2.concordia.ca)

The main areas covered by the present edition are as follows. First, the concept of economic development is defined and its measurement is discussed. This chapter features a case study of the Human Development Index, a case study of international income comparisons, as well as a study of problems arising in the deflation of the national accounts. Second, theories of economic growth are discussed focusing on the best known growth models (Harrod-Domar, the neoclassical growth model), and a short introduction to endogenous growth theory is presented. The case studies in this area cover growth accounting applied to Kenyan data, as well as an analysis of international income convergence. The third chapter deals with the financing of economic growth from domestic sources. It examines how savings, investments and national income can be increased through fiscal, financial and monetary policies. The related case studies cover the Indonesian tax reform, as well as the financial reforms in Chile of the 1980s. Chapter 4 examines how foreign savings can contribute to economic growth and development. Gap models are discussed, together with empirical facts about foreign aid, foreign investment, foreign borrowing and debt. The case studies of this chapter apply the two-gap model to Kenyan data and examine the Brazilian debt problem of the 1980s. The fifth chapter discusses the role of international trade in growth and development, as well as policies and policy reforms toward liberalized trade. Data from Senegal and Mexico are used in the case studies of trade and industrial policy reform in these two countries.

Chapter 6 takes a closer look at the problem of external balance, the exchange rate, its misalignment and devaluation. The related case study deals with devaluation and trade policy reform in Mexico. Regional economic integration and monetary union are discussed in Chapter 7, which also includes case studies of Uganda's benefits from regional trade liberalization, and of the African monetary union of the CFA franc zone. In Chapter 8 the previously discussed policies are reviewed in the context of stabilization and structural adjustment programs, and the role of the IMF is discussed. Ghana's reforms of the 1980s serve as a case study. In Chapter 9, social cost-benefit analysis is introduced, and a particular method of measuring competitiveness and comparative advantage is proposed. This method is then applied in a case study of Indian manufacturing competitiveness in the 1980s. The final chapter deals with privatization and public sector reform, which is applied in a case study of privatization of a Mexican airline.

# Acknowledgements

This volume has benefited from the research assistance of several former students at Concordia University, in particular Lieven Hermans, François Pichette, Mindy Sichel, Miroslav Kucera, Aleksandra Novak and David Zerkler. I also owe gratitude to my own former teachers, the late Professor Benjamin Higgins, who introduced me to the discipline of development economics, and Prof. Gerry Helleiner, who guided me through the Ph.D. programme at the University of Toronto. My colleagues, Professors Bernard Décaluwe at Laval University, André Martens at the University of Montreal, Dirck Stryker at Tufts University and John Cockburn at Laval University encouraged and inspired me in various research and assistance projects in Africa. Finally, my family, to whom I wish to dedicate this book, contributed by bearing with my frequent absences from our family home.

*For Nicolai, Catherine and the memory of Marie-Josée*

# Chapter 1

# Economic Development:
# Concept and Measurement

Many economic concepts are widely used but rarely defined with some degree of precision. Economic development is one of these concepts. Its meaning is best apprehended by comparison with economic growth and by thinking about its measurement. The present chapter is devoted to defining these concepts and to discussing their measurement. The attempt to define development and growth in sections 1.1 and 1.2 is followed by a discussion of the income distribution and poverty in section 1.3, and an examination of the problems arising in international comparisons of income levels in 1.4. The chapter concludes with a short discussion of composite development indicators, notably the Human Development Index, which is examined in more detail in the first of our case studies. The other two case studies of this chapter deal with the purchasing power parity (PPP) approach to international income comparisons, as well as with an approach to overcome certain problems in deflating the national accounts.

## 1.1    The Concept of Economic Development

Economic development is understood to be a process, which leads a country from a state of underdevelopment, characterized by low income and a poor quality of life, to one of higher living standards for a large majority of its people. This rather general definition has a normative connotation, since it describes development as a desirable process, the outcome of which is an increased level of welfare. Its disadvantage lies in its generality, leaving open the question of how exactly the level of development is to be measured. More specific indicators exist, but they tend to narrow down the concept of development. It is therefore necessary to apply several, rather than only one measure.

If the average level of income of a country is taken as an indicator of its standard of living, the question remains whether an increase of the level of income is shared by a large proportion of the population or by only a minority. In other words, it is important to know whether the distribution of income has changed over time and in what direction. Since the average income level hides information about the distribution of income among a country's citizens, a second indicator is needed to describe the distribution of income. In section 1.3 we introduce the most frequently used method of measuring the income distribution, as well as a method of integrating growth and distributional objectives.

Another characteristic of economic development is that improvements of the living standard are normally accompanied by changes in the structure of the economy. Structural changes have become known as development criteria in their own right, for instance the increasing importance of the industrial and service sectors relative that of the primary sector. Economic development can therefore also be described as a process of growth and structural change, where the latter may refer to changes in the sector composition or to other structural effects.

High average income, even if distributed in a socially acceptable way, is not a guarantee for the fulfilment of human needs in areas such as education, health care, longevity, or personal freedom. It has therefore become standard practice to define economic development by reference to sets of indicators measuring these aspects. The Human Development Index, computed and published annually since 1990 by the UNDP, is a composite indicator of several welfare aspects including education, health, and per person income. It is the subject of the first case study, where it is explained in some detail.

The concept of national income as measured in the national accounts is not a perfect measure of material well-being, nor of the level of production, because it fails to include various forms of income that are either not marketed or unrecorded, such as the value of housework, child raising and various activities associated with subsistence agriculture and the informal sector. The level of subsistence and informal sector activities is usually estimated by national statistics bureaus and added on to the national accounts, but many other activities, in particular female work in the household, are not included in the concepts of domestic production and income. This is a shortcoming from the point of view of trying to measure all economic activity, but it is widely accepted because of the difficulty of measuring other activities.

In spite of these limitations, the average or per capita level of income is often used as a broad indicator of the level of development. The reason for this usage is threefold: data availability, relative comparability of this measure across countries, and a strong correlation with other indicators of well-being. Indicators of education and health, for instance, tend to be positively related to the level of per capita income. However, it is always possible to find a group of countries in particular time periods, for which such a correlation is either insignificant or even negative. This point was made by Amartya Sen, who showed that for a group of countries like China, Sri Lanka, Brazil, Mexico and South Africa, the correlation between GNP per head and the life expectancy at birth seemed to be negative (Sen, 1989). For a very large number of countries, however, the correlation between these indicators can be shown to be positive and significant.

Accepting the average level of income as (however imperfect) a measure of the level of development of a country amounts to equating the process of development with that of economic growth. It follows from the earlier discussion that the concept of economic development is a wider and more complex one than that of economic growth. However, economic development rarely occurs without growth. When production and income are stationary, any improvement of the living standard of the poor comes at the expense of others. A simple redistribution of income from the rich to the poor rarely makes a society better off in the longer run.

Finally, a further and very important difference between economic development and growth is the consideration of institutions. The formation of institutions, both private and public, and their governance is a distinguishing feature of economic development. While most traditional approaches in economics are limited to analysing non-institutional factors, attention has recently shifted towards analyzes of institutional growth covering private firms, government, as well as norms and networks of the civil society. This new emphasis in development economics is clearly visible in the fact that two recent World Development Reports of the World Bank (2002 and 2003) are dedicated to building and transforming institutions. The latter Report also contributes to a widening of the concept of economic development by adding the dimension of sustainability.

## 1.2    Measurement of Economic Growth

Economic growth is an increase in real income or production (GDP or GNP) of an economy. In order to result in an increase in living standards, economic growth has to occur in terms of per capita income. In other words, income has to grow faster than the population. When measuring per capita income and its growth, we must first remember the differences between national income, gross national product (GNP), and gross domestic product (GDP), although they do not matter for the present purpose. While GDP is the total value of all economic activities that take place within the geographical frontiers of a country, GNP is the value of production of all factors that are owned by the Nation's citizens. Taking the letter Y for either of these income concepts, N for the size of population, and y = Y/N for per capita income, $g_y = \Delta(Y/N)/(Y/N)$ is the proportional growth rate of per capita income.

Whenever we observe growth over a period of several years, we can express the average annual growth rate in two different ways, the continuous and the discrete growth rate. The continuous growth rate describes a process in which the increment is added continuously to the base value, so that a constant growth rate results in a continuously growing increment. This type of growth is known as continuous exponential growth and is described by the function:

$$(1.1) \quad Y_t = Y_0\, e^{gt}$$

where $Y_0$ and $Y_t$ are income levels in the base year and in year t respectively, and g is the continuous annual growth rate. Its geometric representation is a continuously and exponentially rising curve. Alternatively, we can view growth as a process in which the yearly increment is added to the previous-year value only once a year, so that we obtain a growth function that rises linearly during the year, but the yearly increment becomes larger every year. It obeys the function:

$$(1.2) \quad Y_t = Y_0\,(1 + g)^t$$

where g is the discrete annual growth rate. This process is described by a sequence of straight-line segments with an increasing slope.

In practical growth analysis the analyst faces a series of observations on Y or any other aggregate over a period of time. The first objective is then to express the growth process by a single number, such as the annual average growth rate over the whole period. It is computed by solving either of the expressions 1.1 or 1.2 for g, obtaining the continuous ($g_c$) or the discrete annual growth rate ($g_d$). This procedure amounts to connecting the first-year point with the end-year point by lines that behave differently in the continuous and discrete cases, as described above. In either case, however, one ignores the fluctuations between the two points that are typical for real-world observations. Computing an average of the year-to-year growth rates would lead to a rate that is different, but close to the discrete growth rate obtained from the expression (1.2). One method that one should not use is to divide the total percentage increase of the whole period by the number of years. As the reader can easily observe, this method results in a growth rate that is too high, because it relates to the period base year instead of a constantly growing base. Another problem, which the earlier correct procedures entail, is that the choice of the base and end years obviously has an influence on the average growth rate. If either of them is a true 'outlier', the computed rate does not correspond to the longer-run trend. To overcome this danger, one may choose as beginning and end points three-year averages.

In order to see the difference between the continuous and the discrete growth rates let us assume that national income has grown from 100 to 500 in 20 years, the average annual growth rate is then computed as follows:

$$\text{continuous growth rate: } g_c = 1/t \ln (Y_t/Y_o) = (1/20) \ln 5 = 0.080$$

$$\text{discrete growth rate: } \quad g_d = (Y_t/Y_o)^{1/t} - 1 = 5^{0.05} - 1 = 0.084.$$

The continuous growth rate, which in finance is also referred to as the compound interest rate, is then 8 percent, and the discrete growth rate is 8.4 percent (both rounded).

Now suppose that the population grows at a rate of $g_N = 3$ percent annually while income grows at the rate of $g_Y = 8$ percent. How can we find the annual growth rate of per capita income? The simple but not perfectly correct answer is to simply deduct the population growth rate from the income growth rate: $g_y = g_Y - g_N = 8$ percent - 3 percent = 5 percent. This answer is usually sufficiently accurate as long as the numbers involved are small. For large numbers, that is, larger than approximately 5 percent, however, the accurate growth rate is derived as follows:

$$
\begin{aligned}
(1.3) \quad g_y &= \Delta y/y = (y_t - y_o)/y_o \\
&= (Y_t/N_t - Y_o/N_o)/Y_o/N_o \\
&= (Y_t N_o)/(Y_o N_t) - 1 \\
&= [Y_o(1 + g_Y) N_o]/[Y_o N_o(1 + g_N)] - 1 \\
&= (g_Y - g_N)/(1 + g_N).
\end{aligned}
$$

We see that this result is approximately equal to the simple difference between $g_Y$ and $g_N$ whenever $g_N$ is very small. The reader may also verify that the simplified method is significantly off track whenever $g_N$ is large.

The use of the precise relationship (1.3) is particularly important when we calculate the growth rate of real income in inflationary circumstances. Let us define real income as $Yr = Y/P$, where $P$ is the national price level, for instance measured as the consumer price index or

**Table 1.1    Growth rates of gross national income (GNI), population, price level, and per capita real income in a sample of developing and industrialized countries, 1989-1999 (in percent)**

|  | $g_Y$ | $g_N$ | $g_P$ | $g_{Yr}$ |
|---|---|---|---|---|
| **Africa** | | | | |
| Kenya | 16.0 | 1.7 | 16.2 | -1.9 |
| Ghana | 26.9 | 3.0 | 26.8 | -2.8 |
| Senegal | 7.0 | 2.7 | 4.1 | 0.1 |
| **Latin America** | | | | |
| Mexico | 23.7 | 1.8 | 20.1 | 1.3 |
| **Asia** | | | | |
| India | 16.3 | 1.9 | 9.5 | 4.2 |
| Indonesia | 19.3 | 1.6 | 13.7 | 3.3 |
| **Industrialized** | | | | |
| Canada | 4.0 | 1.1 | 2.2 | 0.6 |
| United States | 5.3 | 1.0 | 3.0 | 1.2 |
| United Kingdom | 5.7 | 0.2 | 3.7 | 1.7 |

*Notes*:    Numbers may not add up due to rounding
Col.1: $g_Y$ = annual growth rate of nominal GNI
Col.2: $g_N$ = annual population growth rate
Col.3: $g_P$ = annual rate of inflation
Col.4: $g_{Yr}$ = annual growth rate of real per capita GNI

*Source*: International Financial Statistics, Yearbook, 2000.

as the GDP deflator. If the growth rate of Y and the annual rate of inflation are given as $g_Y$ and $g_P$, the real income growth rate is then computed as:

$$(1.4) \quad g_{Yr} = (g_Y - g_P)/(1 + g_P).$$

For instance, when $g_Y = 100$ percent and $g_P$ (rate of inflation) = 80 percent, real income growth is only 11 percent rather than 20 percent.

When the growth rates of nominal income ($g_Y$), population ($g_N$), and the price level ($g_P$) are known, the growth rate of real per capita income ($g_{yr}$) is then:

$$(1.5) \quad g_{yr} = (g_Y - g_N - g_P - g_N g_P)/[(1 + g_N)(1 + g_P)],$$

which the reader may derive in the same fashion as (1.3).

Table 1.1 shows the growth rates of nominal, real and real per capita GNI for a sample of developing and industrialized countries. As the reader may verify, the numbers satisfy the relationship of expression (1.5). The large (inflationary) growth rates of nominal income in Kenya, Ghana and Mexico can be taken to demonstrate the importance of using the correct relationship (1.5) instead of the simple approximation.

## 1.3    The Distribution of Income and Poverty

From a development perspective, no rate of economic growth can be deemed satisfactory without consideration of the income distribution and its change over time. We distinguish the functional from the size distribution, where the former relates to the income shares earned by different factors of production, and the latter describes the distribution according to the level of income. The following discussion focuses entirely on the size distribution. In order to describe the size distribution, we need to know what proportion of total national income is earned by various sections of the population, where these sections (for instance quintiles) are ranked according to their average income level. In countries, in which the distribution of income is very unequal, the poorest quintile (20 percent) of the population typically earn only about 5 percent of total income or less, the next 20 percent about 10 percent, and the top 20 percent typically earn about 50 percent of the total or more. When these proportions are shown cumulatively on the vertical axis, and the ordered population proportions on the horizontal axis, we obtain a set of four points which form, when extended from the origin to the north-east corner, the so-called Lorenz curve of income distribution. With more information on even smaller sections of the population, the Lorenz curve becomes increasingly a smooth curve. The more this curve bulges out toward the bottom the more unequal is the income distribution.

The information contained in the Lorenz curve can be translated into a single number, the so-called Gini coefficient, or Gini concentration ratio, by measuring the area between the Lorenz curve and the upward-sloping diagonal, and by dividing this surface (area A in Figure 1.1) by the total surface under the diagonal (area A + B in Figure 1.1):

(1.6)    Gini coefficient = $A/(A + B)$          with $0 \leq G \leq 1$

Information on the income distribution in several developing and high-income countries, including the Gini coefficient and average income levels,

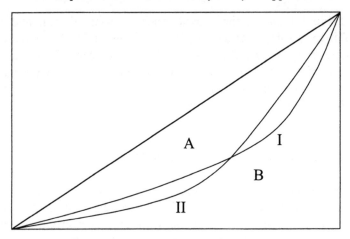

**Figure 1.1    Lorenz curves of two countries with different income distributions**

is shown in Table 1.2. Casual inspection of the data suggests that across countries with different income levels, the Gini coefficient tends to rise with the income level. It is low in the poorest countries, reaches a maximum at the lower middle-income range, and declines with rising incomes in the richer countries. This observation was first postulated by Kuznets (1955) and is known as the inverted U-shape hypothesis of income inequality in the process of development. Although recent studies have thrown some doubt on the empirical support of this hypothesis, there are substantial theoretical arguments, which suggest that the distribution of income tends to become more even at higher income levels. Widespread free education and social programmes, such as unemployment insurance and old age security, as well as progressive income taxation, are major factors that tend to reduce income disparities at a high level of per capita income.

Using the Gini coefficient, or any other similar measure of income inequality, permits us to observe the income distribution of developing countries over longer periods of time. When the Gini coefficient rises we call this a deterioration of the distribution, and an improvement when it declines. This qualification assumes that increased inequality is bad for society per se because it contributes to social conflict. On the other hand, if governments try to achieve greater equality, this policy may lead to the elimination of incentives to work and to raise productivity. Therefore, there may be an optimal level of equality or inequality, which depends on various factors and is not easily determined, not even for any specific society.

**Table 1.2     Income inequality in selected developing and high income countries, 1998**

| | GNP p.c. (U.S. $) | PPP GNP p.c. | 1st quintile | 2nd quintile | 3rd quintile | 4th quintile | 5th quintile | Gini coefficient |
|---|---|---|---|---|---|---|---|---|
| **Low income** | | | | | | | | |
| Burundi | 140 | 561 | 5.1 | 10.3 | 15.1 | 21.5 | 48.0 | 0.43 |
| Burkina Faso | 240 | 866 | 4.6 | 7.2 | 10.8 | 17.1 | 60.4 | 0.55 |
| Vietnam | 350 | 1689 | 8.0 | 11.4 | 15.2 | 20.9 | 44.5 | 0.36 |
| India | 440 | 2060 | 8.1 | 11.6 | 15.0 | 19.3 | 46.1 | 0.38 |
| Honduras | 740 | 2338 | 2.2 | 6.4 | 11.8 | 20.3 | 59.4 | 0.56 |
| **Middle income** | | | | | | | | |
| China | 750 | 3051 | 5.9 | 10.2 | 15.1 | 22.2 | 46.6 | 0.40 |
| Morocco | 1240 | 3188 | 6.5 | 10.6 | 14.8 | 21.3 | 46.6 | 0.39 |
| Thailand | 2160 | 5524 | 6.4 | 9.8 | 14.2 | 21.2 | 48.4 | 0.41 |
| Russian Federation | 2260 | 6180 | 4.4 | 8.6 | 13.3 | 20.1 | 53.7 | 0.49 |
| Mexico | 3840 | 7450 | 3.5 | 7.3 | 12.1 | 19.7 | 57.4 | 0.53 |
| Brazil | 4630 | 6460 | 2.2 | 5.4 | 10.1 | 18.3 | 64.1 | 0.61 |
| **High income** | | | | | | | | |
| United Kingdom | 21410 | 20314 | 6.1 | 11.6 | 16.4 | 22.7 | 43.2 | 0.37 |
| France | 24210 | 21214 | 7.2 | 12.6 | 17.2 | 22.8 | 40.2 | 0.33 |
| Austria | 26830 | 23145 | 6.9 | 13.2 | 18.1 | 23.9 | 38.0 | 0.31 |
| United States | 29240 | 29240 | 5.2 | 10.5 | 15.6 | 22.4 | 46.4 | 0.41 |
| Norway | 34310 | 26196 | 9.7 | 14.3 | 17.9 | 22.2 | 35.8 | 0.26 |

*Source:* World Bank, World Development Indicators 2002.

More relevant than defining an optimal distribution of income is the goal of avoiding extreme or widespread poverty. In this respect, we can see from Figure 1.1 that the Gini coefficient is not an ideal description of the income distribution because it hides the extent of poverty. In Figure 1.1, where two Lorenz curves are shown, clearly the curve of country I reflects a distribution with less poverty than the curve of country II. In country II the poorest 20 and 40 percent of the population are poorer than in country I, whereas its middle-income class is better off than in country I. Nevertheless, the two countries may have the same Gini coefficient, as the size of their areas A is similar.

Governments and other agencies measure the extent of poverty by defining poverty lines, defined as income levels, below which individuals are considered to be poor. Based on such poverty lines, the proportion of the population that lives in poverty can be determined. This method is often referred to as the head count method. The World Bank calculated in 1990 that out of the total population of developing countries, more than one billion, or one third, live in poverty and nearly 20 percent in extreme poverty (World Bank, 1990).

Monitoring the income distribution and poverty is therefore an important task for analysts advising policy makers. It is equally important to define quantitative objectives of economic growth, equity and poverty reduction, to understand the trade-offs between them and to identify the appropriate policy measures. One way of doing this is to monitor each objective separately and to adjust the policies accordingly.

Another and quite interesting way is to integrate growth and distributional objectives into a single target. This method, proposed in a World Bank study, consists of constructing a growth rate target that is based on distributional weights (Ahluwalia and Chenery, 1974).

A growth rate of national income ($g_Y$) can always be interpreted as the weighted average of the growth rates of the incomes earned by different groups of the population. For instance, if we divide the population into five quintiles where income is lowest in the first, and highest in the fifth quintile, then the growth rate of total income ($g_Y$) equals:

$$(1.7) \quad g_Y = g_1 \, w_1 + g_2 \, w_2 + \ldots + g_5 \, w_5$$

where $g_1$ to $g_5$ are the average growth rates of incomes earned in the five population quintiles, and $w_1$ to $w_5$ are the natural weights, that is, the shares in total income of the five groups. If we replace the natural weights by either population weights, that is, $w_1 = w_2 = \ldots = w_5 = 0.2$, or by poverty weights, we obtain different total growth rates which can be used as indicators combining growth and distributional aspects. Poverty weights put strong emphasis on the lowest income groups, for instance $w_1=0.4$, $w_2=0.3$, $w_3=0.2$, $w_4=0.1$ and $w_5=0$. In light of this method it is also evident that the simple GDP growth rate is a target that is biased in favour of the rich, since by definition, the natural weight of the incomes of the rich is a multiple of that of the poor. A government that simply maximises the GDP growth rate may reach this goal most easily by favouring the income growth of the highest income earners. Population or poverty-weighted growth rates permit governments to monitor growth performance in conjunction with performance in terms of distributional objectives.

## 1.4    International Income Comparisons

A country's average income level becomes meaningful for international comparison once converted into an international currency. It is common in international publications to express all incomes in terms of U.S. dollars. The transformation of national currency data into U.S. dollars may be and has traditionally been undertaken using the official exchange rate (E). For the purpose of comparison of living standards, however, this is not satisfactory, since the official exchange rate may either over or understate the real value of a currency in terms of purchasing power. Even if a currency is well-aligned in terms of external balance, the official exchange rate is likely to understate the value of non-tradables, mainly services, because they tend to be relatively cheap in less developed countries, due to their high labour content. Therefore, in order to assign similar values to similar services, one needs to compute a non-observable exchange rate that assigns higher values to non-traded goods and services. The extensive studies of Kravis and associates (1978) have led to the construction of such a method, which is deemed to express the real purchasing power of currencies. For international income comparisons it is now standard practice to use such purchasing power-adjusted exchange rates. They are constructed in the following way.

Suppose we wish to convert the Mexican income level from pesos into U.S. dollars. If we compare the peso and dollar prices of a well-defined, homogeneous and tradable commodity, we obtain an exchange rate that may not differ much from the official rate. If, however, we compare the peso and dollar prices of non-tradable services, such as haircuts and corner store services, we come to a very different rate. The implicit exchange rate, which equals the relative (Mexican to U.S.) price of a well-defined non-traded service, attributes a much higher value to the peso. The purchasing power parity exchange rate is a weighted average of the two implicit rates, those based on tradables and non-tradables. The weights are the quantities of goods and services consumed, which form a basket that is representative of the consumption patterns of the country. Since the two countries involved in the comparison, however, will have different representative consumption baskets, it is necessary to use average quantities of the two baskets for the exchange rate. This is done in the following way. Two exchange rates are computed, one using Mexican quantities and one using U.S. quantities. Using first Mexican quantities we receive:

$$(1.8) \quad E_M = (\Sigma_i\, P_{iM}\, Q_{iM})/(\Sigma_i\, P_{iU}\, Q_{iM})$$

where $P_{iM}$ and $Q_{iM}$ are the prices and quantities of i goods and services of the representative Mexican consumption basket. Using a representative U.S. goods basket we obtain:

$$(1.9) \quad E_U = (\Sigma_i\, P_{iM}\, Q_{iU})/(\Sigma_i\, P_{iU}\, Q_{iU}).$$

In order to accommodate both bundles in the valuation, instead of biasing it versus one or the other, we then take the geometric average of the two exchange rates and call it $E_P$, where the index P refers to the adjustment for purchasing power:

$$(1.10) \quad E_P = \sqrt{(E_M\, E_U)}.$$

The rates $E_M$ and $E_U$ correspond to the Paasche and Laspeyres price indices, respectively, and $E_P$ corresponds to the so-called Fisher index.

The method described was developed by Kravis, Heston and Summers (1978) and is based on an extensive research effort by this group of economists over several years. The above description is a much simplified version of the Kravis method, which reflects the essential ideas, however.

## 1.5    The Income Gap and Convergence

The concept of a gap in terms of per capita income between two countries is useful to answer the question whether income levels have converged or will converge in how much time. The numerical difference in per capita income between two countries is the absolute gap, and the proportion of that difference in terms of one country's income is the relative gap. The arithmetic of growth discussed earlier permits us to answer this and similar questions.

The necessary condition for the reduction of an income gap is of course that the lagging country's growth rate of per capita income must exceed that of the leading country. Assume, for instance, that a less developed country (LDC) with present per capita income of $1,000 achieves seven percent per capita income growth, while a developed country (DC) with per capita income of $20,000 advances at the lower rate of three percent. How many years would it take for the LDC to catch up with the DC?

Equating the per capita income levels in t years and expressing them as functions of present income ($Y_o$) and per capita income growth rates (g) we receive:

$$(1.11) \quad Y_{oL} (1 + g_L)^t = Y_{oD} (1 + g_D)^t$$
$$\text{and } t = \log(Y_{oD}/Y_{oL})/\log[(1+g_L)/(1+g_D)]$$
$$= \log20/\log(1.07/1.03) = 79 \text{ years.}$$

Since three percent per capita income growth in the high-income countries is not unusual (given their low population growth), it is evident that low-income countries will need very high GDP growth, in the order of ten percent, if their population growth continues to be high, that is, in the order of two to three percent, in order to close the income gap in a lifetime. Fortunately, population growth tends to slow down with higher income levels, so that the goal is not totally unrealistic, as the experience of some countries in East Asia shows.

The most interesting question in this respect, however, is whether there is some likelihood for most less developed countries to catch up with the high-income countries. Such a process is known as convergence of international income levels. The empirical evidence of such a process for many countries is not convincing, as we shall see in the next chapter. For a better understanding of the mechanism involved it is useful to analyze first some simple models of economic growth in Chapter 2.

## 1.6     Composite Development Indicators

As we have seen, some aspects of economic development are neither guaranteed by the level of income, and nor are they closely correlated with income. Recognition of this fact has led economists to replace the simple income target with more complex indicators or objective functions of economic development. One of these, the distribution-weighted growth target, was discussed in section 1.3. Another approach advocated by various institutions, including the International Labour Office (ILO), is to focus on the fulfilment of basic human needs. The basic needs approach defines minimum standards in the consumption of basic goods and services, such as staple foods, water, health care, education and housing. Policies are chosen with the goal of achieving these targets, but no single composite indicator exists to quantify whether or not the basic needs targets have been met. Two approaches that integrate several aspects of development into a single indicator are the Physical Quality of Life Index (PQLI) proposed by the Overseas Development Council (Morris, 1979), and the Human Development Index (HDI) computed and published since 1990 by the United Nations Development Programme (UNDP, 1990 and later editions).

In the PQLI, three aspects relevant to the standard of living are considered: life expectancy, infant mortality and literacy. The respective rates are normalized and the indicator is computed as a simple average of these three rates. One may argue that the exclusive focus on health and education captures most of what is important for the standard of living; but, in our view, the physical quality of life includes aspects other than simply health and education, and these should be added to the index, either by including additional measures or by including income.

The Human Development Index (HDI) remedies this problem by considering three aspects of human development: health, education and income. Health is measured by the life expectancy at birth, education through the literacy rate and the rate of school enrollment, and income by a measure of utility of income, thereby capturing the declining marginal utility of income. Certainly, the HDI can be criticized for omitting some aspects and over-emphasizing or double-counting others, but it is a relatively complete measure that makes good use of widely available data. The indicator is *computed* for over 170 countries. Case Study 1 introduces the reader to the technical aspects of computation of the HDI, as well as to the changes in methodology it has undergone since it was first published.

## References

Ahluwalia, M.S. and H. Chenery (1974), 'A Model of Distribution and Growth', in: Chenery et al. (eds.), *Redistribution with Growth*, The World Bank, Oxford University Press.

Kravis, I., Heston, A. and Summers, R. (1978), *International Comparisons of Real Product and Purchasing Power*, Baltimore, Johns Hopkins Press.

Kuznets, Simon (1955), 'Economic Growth and Inequality', *American Economic Review*, 45, no. 1.

Morris, David (1979), *Measuring the Condition of the World's Poor. The Physical Quality of Life Index*, New York, Pergamon Press for the Overseas Development Council.

Sen, Amartya (1989), 'The concept of development', Chenery and Srinivasan (eds.), *Handbook of Development Economics*, vol.1, North Holland, pp. 9-26.

United Nations Development Program (UNDP, 1990), *Human Development Report*, New York, Oxford University Press.

UNDP (1995), *Human Development Report*, New York, Oxford University Press.

World Bank (2002 and 2003), *World Development Reports 2002 and 2003*, Washington, Oxford University Press.

# Case Study 1
# The Human Development Index: Kenya, Mexico and Canada

## Purpose

The purpose of this first case study is to acquaint students with the difficulties of computing indicators of development. By calculating the UNDP-sponsored Human Development Index (HDI) for three countries and two time periods, students will not only understand the mechanics of this indicator but also see its problems and limitations. The HDI is to be computed using the simple method used in 1990 as well as the more sophisticated version of 1992. The three countries are taken from three different income levels, low income (Kenya), middle income (Mexico), and high income (Canada). By computing the index for two time periods, using a slightly different method, one can also make observations about the factors that have led to a different ranking of the countries.

## Method of Analysis

The simple (1990) and more sophisticated (1992) methods for calculating the HDI are explained in this section.

*The original (1990) HDI method*

The human development index is calculated in three steps. The first step is to define a measure of deprivation ($I_{ij}$) that a country suffers in each of the three basic variables – life expectancy ($X_1$) literacy ($X_2$) and the logarithm of real GDP per capita ($X_3$), where GDP per capita is limited to a maximum of \$4,832. This limitation is based on the assumption that income beyond this ceiling does not add to human development. A maximum and a minimum value are determined for each of the three variables, from their values in all countries in the sample. The deprivation measure then places a country in the range of zero to one as defined by the difference between the maximum and the minimum. Thus $I_{ij}$ is the deprivation indicator for the jth country with respect to the ith variable and it is defined as:

$$(1) \qquad I_{ij} = (\max_j X_{ij} - X_{ij}) / (\max_j X_{ij} - \min_j X_{ij})$$

The second step is to define an average deprivation indicator ($I_j$). This is done by taking a simple average of the three indicators:

$$(2) \qquad I_j = (1/3)\Sigma_{i=1..3}I_{ij}$$

The third step is to measure the human development index (HDI) as one minus the average deprivation index:

$$(3) \qquad HDI_j = (1-I_j)$$

*The 1992 HDI method (used until 1998)*

The 1992 method differs from the 1990 one in two ways. First the educational deprivation (formally literacy deprivation) is measured by two educational variables: adult literacy rate and mean years of schooling. Both deprivations are calculated using the deprivation indicator as described in the 1990 method. It is important to note that in this method, the total educational deprivation is derived by taking a weighted average of the two deprivations and assigning a weight of 2/3 to the adult literacy rate and 1/3 to mean years of schooling.

The second change involves income deprivation. This method is based on the premise of diminishing marginal utility of income for human development, but instead of using the log of real GDP per capita to measure income utility, this method uses a more complex formulation for the utility of income. The variable y* is equal to the poverty level, which is common for all countries, and W(y) is the utility or well being derived from income (y). Income is taken as real GDP per capita based on a purchasing power parity (PPP) exchange rate. If y<y*, there is no diminishing marginal utility of income. The country receives the full utility for it's income. If y>y*, the country receives the full utility of income up to y*, plus the incremental marginal utility of income, which diminishes gradually above y*. The precise way of calculating the utility of income is given by the following expressions:

$$
(4) \quad
\begin{aligned}
W(y) &= y & &\text{for } 0 \leq y \leq y^* \\
&= y^* + 2(y-y^*)^{1/2} & &\text{for } y^* \leq y \leq 2y^* \\
&= y^* + 2(y^*)^{1/2} + 3(y-2y^*)^{1/3} & &\text{for } 2y^* \leq y \leq 3y^*
\end{aligned}
$$

and so on. The higher the income relative to the poverty level, the more sharply the diminishing returns affect the contribution of income to human development. This marginal effect is enough, however, to differentiate slightly among industrial countries.

For example, Singapore has a real GDP per capita of $15,108. With the poverty line a $4,829.

$$
(5) \quad
\begin{aligned}
W(y) &= y^* + 2(y^*)^{1/2} + 3(y^*)^{1/3} + 4(y-3y^*)^{1/4} \\
&= 4{,}829 + 2(4{,}829)^{1/2} + 3(4{,}829)^{1/3} + 4(15{,}108-14{,}487)^{1/4} \\
&= 4{,}829 + 139 + 51 + 20 = \$5{,}029
\end{aligned}
$$

The life expectancy deprivation is calculated in the same way as in the 1990 method. The second and third steps as described in the 1990 method also remain unchanged.

*The 1999 HDI method*

The 1999 method differs from the earlier methods in three respects. First, the deprivation index has been replaced by an attainment index, in which the numerator is the difference between the country's actual value and the minimum value. Second, while the treatment of life expectancy is the same as before, the educational attainment combines the adult literacy with a weight of 2/3 and the combined gross enrollment ratio (first, second and third level of schooling) with a weight of 1/3, replacing the mean years of schooling. Third, the treatment of income corresponds to that in the original 1990 method, except that there is no ceiling to welfare derived from income.

**Assigned Questions**

1)    Calculate the Human Development Index (HDI) for Kenya, Mexico and Canada for 1990 and 1999, using the data provided in the table. The HDI indices are shown in the table, to check your answers. Show the main steps of your computations in table format.

2)    Explain how the 1999 method differs from (a) the 1990 method and (b) the 1992 method. Which one of the three methods is the best in your view? Provide arguments.

3)    How much of the change of the HDI value is attributable to the changed method and how much is attributable to the performance of the three countries? Express the changes in percent terms. (Hint: To answer the question adequately, you need to re-compute the 1999 numbers with the 1990 method.)

4)    What are the main sources of the three countries' real change in human development based on the recalculation keeping the method constant?

5)    The Technical Notes of the Human Development Report 2002 include explanations of further additions to the HDI method (indices HP-1, HP-2, GDI and GEM). Explain what the main objectives and disadvantages are of these additions to the HDI methodology.

**Table CS1a  The Human Development Index: Data for Kenya, Mexico and Canada**

|  | Kenya | Mexico | Canada | Max | Min |
|---|---|---|---|---|---|
| **1990** |  |  |  |  |  |
| Life expectancy at birth (years) | 59.0 | 69.4 | 77.0 | 78.4 | 41.8 |
| Adult literacy rate (%) | 60.0 | 90.0 | 99.0 | 100.0 | 12.3 |
| Real GDP per capita (PPP $) | 794 | 4,624 | 4,832 | 4,832 | 220 |
| HDI score | 0.481 | 0.876 | 0.983 |  |  |
| HDI ranking | 89 | 40 | 5 |  |  |
| **1999 (1997 data)** |  |  |  |  |  |
| Life expectancy at birth (years) | 52.0 | 72.2 | 79.0 | 85.0 | 25.0 |
| Adult literacy rate (%) | 79.3 | 90.1 | 99.0 | 100.0 | 0.0 |
| Gross enrollment ratio (%) | 50.0 | 70.0 | 99.0 | 100.0 | 0.0 |
| Real GDP per capita (PPP $) | 1,190 | 8,370 | 22,480 | 40,000 | 100 |
| HDI score | 0.519 | 0.786 | 0.932 |  |  |
| HDI ranking | 136 | 50 | 1 |  |  |

*Source*:   *Human Development Report*, 1990 and 1999.
*Note*:    There are 130 countries in the 1990 HDI sample and 174 in the 1999 sample. The HDI of 1990 uses 100.0 percent as the maximum literacy rate while the 1999 study uses 99.0 percent as the maximum observed literacy rate. This reflects a slight difference in measurement.

**Case Study 1: Solution**

1)    The computations are shown in Table CS1b on page 22.

2)    The 1999 method differs from the original 1990 method in two important respects, the measurement of educational achievement by the literacy rate as well as the enrollment ratio (instead of literacy only), and the measurement of income utility by its logarithm but without the cap applied in 1990. A third change, which has no consequence for the outcome, is the fact that all measurements enter positively into an achievement index, the average of which is the HDI. In the 1990 method, deprivation indices were computed, which, after averaging were deducted from unity to result in the HDI.

The first of these changes was adopted in order to take the differences in human qualification beyond literacy into account. In the 1992 method, this was done by using the mean years of schooling, which in the 1999 method is replaced by the combined enrollment ratio.

The second of these changes, is a return to the simple logarithm of income for its utility, which was also the case in 1990, but without the capping of income at a level of $4832. This cap implied that people do not derive developmental benefits from income above that cap, which is a questionable hypothesis. In the 1992 method the utility or welfare of income was computed by using the Atkinson formula, which was abandoned in later issues. Based on these arguments, it would appear that the 1999 method is superior to both the 1990 and 1992 methods.

3)      By computing the 1999 data with the 1990 method we see how the index would have changed if the same method as in 1990 had been used. This procedure is somewhat problematic because the income cap at $4832 applied in 1990 would need to be inflated by some measure of inflation in order to be realistic.

For Kenya the 9.2% increase of the HDI from 0.476 in 1990 to 0.52 in 1999 is accounted for by 31.7% real increase and a 22.5% decrease due to method change. The method change affected the Kenya index negatively because of two effects: the school enrollment ratio used in the 1999 method was low (50 percent) for this country and the elimination of the income cap led to an increase of Kenya's income deprivation.

For Mexico the 10.1% decline of the HDI from 0.875 in 1990 to 0.787 in 1999 results from a real increase of 2.4% and a 12.5% decline due to the method change. The method change affected Mexico strongly since with the cap in 1990 Mexico had zero income deprivation, whereas in without the cap its income achievement of 0.739 corresponds to a 0.261 deprivation score. The inclusion of school enrollment also lowered its score.

For Canada the change of method has had only a small effect of minus 3.3%, which added to the 2% real decline for a total decline of the HDI of 5.3%. The effect of method change comes entirely from the increase of the income range, which increased Canada's income deprivation from zero to 10%, given the very high level of the income maximum of $40,000.

4)      Considering the 1990 to 1999 change of HDI score that reflects real changes in development, excluding the impact of method change and keeping in mind the limitations of this procedure, we demonstrated above that Kenya increased strongly its development score (by 31.7%), Mexico

also increased it but only slightly (2.4%) and Canada experienced a slight decrease (2%).

For Kenya the increase from 0.476 to 0.627 is explained mainly by the advance in literacy from 60 to 79.3 percent and in per capita income from $794 to $1190, whereas in terms of life expectancy the change of deprivation is minimal.

For Mexico the increase of HDI from 87.5 in 1990 to 89.6 in 1999 is accounted for by a small improvement in health and education, as well as a decline in income deprivation, which, however, is over-stated by the unchanged income cap of $4832.

For Canada, the fall of HDI from 98.3 in 1990 to 96.3 in 1999 is essentially due to increased health deprivation, which results from the rising life expectancy in other countries, especially in Japan.

5)      The additional indices proposed in the Human Development Report of 2002 focus on aspects like standard of living, social exclusion, gender equality and gender empowerment. The HPI-1 index is a poverty index, which measures the deprivation in the three basic dimensions captured in the HDI, life expectancy, education and a decent standard of living, where the latter replaces income by information on population shares not using improved water sources and of underweight children under five. The HPI-2 index adds to the three basic dimensions a further one, that of social exclusion as measured by the rate of long-term unemployment. The GDI index adjusts the average achievement measured by the HDI to reflect the inequalities between men and women in the dimensions of life expectancy, education and a decent standard of living. Finally, the GEM index focuses on women's opportunities, rather than their capabilities. It captures gender inequality in the areas of political participation and decision-making power, economic participation and decision-making power, and power over economic resources.

The advantage of such special indices lies in recording the progress in more advanced aspects of human development. Their disadvantage lies in the fact that they require a large amount of information that is not available in the required format from many countries. This reduces their applicability and the scope for international comparison.

**Table CS1b  The Human Development Index: Solution**

|  | Max | Min | Kenya | Mexico | Canada |
|---|---|---|---|---|---|
| **1990 data & method** | | | | | |
| Life expectancy (years) | 78.4 | 41.8 | 59 | 69.4 | 77 |
| Health deprivation | | | 0.5301 | 0.2459 | 0.0383 |
| Adult literacy (%) | 100 | 12.3 | 60 | 90 | 99 |
| Education deprivation | | | 0.4561 | 0.1140 | 0.0114 |
| Real GDP p.c. (PPP) | 4832 | 220 | 794 | 4624 | 4832 |
| Income deprivation | | | 0.5846 | 0.0142 | 0.0000 |
| Total deprivation | | | 0.524 | 0.125 | 0.017 |
| HDI score | | | 0.476 | 0.875 | 0.983 |
| **1999 data/1990 method** [1] | | | | | |
| Life expectancy (years) | 85 | 25 | 52 | 72.2 | 79 |
| Health deprivation | | | 0.5500 | 0.2133 | 0.1000 |
| Adult literacy (%) | 100 | 0 | 79.3 | 90.1 | 99 |
| Education deprivation | | | 0.2070 | 0.0990 | 0.0100 |
| Real GDP p.c. (PPP) | 4832 | 100 | 1190 | 4832 | 4832 |
| Income deprivation | | | 0.3614 | 0.0000 | 0.0000 |
| Total deprivation | | | 0.373 | 0.104 | 0.037 |
| HDI score | | | 0.627 | 0.896 | 0.963 |
| **1999 data & method** | | | | | |
| Life expectancy (years) | 85 | 25 | 52 | 72.2 | 79 |
| Health achievement | | | 0.450 | 0.787 | 0.900 |
| Adult literacy (%) | 100 | 0 | 79.3 | 90.1 | 99 |
| Literacy achievement | | | 0.793 | 0.901 | 0.990 |
| Gross enrollment (%) | 100 | 0 | 50 | 70 | 99 |
| Enrollment achievement (%) | | | 0.500 | 0.700 | 0.990 |
| Education achievement | | | 0.695 | 0.834 | 0.990 |
| Real GDP p.c. (PPP) | 40000 | 100 | 1190 | 8370 | 22480 |
| Income achievement | | | 0.413 | 0.739 | 0.904 |
| HDI score | | | 0.520 | 0.787 | 0.931 |

---

[1] The income cap or $4832 is applied here, although it would need to be inflated.

# Case Study 2
# International Income Comparisons

## Purpose

How can the GDP levels of different countries be compared when the values are expressed in each nation's domestic currency? The traditional method is to use the official exchange rate to convert the GDP into U.S. dollars. As we saw earlier, however, official exchange rates do not typically reflect the real purchasing power of currencies because they do not attribute similar prices across countries to similar non-traded goods and services. International institutions like the World Bank are therefore using so-called purchasing power parity exchange rates for the conversion and comparison of GDP across countries.

In the present case study we construct such an exchange rate based on the principle of purchasing power parity (PPP). The principle implies that when a PPP-based exchange rate is used for conversion, most goods should sell at the same price in both countries involved in the comparison. In reality, this is hardly ever achievable because prices tend to differ substantially. While traded goods tend to have similar prices using even the official exchange rate, diverging only to the extent of differences in tariffs and non-tariff barriers, non-traded goods, and particularly labour intensive services, tend to be considerably cheaper in low-income countries. A PPP-based exchange rate is therefore a rate that equalizes the value of a basket of goods and services in the two countries of comparison.

The case study proposes to convert the 1992 value of Kenya's GDP in Kenyan shillings (KS) into Canadian dollars. To simplify the task we distinguish only two types of goods, tradables and non-tradables. The prices and quantities of these two goods categories are arbitrarily chosen, but they approximately match the Kenyan and the Canadian GDP, respectively.

## Method of Analysis

The estimated PPP exchange rate can be calculated in three steps. In the first step (Laspeyres index) the exchange rate is calculated using the quantity weights of the first country, and in the second step (Paasche index) the quantity weights of the second country are used. In the third step

(Fisher index) a geometric average of the Laspeyres and the Paasche index is used to determine the PPP exchange rate between the two countries.

Let $I_{kc}$ denote the exchange rate (defined as the price of foreign currency) of country k (Kenya) with respect to country c (Canada) Let i represent the commodity, p the price and q the quantity of the i'th commodity consumed. The three indices are calculated in the following way:

Laspeyres:     $I_{kc} = \Sigma_i \, (p_{ik} \, q_{ic}) / \Sigma_i \, (p_{ic.} \, q_{ic})$
               (using Canadian quantities as weights)
Paasche:       $I_{kc} = \Sigma_i \, (p_{ik} \, q_{ik}) / \Sigma_i \, (p_{ic} \, q_{ik})$
               (using Kenyan quantities as weights)
Fisher:        $I_{kc} = (I_{kc}^{\text{Lasp}} \, I_{kc}^{\text{Paasche}})^{1/2}$

The so computed exchange rate attributes a different value to the Kenyan shilling than the official rate, mainly because it takes non-tradable goods into consideration. The rate can then be used to translate Kenyan income into Canadian dollars.

## Assigned Questions

1)     The Kenyan GDP per capita in 1999 was equal to KS 24,939. Calculate the Canadian dollar value of this income level, using the official exchange rate of 37.5 Kenyan shillings/Canadian dollar.

2)     What are the exchange rates implicit in the prices of tradables and non-tradables? Use the following data for your calculations:
       Price of tradables:      Kenya = 45 KS/unit  Canada = 1 $/unit
       Price of non-tradables:  Kenya = 88 KS/unit  Canada = 20$/unit
       Quantity of tradables:   Kenya = 4.2 billion  Canada = 200 billion
       Quantity, non-tradables: Kenya = 1 billion     Canada = 15 billion
       Notice that the price of tradables in Kenya of 45 KS is equal to the exchange rate of 37.5 KS times the Canadian price of one dollar plus a margin of 20 percent. This margin reflects the fact that there are higher tariffs in Kenya, and this causes the price of tradables to increase accordingly.

3)     Using the Laspeyres, Paasche and Fisher indices, calculate the PPP exchange rate for Kenya based on the two categories of goods and services, tradables and non-tradables.

4)     Calculate the Canadian dollar value of the Kenyan GDP per capita using the PPP exchange rate. Why is it larger than the one you have computed in question (1)?

5)     Would you recommend the Kenyan government to adopt this PPP-based rate as the official exchange rate? Why or why not?

# Case Study 3
# Deflation of National Accounts

## Purpose

The main problem in deflation of national account aggregates is how to deflate non-commodity flows such as value added (GDP) or foreign capital inflows. This problem is illustrated easily by deflating the nominal value of the trade balance. The quick and easy way of doing this is to use the GDP deflator to deflate all values into real terms. However, export and import prices tend to change at rates that differ and also differ from the GDP deflator. Therefore, using the GDP deflator for the deflation of trade flows is imprecise. We therefore use the import price index (Pm) and the export price index (Px) to deflate imports and exports respectively. It may then happen that for some years a nominal trade surplus turns into a real trade deficit. In other words, it is possible to arrive at the undesirable situation where $F=M-X>0$ and $F'=M'-X'<0$, where primed variables are in real terms. Although this result is perfectly consistent with the idea of expressing all present flows in terms of past prices, it raises the question of what prices represent a more valid valuation of the real flows, past or present prices. In order to avoid this ambiguity it is common to express this flow in constant prices and to introduce a term reflecting the effect of the price change. One of the methods dealing with this problem is the one proposed by Burge and Geary (1957).

The Burge-Geary method solves this problem by introducing a slack variable term, Z', which is a measure of the terms of trade gain or loss. This method is attractive because it is simple to use and it gives consistent values for nominal and real foreign capital inflows. That is, if nominal foreign capital inflows are positive, real foreign capital inflows will also be positive. The discrepancy between the two is captured in the slack variable term, Z'.

In this exercise, Kenyan imports and exports for the years 1972 to 1992 will be converted from nominal to real terms. The import and export price indices use 1982 as the base year.

## Method of Analysis

The Burge-Geary method consists of the following assumption and computation. Foreign capital inflows (F) are in a simplified model of the balance of payments, assuming that the trade balance and the current account are equal, given by:

$$M - X = F$$

Real Imports and exports are obtained by using import and export price indices (Pm and Px).

$$M/Pm - X/Px = M' - X'$$

Real capital inflows (F') are defined as F/Pf, where Pf is the non-commodity flow price index. Following Burge and Geary, Pf is determined in the following way:

for F>0 (M>X), Pf=Pm.
for F<0 (M<X), Pf=Px.

This definition of F' assumes that F' will always have the same sign as F. However F' is unequal to M'-X'. The difference (Z') is a slack term representing the value of changing terms of trade.

$$M/Pm - X/Px = F/Pf + Z' \qquad \text{or} \quad M' - X' = F' + Z'$$

where Z' is determined in the following way:

for M>X $\qquad$ Z' = M/Pm - X/Px - F/Pm
replacing F by M-X: Z' = -X' (1-Px/Pm)

for M<X $\qquad$ Z' = M/Pm - (X/Px - F/Px)
replacing F by M-X: Z' = M' (1-Pm/Px)

In the case of a terms of trade gain (Px>Pm), Z' is positive and in the case of a terms of trade loss (Px<Pm), Z' is negative.

## Assigned Questions

1) Convert the import and export price indices, which are given for the base year of 1982, such that the base year becomes 1972, that is, the 1972 import and export price indices should be equal to 100.
2) Use the Burge-Geary method to deflate imports, exports and the current account balance using the price indices with base year 1972.
3) Calculate the value of Z' and interpret its meaning.
4) Has Kenya experienced a terms of trade gain or loss in every year of the study period (1972-1992)? Explain your answer.
5) Explain the difference between the nominal and the real values of imports, exports and foreign capital inflows.

**Table CS3a  Data for the deflation of national accounts: Kenya**

| Year | GDP | GDP Defl. | Imports | Imports Defl. | Exports | Exports Defl. |
|------|------|------|------|------|------|------|
| 1972 | 663.5 | 34.9 | 197.8 | 15.0 | 127.8 | 22.5 |
| 1973 | 755.0 | 38.1 | 228.5 | 8.2 | 174.5 | 25.7 |
| 1974 | 900.3 | 44.1 | 383.9 | 26.9 | 228.8 | 34.3 |
| 1975 | 1,087.8 | 51.8 | 362.6 | 41.2 | 230.4 | 39.6 |
| 1976 | 1,313.6 | 60.0 | 407.0 | 47.8 | 335.4 | 53.5 |
| 1977 | 1,683.8 | 71.1 | 531.4 | 52.2 | 480.3 | 76.0 |
| 1978 | 1,833.5 | 71.9 | 661.1 | 56.9 | 370.0 | 64.2 |
| 1979 | 2,033.2 | 76.0 | 620.2 | 63.2 | 385.5 | 68.5 |
| 1980 | 2,298.4 | 82.6 | 959.0 | 75.1 | 487.6 | 82.4 |
| 1981 | 2,659.5 | 90.2 | 932.4 | 89.0 | 513.9 | 91.0 |
| 1982 | 3,049.3 | 100.0 | 900.3 | 100.0 | 545.7 | 100.0 |
| 1983 | 3,473.7 | 110.6 | 905.6 | 140.0 | 633.1 | 88.0 |
| 1984 | 3,876.2 | 122.9 | 1,097.2 | 143.0 | 754.8 | 154.0 |
| 1985 | 4,423.8 | 133.5 | 1,196.0 | 173.0 | 785.1 | 151.0 |
| 1986 | 5,115.0 | 146.2 | 1,337.9 | 187.0 | 958.0 | 174.0 |
| 1987 | 5,648.2 | 154.0 | 1,430.9 | 185.0 | 753.4 | 138.0 |
| 1988 | 6,480.6 | 168.0 | 1,765.1 | 209.0 | 917.7 | 165.0 |
| 1989 | 7,387.8 | 182.3 | 2,238.6 | 246.0 | 999.8 | 171.0 |
| 1990 | 8,377.8 | 198.4 | 2,545.6 | 287.0 | 1,232.4 | 178.0 |
| 1991 | 9,521.4 | 220.8 | 2,645.9 | 318.0 | 1,533.8 | 227.0 |
| 1992 | 11,088.4 | 256.2 | 2,954.9 | 369.0 | 1,708.1 | 254.0 |

**Case Study 3: Solution**

1)      The re-scaled import and export price indices (Pm' and Px') show that import prices have risen much more (from 100 to 2460) than export prices (from 100 to 1128.9).

2)      The deflated (real) imports and exports are shown as M' and X', respectively. Net real imports are shown as M'-X'. Comparing them with net nominal imports (M − X)) in the next column shows that in several years net real imports were negative, while they were nominally positive. In the following column real capital imports (F') are computed alternatively, using the Burge-Geary method, that is, dividing (M −X) by Pm' whenever positive and by Px' whenever negative.

3)      The slack term is shown in the second column from the right hand side. It is computed as Z' = -X' (1-Px/Pm) since nominal imports always exceed exports. The slack term represents the terms of trade gain or loss.

4)      Has Kenya experienced a terms of trade gain or loss in every year of the study period? The numbers in the column of Z' may suggest that there was a ToT loss every year. But this would be the wrong conclusion, because the slack term Z' appears in index form. Therefore the yearly ToT gain or loss can be seen only when taking the difference from one your to the next. This is shown in the last column as $Z'_t - Z'_{t-1}$. As a result we can see that Kenya has experienced ToT losses only in 14 out of 20 years and ToT gains in 6 years. The highest ToT gain appears to have occurred in 1984.

5)      While imports and exports are commodity flows, their real values can be obtained by using the price indices (deflators) that relate to them. This is impossible for capital inflows, which is a non-commodity flow. It equals net imports through the balance of payments equation and is obtained as a residual from this balance equation. The deflation of non-commodity flows is therefore problematic and requires assumptions, such as the Burge-Geary method.

**Table CS3b    Deflation of national accounts in Kenya: Solution**

| Year | M | Pm' | M' | X | Px' | X' | M'-X' | F=M-X | F'=F/Pf | Z' | Z't-Zt-1 |
|------|------|--------|-------|--------|--------|-------|-------|--------|---------|-------|---------|
| 1972 | 197.8 | 100.0 | 197.8 | 127.8 | 100.0 | 127.8 | 70.0 | 70.0 | 70.0 | 0.0 | |
| 1973 | 228.5 | 121.3 | 188.3 | 174.5 | 114.2 | 152.8 | 35.6 | 54.0 | 44.5 | -9.0 | -9.0 |
| 1974 | 383.9 | 179.3 | 214.1 | 228.8 | 152.4 | 150.1 | 64.0 | 155.1 | 86.5 | -22.5 | -13.6 |
| 1975 | 362.6 | 274.7 | 132.0 | 230.4 | 176.0 | 130.9 | 1.1 | 132.2 | 48.1 | -47.0 | -24.5 |
| 1976 | 407.0 | 318.7 | 127.7 | 335.4 | 237.8 | 141.1 | -13.3 | 71.6 | 22.5 | -35.8 | 11.2 |
| 1977 | 531.4 | 348.0 | 152.7 | 480.3 | 337.8 | 142.2 | 10.5 | 51.1 | 14.7 | -4.2 | 31.6 |
| 1978 | 661.1 | 379.3 | 174.3 | 370.0 | 285.3 | 129.7 | 44.6 | 291.1 | 76.7 | -32.1 | -28.0 |
| 1979 | 620.2 | 421.3 | 147.2 | 385.5 | 304.4 | 126.6 | 20.6 | 234.7 | 55.7 | -35.1 | -3.0 |
| 1980 | 959.0 | 500.7 | 191.5 | 487.6 | 366.2 | 133.1 | 58.4 | 471.4 | 94.2 | -35.8 | -0.6 |
| 1981 | 932.4 | 593.3 | 157.1 | 513.9 | 404.4 | 127.1 | 30.1 | 418.5 | 70.5 | -40.5 | -4.7 |
| 1982 | 900.3 | 666.7 | 135.0 | 545.7 | 444.4 | 122.8 | 12.3 | 354.6 | 53.2 | -40.9 | -0.5 |
| 1983 | 905.6 | 933.3 | 97.0 | 633.1 | 391.1 | 161.9 | -64.8 | 272.5 | 29.2 | -94.0 | -53.1 |
| 1984 | 1097.2 | 953.3 | 115.1 | 754.8 | 684.4 | 110.3 | 4.8 | 342.4 | 35.9 | -31.1 | 62.9 |
| 1985 | 1196.0 | 1153.3 | 103.7 | 785.1 | 671.1 | 117.0 | -13.3 | 410.9 | 35.6 | -48.9 | -17.8 |
| 1986 | 1337.9 | 1246.7 | 107.3 | 958.0 | 773.3 | 123.9 | -16.6 | 379.9 | 30.5 | -47.0 | 1.9 |
| 1987 | 1430.9 | 1233.3 | 116.0 | 753.4 | 613.3 | 122.8 | -6.8 | 677.5 | 54.9 | -61.8 | -14.7 |
| 1988 | 1765.1 | 1393.3 | 126.7 | 917.7 | 733.3 | 125.1 | 1.5 | 847.4 | 60.8 | -59.3 | 2.5 |
| 1989 | 2238.6 | 1640.0 | 136.5 | 999.8 | 760.0 | 131.6 | 4.9 | 1238.8 | 75.5 | -70.6 | -11.3 |
| 1990 | 2545.6 | 1913.3 | 133.0 | 1232.4 | 791.1 | 155.8 | -22.7 | 1313.2 | 68.6 | -91.4 | -20.8 |
| 1991 | 2645.9 | 2120.0 | 124.8 | 1533.8 | 1008.9 | 152.0 | -27.2 | 1112.1 | 52.5 | -79.7 | 11.7 |
| 1992 | 2954.9 | 2460.0 | 120.1 | 1708.1 | 1128.9 | 151.3 | -31.2 | 1246.8 | 50.7 | -81.9 | -2.2 |

# Chapter 2

# Economic Growth and its Determinants

The analysis of economic growth has three purposes: (a) the measurement of the growth of various aggregates of the economy; (b) the identification and measurement of its determinants or sources; and (c) the prediction of future growth by help of growth models. We are interested in answering questions such as: What determines economic growth? Which factors make the most important contributions to growth, the factors of production or technical change? How can we predict economic growth? We have already seen in Chapter 1 how growth is measured, and will turn our attention now to models of growth. At first we discuss simple production function models, which allow us to analyze growth in terms of factor contributions and technical change under the name of growth accounting. In the next section we examine full-fledged macro models, which endogenize the accumulation of capital. Two members of this family are introduced, the Harrod-Domar model with fixed coefficients and the neoclassical (Solow) model, which allows for substitution between capital and labour. A short review of modern growth theory, often referred to as endogenous growth, concludes the theory, which is being applied in the last section to examine whether the international long-run experience with economic growth supports the hypothesis of convergence of income levels.

## 2.1    Production Function Models

The question of what determines economic growth can be approached in various ways. In the production function approach we envisage the growth process entirely from the supply side. The growth of production is then described in the same way as the level of production, that is, by the combination of factors of production and their increase. In a general form we write a production function as a relationship between the quantity of output (Q) and the quantity of factor inputs, such as labour (L) capital (K) and technology (T).

$$(2.1) \quad Q = F(L, K, T)$$

While the quantities of labour and capital can be measured, notwithstanding some formidable problems of measurement, this is not possible for technology because a technology is simply the way the factors of production are being combined. It has no specific dimension, except if one considers the passing of time as a typical determinant of technical change. It is also understood in the above production function, that each of the variables relates to the same time period. We omit here for simplicity the time subscripts t.

A particular and very popular production function is the so-called Cobb-Douglas function which has the following form:

$$(2.2) \quad Q = T\,L^{\alpha}\,K^{\beta}.$$

This production function assumes that the factor inputs determine the output quantity in a multiplicative form. The exponents $\alpha$ and $\beta$ are elasticities of output with respect to inputs. If the exponents add up to one the function exhibits constant returns to scale, that is, whenever labour and capital inputs are doubled or tripled, the output is doubled or tripled as well. The constant T is a measure of total factor productivity, since it equals output per unit of combined factor inputs. It can also be thought of as the level of technology, as we have called it initially.

The setting of T = constant is obviously not a useful assumption because neither the level of technology nor the factor productivity remain typically constant over time. If we allow T to increase over time, however, the output will more than double over time when factor inputs double, although the function has constant returns to scale. The additional increase in output then comes from the increase in T which we call technical change or, if positive, technical progress. One way of measuring technical change is therefore to hold the variable T constant, but to attach an exponential growth coefficient to it, so that the technical change is expressed as a constant rate. The function then takes the following form:

$$(2.3) \quad Q = T\,e^{gt}\,L^{\alpha}\,K^{\beta}$$

where t is an index of time, g is the rate of technical change and e is the basis of the natural logarithm (= 2.7183).

In order to compute the percentage growth rate of Q we need to either take the logarithm of equation 2.3 and differentiate it with respect to time t, or, using the discrete rather than continuous growth rate, take first differences, for instance $\Delta Q$ for Q, and divide the whole equation by Q. The latter procedure is rather tedious because it involves not just one but several interaction terms (see our earlier discussion of computing growth rates when increments are large); therefore we shall assume that all variables grow in small annual increments, and apply the former procedure. This permits us to express the growth rate of Q in the following way:

$$(2.4) \quad g_Q = dQ/(dt\ Q)$$
$$= \alpha\ g_L + \beta\ g_K + g_T$$

where $g_T$ is the growth rate of total factor productivity (TFP), or the rate of technical change, and $g_L$ and $g_K$ are the growth rates of labour and capital input, respectively.

One may also want to estimate the growth of labour productivity (Q/L) which is easily done by using a Cobb-Douglas function. Based on the assumption of constant returns to scale, that is, $\alpha + \beta = 1$, equation 2.3 can be rewritten as:

$$(2.5) \quad Q/L = T\ e^{gt}\ (K/L)^{\beta}.$$

This means that the labour productivity depends on the capital/labour ratio and the rate of technical change. The growth rate version of this function is then:

$$(2.6) \quad g_{Lp} = g_Q - g_L$$
$$= g_T + \beta g_{KL}$$
$$= g_T + \beta(g_K - g_L)$$

where $g_{Lp}$ is the growth rate of labour productivity, and $g_{KL}$ is the growth rate of the capital/labour ratio, equal to the growth rate of capital minus that of employed labour.

If we assume in addition perfect competition, so that the factors of production earn their marginal products, then the exponents $\alpha$ and $\beta$ are not only output elasticities but also equal to the factor shares of output. This is easily seen by re-writing, for instance, the output elasticity of labour as:

$$(2.7) \quad \alpha = (\partial Q/Q)/(\partial L/L)$$
$$= (\partial Q/\partial L)\ L/Q.$$

Noting that $(\partial Q/\partial L)$ L is equal to labour times its marginal product equal to labour's earnings under perfect competition, $\alpha$ is then labour's proportional share of output.

This assumption and interpretation of α and ß permits us to use the equations 2.4 and 2.6 in a very convenient fashion. We can calculate from the data the average factor shares, α and ß, over time and compute then the growth rate of TFP as a residual, based on the measured growth rates of capital and labour input. This procedure emphasizes the residual nature of $g_T$, which captures all factors influencing Q other than the quantities of factor inputs. The interpretation of $g_T$ as rate of technical change is therefore an overstatement and deserves further consideration. Before we look in more detail at the nature of technical change, let us see another way of estimating its rate.

An alternative method of finding the growth rate of TFP is to estimate the whole production function by way of regression analysis. Equation 2.3 can be estimated in linear form as:

$$(2.8) \quad \ln Q = \ln T + \alpha \ln L + \text{ß} \ln K + gt$$

where lnT is a constant and α, ß and g are the regression coefficients of the variables L, K and t. This procedure should ideally give similar results as the former procedure, but it respects more the vagaries of the data. For instance it can happen that the coefficients α and ß do not sum up to one, or that one or more of the coefficients are revealed statistically insignificant. The former problem means that the data do not support the hypothesis of constant returns to scale. The latter problem is more serious and puts into doubt the adequacy of the chosen production function. For instance, the assumed constancy of the coefficients, especially that of constant factor shares, may not be compatible with the data. One may have to look for another functional form that better matches the data. In addition to these limitations, one can have doubts about the reliability of the measurements of factor inputs, especially that of capital.

## 2.2     The Nature of Technical Change

Starting from the method of estimating the rate of technical change explained above, let us now see what elements the TFP growth rate captures and which of these elements can be truly considered as technical change. First, the $g_T$ captures the differences in factor utilization. If workers or machines are employed but remain partially idle, this would show up as a low $g_T$, although it is inefficiency rather than slow technical progress. In the narrower sense of the term, technical change is only that part of TFP increase that is caused by improved methods of combining the factors, and improved methods imply additional knowledge. Even improvements in the quality of factors, such as education and training in the case of labour, and improved technical characteristics of machines in the case of capital, require a somewhat wider definition of technical change. Such a wider definition includes both, embodied and disembodied technical change. Education and training are typically embodied in labour, new technical characteristics are embodied in capital, and disembodied change is essentially the addition of pure knowledge.

In order to account for such improvements of the factor quality in our analysis, we could proceed in the following way. For labour we could, for instance, distinguish different categories of labour, such as skilled and unskilled workers, and possibly other categories of labour quality. This approach is used in our analysis of technical change in the manufacturing sector of Kenya (Siggel, 1993), on which Case Study 5 is based. Another approach would be to construct a labour quality variable LQ and measure its rate of growth over time as $g_{LQ}$. If this LQ variable applies multiplicatively to the factor input L, then the contribution of labour-embodied technical change to TFP growth would be found in an extension of equation 2.4 as $\alpha\, g_{LQ}$.

A similar adjustment could be made for capital-embodied technical change. This was attempted first by Solow (1960), who referred to the quality-weighted capital stock as vintage. Capital stock not only depreciates by use but also becomes obsolete. A later vintage of capital equipment may not necessarily show up as more expensive capital stock, but it may nevertheless be a more potent factor of production. Without going into details of how these ideas are best modelled in the production function, we can conclude that the TFP growth rate net of embodied technical change, which we may call disembodied technical change, must be smaller than the rate computed without such consideration. It is clear also that the quantification of embodied technical change requires fairly sophisticated and reliable data.

Finally, technical change may also be analyzed according to its effect on the factor inputs. For instance, we know that technical progress tends to reduce the labour requirements per unit of output. The kind of technical change we have introduced in equation 2.3 can be called neutral technical change, because it enhances output without a bias toward any of the factor inputs. Several authors, especially Hicks (1932) and Harrod (1948) have provided alternative definitions of the neutrality and bias in technical progress. Focusing only on Hicks' definition here, neutrality is defined by him as given if the marginal rate of technical substitution (MRTS) remains constant as long as the capital/labour ratio also remains constant. Therefore, if technical change is shown diagrammatically as an inward shift of the production isoquant in Figure 2.1, it is neutral in the Hicksian sense if the isoquant maintains its slope along any ray from the origin such as the one marked as $(K/L)_A$. According to Hicks, technical change is labour-saving if the MRTS is lower on the new isoquant along

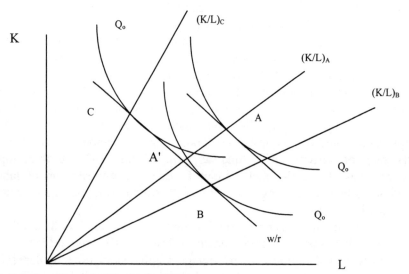

**Figure 2.1    Biases of technical change**

any ray from the origin. It is capital-saving if the MRTS along any ray increases when the isoquant shifts inward. The Hicksian definition is the most straightforward of various definitions of neutrality and bias. The reader can easily verify that under labour-saving technical progress a firm facing the same relative factor prices as before would choose a more capital-intensive technique (C) after the change than before (A). Alternatively, it would choose a technique of the same capital/labour ratio (A') only if the relative price of labour was lower than before, that is, $(w/r)_1 < (w/r)_0$.

## 2.3    Empirical Evidence and Policy Conclusions

The analysis of the sources of growth has been undertaken in many studies, both at the single-country and the international (across-country) levels. Although the former category of studies is more meaningful in terms of policy conclusions, let us see here only the results of international studies which provide more general results. Perhaps the most interesting and fairly recent international study is the one by Chenery (1986), which compares three groups of countries with each other, 12 developed economies (DEs), 20 developing economies (LDEs) and 7 centrally planned economies (CPEs). Table 2.1 reproduces only the results for the country group averages and uses the names of variables used in the present discussion.

**Table 2.1**   **Growth rates of value added ($g_v$), inputs ($g_k$, $g_i$) and total factor productivity ($g_T$) (in percent) in developed economies (DEs), less developed economies (LDEs) and centrally planned economies (CPEs)**

|  | Value added growth | Factor growth | | | TFP growth | | Factor shares | |
|---|---|---|---|---|---|---|---|---|
|  | $g_V$ | $g_K$ | $g_L$ | share | $g_T$ | share | $\alpha$ | $\beta$ |
| DEs | 5.4 | 5.2 | 1.1 | 0.51 | 2.7 | 0.49 | 0.62 | 0.38 |
| LDEs | 6.3 | 5.5 | 3.3 | 0.69 | 2.0 | 0.31 | 0.55 | 0.45 |
| CPEs | 8.2 | 8.0 | 4.5 | 0.65 | 2.5 | 0.35 | 0.60 | 0.40 |

*Source*: Chenery (1986).

As the table shows, TFP growth plays a much more important role in developed economies (nearly 50 percent) than in developing economies (31 percent). The greater importance of factor growth in less developed economies (LDEs) is expected, given their initial capital scarcity, as well as their rapid population growth. The results for the CPEs, which exclude China, refer to the 1950s and 1960s, that is, long before their economies broke down. Although the data of DEs and LDEs are more recent, none of them go beyond 1974. The findings of this study are consistent, although not equal, with those of Madison (1970), Nadiri (1972) and The World Bank (1991). While policy conclusions are more meaningful when based on single-country studies, one may nevertheless conclude that investment and capital accumulation do play an important role in the growth of production in developing countries, a greater role than that of TFP growth which, however, is not negligible either.

## 2.4    Macroeconomic Growth Models

The analysis of growth based on production functions can be and has been applied not only at the level of industries or sectors but also at the level of total GDP. Nevertheless, its nature is microeconomic and partial in that it considers only the process of production, that is, the supply side, and identifies the factors of production as sources of growth. Macroeconomic growth models, on the other hand, explore the relationship between typical macroeconomic variables such as investment and saving and integrate both supply and demand. They focus on the generation of savings, the transformation of savings into investments and the use of new capacity in the generation of output, as well as on the demand for new output, so that internal and external equilibria are achieved.

The simplest of this kind of models is the Harrod-Domar model which owes its name to two important and more or less simultaneous publications by Roy E. Harrod (1948) of Cambridge University and Evsey D. Domar (1946) of the M.I.T. While the two authors pursued slightly different ideas, the essence of their thinking combines to what we refer to as Harrod-Domar model.

*2.4.1    The Harrod-Domar (HD) Model*

The basic assumptions of this closed-economy model are as follows:

First, the economy generates savings (S) at a constant proportion (s) of national income (Y):

(2.9)    $S = s\,Y$

where s is the marginal and average savings ratio. Second, the economy is in equilibrium, that is, planned savings and planned investments are equal:

(2.10)   $I = S.$

Third, investments are determined by the expected increase in national income ($\Delta Y$) and a fixed technical coefficient v, which is called Incremental Capital Output Ratio (ICOR):

(2.11)   $I = v\,\Delta Y$

When putting equations 1 to 3 together in such a way as to solve for $g_Y = \Delta Y/Y$, which is the growth rate of national income, we obtain:

(2.12)   $g_Y = s/v.$

This result means that the economy can grow at a rate determined by the parameters s and v if all the underlying assumptions are fulfilled. There are two further implications of these assumptions. First, the fixed ICOR implies that there is a fixed relationship between the amount of capital stock in the economy and the output it generates. In other words, the underlying production function is of the fixed-proportion or Leontief type. Second, since labour does not appear anywhere in this model, it is assumed that labour is not a constraining factor, or that labour is always sufficiently available.

In order to see how this model works, let us use a numerical example of a closed economy with national income and production in the base year of $Y = 1000$, a savings ratio of $s = .2$ and an ICOR of $v = 4$. The growth process is shown in Table 2.2. In this model every variable grows at the same rate so that demand and supply remain in equilibrium. This is a form of balanced growth. The 20 percent of national income that are saved are transformed into investment, which generate 5 percent new output capacity, given an ICOR of 4. We assume also that the new output capacity generated by the investments in every year is being used for production only in the following year. The model also shows that it involves another implicit assumption, namely that all investment goods needed for the capacity expansion are domestically available and that the consumption and investment goods sectors correspond, in terms of their size, to the size of consumption and investment. We shall return to this numerical framework when discussing policies for increasing economic growth in the next lecture.

**Table 2.2    Macroeconomic growth in the Harrod-Domar model**

| Year | Nat. income and output | Allocation of income | | Investment | Capital stock | |
|------|------------------------|------|------|------------|-------|-------|
| | $Y$ | $C$ | $S$ | $I$ | $K_o$ | $K_1$ |
| 1 | 1000 | 800 | 200 | 200 | 4000 | 4200 |
| 2 | 1050 | 840 | 210 | 210 | 4200 | 4410 |
| 3 | 1102.5 | 882 | 220.5 | 220.5 | 4410 | 4631 |

One of the critical assumptions in the Harrod-Domar model is the one of sufficient availability of labour. This assumption allows us to focus entirely on the process of capital accumulation and to leave the labour market aside. The problem with this approach is that full employment of labour can be assured only if quite accidentally the growth rate of output and employment equals that of the labour force, which is an unlikely coincidence in the real world. If the labour force grows at a different rate than output and capital, on the other hand, two alternative outcomes are possible. Either unemployment will increase or labour will become so scarce that the growth rate warranted by s and v cannot be sustained.

It is clear that this problem stems from the assumption of a fixed capital coefficient (ICOR) which is linked to the assumption of unlimited availability of labour. In order to eliminate this problem, it is useful to replace the underlying fixed-coefficient production function by a more flexible one that contains both capital and labour inputs. Let us see then what form the growth model takes if we replace the fixed capital coefficient by a neoclassical production function permitting the substitution of capital for labour. The result is the well-known neoclassical growth model pioneered by Solow (1956).

### 2.4.2 The Neoclassical Growth Model

The main building block of this growth model is the neoclassical production function, which we can write here in its most general form:

$$(2.13) \quad Y = F(L, K)$$

where Y is gross national product (GNP) or national income, L and K are labour and capital inputs, and the time subscripts are omitted for simplicity. Assuming also constant returns to scale (CRTS), we can rewrite this function as an expression of labour productivity:

$$(2.14) \quad y = Y/L = f(k)$$

where y is labour productivity, f(k) equals F(K/L, 1) and K/L is the capital-labour ratio. This function is drawn in Figure 2.2, which shows the whole

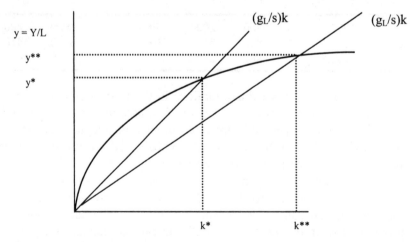

**Figure 2.2  The neoclassical growth model**

model and its quilibrium solution. The declining slope of the function follows from the CRTS assumption. If a proportional increase in factor inputs leads to the same proportional increase in output, then the labour productivity remains the same as long as the capital/output ratio remains constant. If, however, the K/L-ratio increases, then labour productivity must also increase, but at a declining rate because as more and more capital is combined with labour, its marginal contribution to output is getting smaller. Saving in this model is determined by the same simple function as in the Harrod-Domar model:

(2.15)  $S = s\,Y$.

The third component of this model is a function that determines the growth of labour using a simple exponential growth function:

(2.16)  $L = L_o\,e^{gt}$

where $L_o$ is the amount of labour in the base period and $L$ is its level at time t, and $g_L$ is the annual growth rate of labour. Finally, we assume macroeconomic equilibrium in this closed economy by writing:

(2.17)  $S = I$,

where I is for simplicity assumed to correspond to the net increase in capital stock:

(2.18)  $I = dK$.

In other words, there is no depreciation of capital stock and all investment increases the capital stock. In reality, this assumption is easily modified by introducing a depreciation term.

To determine the steady state equilibrium growth path, we ask the question whether there are levels of y and of k that remain constant while labour grows at the exogenous rate $g_L$, and capital grows through saving and investing in the stated manner. For K/L to remain constant it is necessary that $dk/k = 0$, or equivalently, that $dK/K - dL/L = 0$. Obviously, capital and labour must grow at the same rate. Replacing dK/K by sy/k, using equations 2.15, 2.17 and 2.18, y by f(k) and dL/L by $g_L$, we obtain:

(2.19)  $s\,y/k = s\,f(k)/k = g_L$.
or,      $f(k) = (g_L/s)\,k$

where $(g_L/s)$ k is shown as a straight line from the origin in diagram 2.1, since $g_L/s$ is assumed to be constant. The intersection of this line with the labour productivity function $f(k)$ shows the equilibrium levels of Y/L and K/L, $y^*$ and $k^*$, which remain constant while the economy grows at the rate g determined by the growth of labour. The equilibrium capital/output ratio, $v^*$, can be obtained as $k^*/y^*$. In comparison with the Harrod-Domar model we can write the equilibrium growth rate also as:

$$(2.20) \quad g_Y = g_L = s/v^*$$

which shows the similarities and differences between the two models. While Harrod-Domar growth is strictly capital-determined growth, neoclassical growth is labour-determined, to which capital growth adjusts. This conclusion is important for policy purposes. It implies that in an economy with capital-labour substitution, governments cannot accelerate indefinitely the growth of labour productivity and per capita income by raising the savings rate. If saving can be increased, this will simply lead to a higher equilibrium level of k and y, and output and factor growth will then continue to grow at the same pace. This is a somewhat surprising result, since our understanding of the Harrod-Domar model leads us to expect that a higher savings ratio may imply a higher growth rate. But in the neoclassical model one must remember that increased saving leads to higher capital intensity (k) and labour productivity (y) with k increasing more than y, so that the ICOR (v) also increases. This is shown in Figure 2.1 by the new equilibrium $k^*$ and $y^*$ for an increased savings ratio (s').

### 2.4.3    Comparisons between the HD and Neoclassical Models

In order to see how neoclassical growth works and how many years it takes to reach the steady-state equilibrium path, it is useful to set up a table similar to Table 2.2. This is done in Table 2.3, where the increases in capital, labour and national income are generated by using the assumptions underlying the model and where the model is simulated for a large number of years until the variables y and k have nearly attained their steady-state equilibrium values.

The base-year (t = 0) values of K, L and Y are arbitrarily chosen such that they obey the Cobb-Douglas function $Y=0.25*L^{\alpha}K^{(1-\alpha)}$, with constant returns to scale (CRTS). The values of the following years are generated by letting labour grow at its exogenously determined rate of 3 percent and by transforming domestic savings, which are assumed to equal 30 percent of Y, into investments and additional capital stock. The GDP (Y) can then be computed according to the production function, and its growth rate is shown in the last column. As the reader can see in Table 2.3, capital grows at 7.5 percent in the first year, but this rate declines over time since it is not matched by equal growth of labour. All growth rates converge towards 3 percent, the growth rate of labour, and k and y converge towards their steady-state equilibrium values of 6.25 and 0.625, respectively. These equilibrium values of k and y can be obtained by solving the system of two equations, $y=0.25 \, k^{1/2}$ and $y=0.03k/0.3$.

**Table 2.3    Convergence towards steady-state growth in the neoclassical model**

| t | K | L | Y | I=S =dK | k=K/L | y=Y/L | dK/K | dY/Y |
|---|---|---|---|---|---|---|---|---|
| 0 | 4000 | 4000 | 1000 | 300 | 1 | 0.25 | - | - |
| 1 | 4300 | 4120 | 1052.3 | 315.7 | 1.044 | 0.255 | 0.075 | 0.052 |
| 2 | 4615.7 | 4243.6 | 1106.4 | 331.9 | 1.088 | 0.261 | 0.073 | 0.051 |
| 3 | 4947.6 | 4370.9 | 1162.6 | 348.8 | 1.132 | 0.266 | 0.072 | 0.051 |
| ~ | | | | | | | | |
| 300 | $164.7 \, 10^6$ | $26.7 \, 10^6$ | $17.1 \, 10^6$ | $5.1 \, 10^6$ | 6.156 | 0.620 | 0.030 | 0.030 |

It is important to see that the growth process generated in this manner converges towards the steady-state equilibrium growth path, which is not the case in the Harrod-Domar model. The attainment of such an equilibrium growth path through convergence is due to the substitution of capital for labour introduced with the neoclassical production function. It is also important to see that this convergence process takes a lot of time, more than 300 years in our numerical example. This makes it evident that real-world economies are always in the adjustment process and are unlikely to follow a steady-state growth path. For the purpose of prediction, it is therefore more appropriate to simulate the path of adjustment towards steady-state equilibrium than to assume growth according to the equilibrium path. This conclusion emphasizes the importance of the production function as a forecasting device.

## 2.5    Neoclassical Growth and the Stylized Facts of Economic Growth

One problem with neoclassical equilibrium growth, just as with Harrod-Domar growth, is that it contradicts the well-known fact that, over time, both capital and output tend to grow faster than labour. This is known as a stylized fact of growth. To allow for this observation, we must introduce technical change into the neoclassical model. One way of doing this is to redefine labour as effective labour (E) which equals the quantity of labour times an exponential coefficient of technical change:

$$(2.21) \quad E = L \, e^{\tau t} = L_0 \, e^{(g_L + \tau) t}$$

where $g_L$ is the growth of labour and $\tau$ is the rate of technical change. If technical change of this kind occurs, capital and output can grow at the rate of $(g_L + \tau)$, while labour productivity and the capital/labour ratio grow at the rate $\tau$. The nature of this kind of technical progress is therefore labour-saving. This modification reconciles the neoclassical growth model with the stylized facts of macroeconomic growth. However, even without technical change, that is, TPF growth equal to zero, it would be wrong to conclude that increased saving has no effect on economic growth. To be sure, the equilibrium growth rate does not increase, but the adjustment from low to higher K/L ratios and labour productivity is also economic growth and accounts for most of the rise in living standards.

In retrospect, we conclude that the neoclassical growth model helps us to visualize a growth process that does not focus on capital accumulation only, but that also considers the growth of the labour force. By permitting the substitution of capital for labour, it introduces an important stylized fact of longer-run economic growth.

## 2.6     Endogenous Growth

One of the shortcomings of neoclassical growth models is the fact that they assume technical change to be determined exogenously. Since technical change plays a crucial role in raising productivity and per capita income, and since it depends in turn on economic conditions, it is important to let it be determined by the model. This purpose is the essence of various endogenous growth models and approaches, two of which are briefly described here.

An endogenous growth model that stresses the importance and growth of human capital was formalized by Lucas (1988), using earlier work by Uzawa. The Lucas-model uses the production function $Y = AK^\alpha (uhL)^{1-\alpha}$, where 'h' represents the amount of human capital per worker and 'u' is the share of human capital that is devoted to production. The share '1-u' is used for the accumulation of human capital (e.g. education, training, etc.). There is thus a trade-off between devoting human capital for current production and devoting it to the accumulation of human capital, which allows higher future production. In the long run, the more people are willing to postpone current production (and consumption), the higher economic growth will be.

In the neoclassical growth model, long run growth of per capita income is determined by the growth of technology. Romer (1990) tries to explain this technological growth with a three-sector model, where patents play an essential role. In the Romer-model, new technologies are developed in the research sector, which sells patents of these technologies to the intermediate goods sector. The intermediate goods sector produces machinery and sells them to the final goods sector. As in the Solow model, long run economic growth is determined by the growth of technology. The fact that patents give their owners monopoly power, is the major incentive for the development of new technology and economic growth. The Romer model stresses the importance of property rights, but its implications mainly apply to developed countries, as they are the ones who actually develop new technologies. Rather than create new technologies, developing countries adopt existing technologies. Following neoclassical growth, long run economic growth would then be determined by the rate of technology adoption. Economic growth of developing countries can be seen as determined by barriers to technology adoption and the share of skilled labour that is allocated to technology adoption.

## 2.7    Convergence Once Again

In the first chapter we examined the gap in per capita income between the poor and the rich countries and asked the question of whether this gap is likely to narrow down for most countries. This process of a narrowing gap may be referred to as international convergence of income levels. Clearly, it is a major goal of development policies at the international level. The concept of convergence can also apply to a single country, where convergence of income levels between rich and poor individuals or groups, or between rich and poor regions, is an improvement of the income distribution.

In addition to the international convergence of income levels, we have also encountered, in the present chapter, the internal convergence of growth models towards their steady-state equilibrium paths. The neo-classical growth model a la Solow taught us that, unlike the Harrod-Domar growth process, an increase of the propensity to save does not lead to a higher growth rate, but only to a level effect in form of higher levels of labour productivity, per capita income and the capital-labour ratio. We saw that in this model the steady-state growth rate is determined by the growth rate of labour, which is assumed to be exogenous. Capital growth may differ from the growth rate of labour, but it slowly adjusts until it equals that of labour. This process is called model convergence and it differs from the previously discussed concept of international convergence in that it follows a predictable pattern. Assuming that the population growth rate and savings rate remain constant, the growth rate of capital adjusts in a way that is unambiguously determined. The process of convergence is extremely long, however, so that one may conclude that in real-world growth, countries will never reach steady-state equilibrium, but constantly converge towards steady-state equilibria, which, in turn, change due to changes in the parameter values of saving and population growth. A simple exercise in simulation of the Solow model shows that it takes always more than 100 years to converge from the initial conditions towards steady-state equilibrium.[1] In any realistic long-term planning model with a time horizon of 25 or 30 years, one would always be in the state of convergence rather than steady-state equilibrium, even if the main parameters are kept constant. Most likely, however, parameter values would also change, so that the converging economy would see its convergence target change as well.

What the foregoing discussion suggests is that international convergence of growth towards similar levels of income can hardly be predicted by reference to the process of model convergence, because the necessary assumptions of equal savings and population growth rates, as well as their stability over longer periods of time, are unrealistic. Some authors have described the international convergence as an application of model convergence, referring to it as unconditional convergence, as opposed to conditional convergence, which is the single-economy convergence towards its steady-state equilibrium growth rate (cf. Ray, 1998). The historical evidence of international (or unconditional) convergence has been examined in various studies, which have led to different conclusions concerning the state of income differentials.

The study of Baumol (1986) used data of 16 countries from Maddison (1991) and concluded in favour of international convergence. The 16 countries (Australia, Austria, Belgium, Canada, Denmark, Finland, France, Germany, Italy, Japan, the Netherlands, Norway, Sweden, Switzerland, the U.K. and the U.S.A.) had all reached similar income levels

---

[1]  The reader may want to simulate the simple Solow model with parameter values and initial conditions as follows: $y=\frac{1}{4}(k)^{1/2}$, $g_L=0.03$, $s=0.10$, $K_o=4000$, $L_o=4000$, and no technical change for simplicity. In this case the initial growth rate of capital is 2.5 percent. Its adjustment to approximately 3 percent (2.9 percent) would take 120 years.

by 1979, while their 1870 income levels were quite different. Obviously, the selection of this sample is biased in favour of the convergence hypothesis. The selection bias leads to a strong negative correlation between income levels and growth rates. In other words, the poorer countries of the sample grew faster than richer countries.

A much larger data set (of 102 countries in the period between 1960 and 1985) was used in the study by Parente and Prescott (1993), who measured the relative income of each country, relative to U.S. income. They computed the standard deviation of income levels over time and found that it increased by nearly 20 percent during the study period. The conclusion of this study is that an unbiased sample does not exhibit a negative correlation between income levels and growth rates, implying that international convergence is not supported by empirical evidence.

## References

Baumol, W.J. (1986), 'Productivity Growth, Convergence, and Welfare: What the Long-run Data Show', *American Economic Review*, 76, 1072-1082.

Chenery, H. (1986), 'Growth and Transformation', H. Chenery et al. (eds.), *Industrialization and Growth*, Oxford University Press, 13-36.

Domar, E.D. (1946), 'Capital Expansion, Rate of Growth, and Employment', *Econometrica*, vol.14, April, 137-147.

Harrod, R.F. (1948), *Towards a Dynamic Economics*, Macmillan.

Hicks, J.R. (1963), *The Theory of Wages*, Second Edition, Macmillan.

Leontief, W.W. (1951), *The Structure of the American Economy 1919-1939*, Oxford University Press.

Lucas, R.E. (1988), 'On the Mechanics of Economic Development', *Journal of Monetary Economics*, 22, 3-43.

Maddison, A. (1991), *Dynamic Forces in Capitalist Development: A Long-Run Comparative View*, Oxford, New York: Oxford University Press.

Parente, S.L. and E.C. Prescott (1993), 'Changes in the Wealth of Nations', *Federal Reserve Bank of Minneapolis Quarterly Review*, 17, 3-16.

Ray, D. (1998), *Development Economics,* Princeton University Press.

Romer, P. (1990), 'Endogenous Technical Change', *Journal of Political Economy*, 98, S71-101.

Siggel, E. (1991), 'Recent Industrial Growth and Development in Kenya: Constraints and Prospects for the Future', P. Das Gupta (ed.), *Issues in Contemporary Economics*, Macmillan and the International Economics Association, vol.3, 291-311.

Solow, R.M. (1955-56), 'The Production Function and the Theory of Capital', *Review of Economic Studies*, XXIII, 15, 101-108.

Solow, R.M. (1960), 'Investment and Technical Progress', K.J. Arrow et al. (eds.), *Mathematical Methods in the Social Sciences*, Stanford University Press, 89-104.

Solow, R.M. (1962), 'Technical Progress, Capital Formation and Economic Growth', *American Economic Review*, Papers and Proceedings, LII,2, 76-86.

# Case Study 4
# International Convergence of Income Levels

As we have seen earlier, some empirical evidence of international convergence of incomes per capita exists. It is unclear, however, whether this evidence is sufficiently unbiased to support the claim that there is a tendency for average incomes to converge internationally. In the present case study we shall re-examine this question, using two data sets of GDP per capita between 1950 and 1992 of ten countries in each set. The first set refers to ten developed countries including Australia, Austria, Belgium, Canada, France, the Netherlands, Switzerland, Sweden, the U.K. and the U.S.A. The second set consists of mainly developing countries and includes Bolivia, Chile, India, Japan, Kenya, Pakistan, Philippines, Thailand and Uganda.

The theoretical basis of the convergence hypothesis rests on two observations: first, that per capita income rises with the accumulation of capital, both human and physical. Second, as capital accumulates it faces declining marginal returns, implying diminishing incentives for capital owners to continue to accumulate. In other words, capital accumulation tends to slow down. Therefore poor countries should grow faster than rich countries, until in the long run all countries reach the same level and growth rate of income. This process is called convergence. In this case study we examine whether there is any empirical evidence of convergence.

For further reading on the subject refer to 'Changes in the wealth of Nations' by Parente and Prescott, Federal Reserve Bank of Minneapolis Quarterly Review, 17(2), 1993 and Stanley Fischer, 'Globalization and its Challenges', American Economic Review, Papers and Proceedings, Richard T. Ely Lecture, May 2003, vol.93, No. 2.

**Assigned Questions**

1)   Take the natural logarithm (ln) of the data of both sets of countries and plot them in two diagrams featuring the years on the horizontal axis and ln(GDP per capita) on the vertical axis. What is the effect of taking ln on the time paths of income and what happens to the absolute and relative gap between income levels?

2)   Determine the range (max – min) of ln (GDP per capita) in both sets of countries and examine whether the range narrows or widens. What do you conclude about convergence?

3)   Compute the average annual growth rate (continuous) of GDP per capita (in terms of percent, rounded to one decimal) in all 20 countries and interpret its meaning in the diagrams. What would be a sufficient condition with regard to growth rates of a group of countries to converge in terms of per capita income? Distinguish the case of two countries from the case of a group of several or many countries.

4)   Compute the standard deviation of the distribution of income levels in each set of countries for the whole time period. Is the standard deviation a useful measure to describe convergence or divergence of income levels of a group of countries?

5)   Which countries in the two groups have experienced convergence of their income levels? Base your answer on the measure that you have concluded to be most meaningful.

6)   What is the main argument of Stanley Fischer with respect to convergence and globalization?

**Table CS4a    Real GDP per capita in a sample of high-income countries**

| Year | Australia | Austria | Belgium | Canada | France | Netherlands | Switzerland | Sweden | UK | USA |
|---|---|---|---|---|---|---|---|---|---|---|
| 1952 | 1563 | 745 | 1147 | 1638 | 1058 | 1067 | 1685 | 1489 | 1300 | 2230 |
| 1953 | 1715 | 773 | 1156 | 1664 | 1093 | 1157 | 1751 | 1517 | 1382 | 2310 |
| 1954 | 1811 | 848 | 1203 | 1597 | 1143 | 1251 | 1858 | 1622 | 1439 | 2271 |
| 1955 | 1840 | 958 | 1276 | 1706 | 1202 | 1336 | 1958 | 1683 | 1497 | 2443 |
| 1956 | 1889 | 1029 | 1362 | 1868 | 1313 | 1448 | 2117 | 1786 | 1571 | 2528 |
| 1957 | 1934 | 1131 | 1430 | 1910 | 1416 | 1517 | 2233 | 1899 | 1658 | 2614 |
| 1958 | 2061 | 1209 | 1442 | 1925 | 1481 | 1490 | 2190 | 1974 | 1708 | 2608 |
| 1959 | 2195 | 1264 | 1479 | 1979 | 1541 | 1581 | 2375 | 2094 | 1794 | 2772 |
| 1960 | 2241 | 1462 | 1590 | 2004 | 1669 | 1748 | 2598 | 2212 | 1901 | 2838 |
| 1961 | 2209 | 1552 | 1671 | 2027 | 1760 | 1805 | 2808 | 2339 | 1971 | 2884 |
| 1962 | 2366 | 1599 | 1778 | 2161 | 1877 | 1892 | 2930 | 2454 | 2013 | 3059 |
| 1963 | 2545 | 1677 | 1845 | 2266 | 1976 | 1972 | 3043 | 2592 | 2105 | 3179 |
| 1964 | 2708 | 1791 | 1990 | 2407 | 2129 | 2161 | 3207 | 2785 | 2235 | 3349 |
| 1965 | 2733 | 1871 | 2082 | 2560 | 2243 | 2289 | 3300 | 2912 | 2310 | 3581 |
| 1966 | 2923 | 2029 | 2205 | 2777 | 2428 | 2411 | 3459 | 3054 | 2439 | 3876 |
| 1967 | 3073 | 2141 | 2349 | 2916 | 2604 | 2601 | 3650 | 3228 | 2578 | 4051 |
| 1968 | 3461 | 2325 | 2541 | 3150 | 2820 | 2890 | 3904 | 3477 | 2778 | 4373 |
| 1969 | 3752 | 2538 | 2842 | 3412 | 3154 | 3182 | 4252 | 3800 | 2925 | 4667 |
| 1970 | 4065 | 2825 | 3213 | 3693 | 3515 | 3536 | 4719 | 4186 | 3184 | 4933 |
| 1971 | 4294 | 3094 | 3454 | 4039 | 3833 | 3803 | 5123 | 4393 | 3400 | 5289 |

| Year | | | | | | | | | | |
|---|---|---|---|---|---|---|---|---|---|---|
| 1972 | 4697 | 3434 | 3818 | 4442 | 4160 | 4114 | 5502 | 4703 | 3706 | 5755 |
| 1973 | 5158 | 3832 | 4317 | 5066 | 4645 | 4548 | 5910 | 5181 | 4123 | 6373 |
| 1974 | 5603 | 4339 | 4906 | 5858 | 5093 | 5112 | 6542 | 5729 | 4337 | 6830 |
| 1975 | 6229 | 4793 | 5245 | 6417 | 5565 | 5609 | 6871 | 6596 | 4824 | 7349 |
| 1976 | 6693 | 5275 | 5850 | 7199 | 6102 | 6197 | 7277 | 6981 | 5234 | 8120 |
| 1977 | 7005 | 5821 | 6268 | 7774 | 6675 | 6697 | 7856 | 7148 | 5736 | 8969 |
| 1978 | 7870 | 6322 | 6895 | 8573 | 7432 | 7311 | 8680 | 7765 | 6455 | 10015 |
| 1979 | 8730 | 7199 | 7654 | 9829 | 8325 | 8020 | 9434 | 8658 | 7266 | 11045 |
| 1980 | 9822 | 8092 | 8638 | 11108 | 9095 | 8837 | 10672 | 9661 | 7993 | 11889 |
| 1981 | 10798 | 8719 | 9107 | 12498 | 9880 | 9590 | 11944 | 10527 | 8604 | 13190 |
| 1982 | 11047 | 9461 | 9865 | 12524 | 10715 | 10098 | 12744 | 11186 | 9286 | 13558 |
| 1983 | 12111 | 10042 | 10232 | 13310 | 11114 | 10499 | 13306 | 11772 | 9979 | 14457 |
| 1984 | 12935 | 10499 | 10800 | 14501 | 11552 | 11088 | 13917 | 12739 | 10526 | 15879 |
| 1985 | 13583 | 11131 | 11285 | 15589 | 12206 | 11539 | 14864 | 13451 | 11237 | 16570 |
| 1986 | 13811 | 11680 | 12091 | 16305 | 13051 | 12402 | 16162 | 14392 | 11942 | 17511 |
| 1987 | 14987 | 12353 | 12923 | 17637 | 13776 | 12841 | 17221 | 15294 | 12935 | 18435 |
| 1988 | 16486 | 13344 | 14128 | 19153 | 14871 | 13668 | 18194 | 16243 | 14120 | 19706 |
| 1989 | 17315 | 14350 | 15304 | 20360 | 15880 | 14753 | 19322 | 17185 | 15069 | 20964 |
| 1990 | 17517 | 15560 | 16533 | 20752 | 16956 | 16096 | 20729 | 18024 | 15741 | 21827 |
| 1991 | 17914 | 16355 | 17378 | 20534 | 17647 | 16896 | 21427 | 18418 | 15991 | 22204 |
| 1992 | 18500 | 16989 | 18091 | 20970 | 18232 | 17373 | 21631 | 18387 | 16302 | 23220 |

*Source*: Penn World Tables.

**Table CS4b  Real GDP per capita in a sample of low-income countries**

| Year | Bolivia | Chile | India | Japan | Kenya | Mexico | Pakistan | Philippines | Thailand | Uganda |
|------|---------|-------|-------|-------|-------|--------|----------|-------------|----------|--------|
| 1952 | 327 | 644 | 145 | 427 | 162 | 584 | 154 | 212 | 198 | 151 |
| 1953 | 275 | 687 | 152 | 456 | 156 | 559 | 157 | 237 | 184 | 138 |
| 1954 | 280 | 659 | 159 | 481 | 174 | 605 | 158 | 250 | 196 | 137 |
| 1955 | 283 | 677 | 162 | 519 | 186 | 637 | 151 | 260 | 181 | 141 |
| 1956 | 290 | 689 | 171 | 573 | 188 | 676 | 162 | 277 | 190 | 148 |
| 1957 | 293 | 743 | 176 | 636 | 196 | 732 | 166 | 288 | 215 | 159 |
| 1958 | 301 | 771 | 190 | 684 | 191 | 758 | 164 | 300 | 224 | 152 |
| 1959 | 298 | 759 | 193 | 751 | 186 | 761 | 177 | 315 | 245 | 155 |
| 1960 | 316 | 837 | 211 | 860 | 205 | 798 | 191 | 327 | 274 | 159 |
| 1961 | 323 | 878 | 210 | 983 | 182 | 817 | 202 | 333 | 285 | 159 |
| 1962 | 350 | 917 | 217 | 1059 | 192 | 842 | 212 | 355 | 296 | 165 |
| 1963 | 364 | 944 | 236 | 1174 | 202 | 891 | 226 | 365 | 311 | 170 |
| 1964 | 377 | 975 | 248 | 1331 | 205 | 971 | 241 | 364 | 330 | 177 |
| 1965 | 412 | 1029 | 225 | 1399 | 205 | 1015 | 285 | 378 | 359 | 179 |
| 1966 | 443 | 1145 | 203 | 1584 | 231 | 1081 | 302 | 397 | 404 | 194 |
| 1967 | 462 | 1174 | 225 | 1805 | 243 | 1155 | 323 | 427 | 425 | 195 |
| 1968 | 520 | 1238 | 244 | 2109 | 259 | 1267 | 348 | 465 | 462 | 204 |
| 1969 | 544 | 1354 | 267 | 2427 | 275 | 1348 | 346 | 502 | 514 | 221 |
| 1970 | 619 | 1436 | 297 | 2835 | 250 | 1481 | 400 | 532 | 586 | 231 |
| 1971 | 660 | 1614 | 317 | 3071 | 327 | 1640 | 393 | 567 | 589 | 252 |

| 1972 | 691 | 1665 | 323 | 3448 | 375 | 1796 | 376 | 605 | 634 | 261 |
|------|-----|------|-----|------|-----|------|-----|-----|-----|-----|
| 1973 | 778 | 1672 | 342 | 3890 | 376 | 1983 | 402 | 677 | 740 | 269 |
| 1974 | 908 | 1824 | 366 | 4118 | 432 | 2277 | 457 | 768 | 804 | 288 |
| 1975 | 955 | 1597 | 432 | 4567 | 458 | 2590 | 484 | 857 | 900 | 312 |
| 1976 | 1083 | 1701 | 456 | 5008 | 476 | 2773 | 526 | 936 | 1011 | 338 |
| 1977 | 1167 | 1942 | 516 | 5548 | 551 | 2904 | 582 | 1025 | 1149 | 361 |
| 1978 | 1252 | 2219 | 565 | 6278 | 608 | 3314 | 653 | 1136 | 1311 | 331 |
| 1979 | 1414 | 2648 | 583 | 6996 | 675 | 3925 | 744 | 1298 | 1522 | 323 |
| 1980 | 1570 | 3080 | 683 | 7809 | 716 | 4757 | 866 | 1448 | 1700 | 264 |
| 1981 | 1720 | 3479 | 769 | 8830 | 743 | 5562 | 925 | 1572 | 1878 | 529 |
| 1982 | 1697 | 3146 | 843 | 9582 | 779 | 5442 | 1007 | 1716 | 1980 | 507 |
| 1983 | 1708 | 3039 | 923 | 10107 | 782 | 5065 | 1086 | 1723 | 2242 | 546 |
| 1984 | 1721 | 3270 | 974 | 10840 | 814 | 5349 | 1163 | 1581 | 2377 | 560 |
| 1985 | 1754 | 3467 | 1050 | 11771 | 794 | 5621 | 1262 | 1542 | 2463 | 540 |
| 1986 | 1688 | 3654 | 1121 | 12663 | 886 | 5306 | 1310 | 1568 | 2586 | 516 |
| 1987 | 1728 | 4053 | 1190 | 13645 | 935 | 5484 | 1390 | 1706 | 2878 | 526 |
| 1988 | 1774 | 4519 | 1322 | 15028 | 995 | 5769 | 1502 | 1861 | 3279 | 558 |
| 1989 | 1832 | 5134 | 1406 | 16213 | 1043 | 6281 | 1591 | 1993 | 3720 | 601 |
| 1990 | 1890 | 5279 | 1505 | 17625 | 1080 | 6896 | 1661 | 2112 | 4270 | 625 |
| 1991 | 2007 | 5675 | 1552 | 19173 | 1125 | 7405 | 1728 | 2128 | 4659 | 665 |
| 1992 | 2066 | 6326 | 1633 | 19920 | 1176 | 7867 | 1793 | 2172 | 5018 | 654 |

*Source:* Penn World Tables.

# Case Study 5
# Sources of Growth in Kenya's Manufacturing Sector

## Purpose

This case study analyzes the sources of manufacturing growth from the supply side, as opposed to the demand side. Using a simple neoclassical production function, it examines the relative importance of the change in factor inputs, capital and labour, as well as of total factor productivity (TFP), in the growth of value added in Kenyan manufacturing between 1972 and 1991. Unfortunately, more recent data are not available for the capital stock. Capital stock data are always difficult to come by, but they were generated for Kenya through the Long-range Planning Project in the early 1990s. Even for this period from 1972 to 1991, the relative importance of the sources of growth is a question of considerable interest because the sources of growth have different implications for the development of an economy. While strong growth of labour input helps in the reduction of unemployment, capital expansion usually augurs modernization, but it can also lead to unused capacity. Productivity increase, on the other hand suggests that the existing capacity is being used more efficiently and/or that factors are being made more productive. The analysis, therefore tells us more about the nature of the observed growth. For policy purposes it is also important to know the relative importance of the past sources of growth, because the encouragement of growth may require quite different policy instruments, depending on which of the potential sources needs to be stimulated most. For instance, the presence of excess capacity after a period of low TFP and high capital growth may indicate that factor reallocation and efficiency growth should have priority over pure investment incentives.

## Background: Kenya's Manufacturing Sector

In spite of relative political stability and favourable economic growth in Kenya since its independence in 1962, annual income per person is still (in 2001) low at approximately $350, or $1,020 in terms of PPP), putting Kenya into the category of the poorer developing countries. Several reasons can be found for this state of affairs, in particular high population growth, limited natural resources (less than 20 percent of the territory is arable land) and a structure of the economy that makes the country strongly dependent on natural resources (agriculture and tourism). Only about 13 percent of Kenya's total GDP is produced by the manufacturing sector.

In the 1970s real annual growth in manufacturing was nearly 10 percent, but in the 1980s the average rate declined to around 4.5 percent. The sector has grown more rapidly than any other, increasing its share of GDP from 8 percent in 1964 to 13 percent in 1985. Given the land and water constraints on agriculture, urban and industrial growth seem to be of great importance for Kenya's future development. The urban labour force has increased rapidly, driven by population growth estimated as between 3.7 and 4.0 percent in the 1970s, and by rural-urban migration. As for capital, its growth has been relatively rapid, with a non-negligible share of foreign investment, but there has been evidence of excess capacity in many manufacturing firms. The importance of manufactured exports has declined dramatically, especially after the break-up of the East African Community in 1977. In 1967 exports accounted for 31 percent of manufactured output, in 1973 for 23 percent, and in 1985 for only 8 percent.

**Method of Analysis**

The case study of the sources of growth proceeds in two stages, first the computation of the relative shares of capital, labour and technical change in value-added growth, using a neoclassical production function in the procedure known as growth accounting. Second, the econometric estimation of parameter values of this production function. It is expected that the second stage of the procedure throws some doubts on the validity of the assumptions underlying the first stage of analysis.

*Growth accounting*

In the first stage, two of the three growth components are computed, based on the observed rates of growth of factor input, and the third component, change in total factor productivity (TFP), also referred to as technical change, is obtained as a residual. In this method we assume the existence of a general neoclassical production function with three arguments, labour, capital and time.

(1)     $VA = F(K,L,t)$

The sources of growth equation can be derived by differentiating and rearranging the production function with respect to time:

$$(2) \qquad GVA = GTFP + a \ GL + b \ GK$$

where   GTFP  = annual growth rate of total factor productivity
           GVA  = annual growth rate of value added
           GL     = annual growth rate of labour
           GK     = annual growth rate of capital
           a        = labour's share of value added
           b        = capital's share of value added

When the growth rates for value added, labour and capital, as well as the income shares of labour and capital are known, TFP growth can be calculated as a residual:

$$(2a) \qquad GTFP = GVA - a \ GL - b \ GK$$

To calculate growth rates we can use the continuous (compound) growth rate formula or, alternatively, the discrete rate assuming yearly compounding. The former of these rates will be used here:

$$(3) \qquad GVA = 1/t \ \ln (VA_t/VA_o)$$

where   t       = time
           $VA_t$   = value added at time t
           $VA_o$   = value added at time t=0

Labour and capital growth rates (GL and GK) can be calculated using the corresponding formulae, based on data for labour and capital inputs. Labour and capital shares are calculated assuming perfect competition (MPL = wage and MPK = rent). It is also assumed that the factor shares are constant over time.
      To compute the labour share, we divide the total wage bill by value added.

$$(4) \qquad (w \ L) / VA = a$$

Since under constant returns to scale, which are also assumed here, the labour and capital share sum to one (a + b = 1), we can obtain the capital share by subtracting the labour share from 1. Given the labour and capital shares for each year, their period average are then computed and taken as representative for the whole study period.

The computation of equation (2a) leads then to the growth rate of TFP, which, together with the factor growth components, represent the sources of growth of value added. We can express them as a percentage of total growth of value added. For example the proportional contribution of GTFP is calculated by dividing GTFP by GVA. The proportional contributions of labour and capital to value added growth are calculated in the same manner. The growth components of value added sum up to 100 percent.

*Parameter estimation*

In the second stage of analysis the parameter values of the production function are tested against the available data. Here it is useful to adopt a functional form, for instance, the Cobb-Douglas form:

(5) $\quad VA = A\,L^{\alpha}\,K^{\beta}\,e^{gt}$

This function is then estimated in its linear logarithmic form, taking first the natural logarithm of both sides:

(5a) $\quad \ln VA = \ln A + \alpha \ln L + \beta \ln K + g\,t$

It must be remembered that the parameters of this production function, $\alpha$, $\beta$ and $g$ correspond to those in the growth accounting approach, but $\alpha$ and $\beta$ play a different role than a and b in growth accounting. Since we are not making assumptions about perfect competition and returns to scale, $\alpha$ and $\beta$ are not factor shares, but elasticities of output (VA) with respect to capital and labour. The parameter $g$ is, as in growth accounting, the annual average growth rate of TFP, since t is an index of time in terms of years.

**Assigned Questions**

*Stage 1: Growth accounting*

i)      Compute the average annual growth rates of value added, capital and labour, for three periods. The first period is the whole period, from 1973 to 1990, the second one is the sub-period from 1973 to 1981, and the last one is the sub-period from 1981 to 1990. In order to avoid the influence of outlying values as starting or end points, use the 1972/1973/1974 average for the starting year (1973), the

1980/1981/1982 average for the middle year (1981) and the 1989/1990/1991 average for the end year (1990).

ii)      Compute the average values of the factor shares (a and b) for the three periods. Are they constant, as assumed by the production function?

iii)    Compute the average annual growth rate of total factor productivity in percent in the three periods, using the growth accounting equation. Also express them as a percentage of value-added growth.

iv)     Compare your results with the expected ones based on the work by Chenery, as shown in Table 2.1.

*Stage 2: Econometric analysis of the production function*

v)      Estimate the TFP growth rate for the period 1972 to 1991 by regressing the Cobb-Douglas production function.

vi)     Interpret the values for the three coefficients ($\alpha$, $\beta$ and $g_t$) and compare them with the three corresponding coefficients (a, b and $g_t$) calculated in Stage 1. How significant is the econometric result?

vii)   Test the existence of constant returns to scale.

viii)  In which of the two methods do you place more confidence?

## Table CS5   Manufacturing production in Kenya

| Year | VA | Labour | Capital | Labour Earnings |
|------|--------|--------|---------|-----------------|
| 1972 | 165.68 | 84.80  | 603.00  | 32.20  |
| 1973 | 189.51 | 94.50  | 701.00  | 38.70  |
| 1974 | 200.68 | 101.30 | 797.00  | 44.30  |
| 1975 | 208.71 | 100.70 | 845.00  | 50.20  |
| 1976 | 237.91 | 108.80 | 889.00  | 57.70  |
| 1977 | 275.89 | 117.90 | 942.00  | 69.20  |
| 1978 | 310.51 | 130.10 | 1017.00 | 80.20  |
| 1979 | 333.97 | 138.40 | 1110.00 | 90.10  |
| 1980 | 351.47 | 141.30 | 1187.00 | 106.20 |
| 1981 | 364.13 | 146.30 | 1233.00 | 122.20 |
| 1982 | 372.32 | 146.80 | 1276.00 | 136.10 |
| 1983 | 389.07 | 148.80 | 1274.00 | 149.40 |
| 1984 | 405.84 | 153.10 | 1287.00 | 168.70 |
| 1985 | 424.07 | 159.50 | 1285.00 | 188.20 |
| 1986 | 448.67 | 163.90 | 1283.00 | 205.50 |
| 1987 | 474.34 | 169.20 | 1300.00 | 233.60 |
| 1988 | 502.80 | 174.10 | 1322.00 | 252.30 |
| 1989 | 532.47 | 182.80 | 1365.00 | 306.80 |
| 1990 | 560.34 | 187.70 | 1404.00 | 345.10 |
| 1991 | 581.63 | 188.90 | 1461.00 | 376.00 |

*Note*:   Value added (VA), capital stock and labour earnings are all in million 1982 constant Kenyan pounds (K£). Labour is expressed in thousands of worker years.

*Source*:   Historical Economic Data for Kenya, 1972-1992, Ministry of Planning and National Development, Technical Paper 94-01.

**Case Study 5: Solution**

*Stage 1: Growth accounting*

i)      Average annual growth rates in percent:

|                        | 1973-1981 | 1981-1990 | 1973-1990 |
|------------------------|-----------|-----------|-----------|
| growth of value added  | 8.4       | 4.8       | 6.5       |
| growth of labour       | 5.5       | 2.8       | 4.1       |
| growth of capital      | 7.1       | 1.5       | 4.1       |

ii)     Average factor shares:

|                      | 1973-1981 | 1981-1990 | 1973-1990 |
|----------------------|-----------|-----------|-----------|
| Labour's share (a)   | 0.26      | 0.46      | 0.38      |
| Capital's share (b)  | 0.74      | 0.54      | 0.62      |

The numbers show that, contrary to the assumption of the growth accounting model, the factor shares are not constant. Labour's share has continuously increased and capital's share has declined.

iii)    Average annual growth rates of total factor productivity:

|                    | 1973-1981 | 1981-1990 | 1973-1990 |
|--------------------|-----------|-----------|-----------|
| in percent         | 1.8       | 2.7       | 2.4       |
| as proportion of   |           |           |           |
| value added growth | 0.21      | 0.56      | 0.37      |

iv)     While Chenery found that TFP growth in less developed economies typically accounted for 31percent, Kenya's performance in the 1970s was lower (21 percent), but higher in the 1980s (56 percent). This can be explained, at least partially, by the fact that Kenya experienced strong investment and employment growth in manufacturing in the 1970, even generating excess capacity. In the 1980s investment was sluggish and capacity utilization increased, so that the residual TFP growth also increased as a proportion of value added growth. The average for the whole period is in a similar order of magnitude (slightly higher) as Chenery's finding.

*Stage 2: Econometric estimation of the production function*

v)     In order to apply Ordinary Least Squares analysis, the Cobb Douglas production function is expressed in log linear form as:

ln VA = constant + a ln L + b ln K + $g_t$.

The parameter values are estimated as:

|  | coefficients | standard errors | t-statistics |
|---|---|---|---|
| Constant | -0.82 | 0.358 | -2.28 |
| Capital (β) | -0.03 | 0.095 | -0.28 |
| Labour (α) | 1.37 | 0.168 | 8.10 |
| TFP growth | 0.0098 | 0.0038 | 2.53    $R^2 = 0.998$ |

In order to make sure that this result is not based on spurious correlation, the equation is regressed in form of first differences, which yields very similar coefficients (α = 1.06 with t = 5.7 and $R^2$= 0.754). The original equation is maintained, however, so that it remains comparable to the growth accounting equation.

vi)    The message provided by the statistical analysis differs substantially from that of the growth accounting analysis. The labour coefficient, which is statistically significant and larger than one, suggests that the output (value added) is highly elastic with respect to labour. Value added is essentially driven by the employment of labour. Capital does not play a statistically significant role in explaining value added growth. This is not totally surprising, since investments can hardly be expected to be result in increased production during the same year. A lagged production function may provide better results.

       While the growth accounting exercise suggested TFP growth of 2.4 percent, the econometric estimate of TFP growth is only one percent (rounded), but mildly significant.

vii)   Since adding the values of α and β gives a value larger than one, the hypothesis of constant returns to scale is not supported by the data.

viii)  The production function used in the growth accounting method relies on very strong assumptions: Constant returns to scale, perfect competition and constant shares of labour and capital. Since these are not supported by the data, it would seem to be reasonable to have more trust in the econometric results, in spite of its weak significance of some coefficients, because this analysis is based on less restrictive assumptions.

# Chapter 3

# Financing Economic Growth from Domestic Sources

According to the traditional view point, economic growth depends to a large extent on capital accumulation. When productive capacity is generated by investing capital, it constitutes the essential ingredient for increased production and incomes. We see that other factors like labour, skills and technology are also important. Unskilled labour is usually available, but skills and technology must be acquired by education and training or, in the short run, by importing them, just like capital goods that are imported when they are not available locally. Indeed, highly skilled workers and managers are often hired from abroad by firms in developing countries, and technologies are purchased or otherwise transferred. This means that, to a large extent, the short-run problem of generating economic growth is equivalent to the problem of financing it. But even if a country can produce every input necessary for economic growth, it still needs to finance the required investments. The question is then how to increase the financial means available for investment and growth. We address this question in the present chapter by focusing on domestic sources of finance before we consider external sources in the next chapter. After a brief discussion of the determinants of growth in the short and medium run in section 3.1, we examine the possibilities of raising the propensity to save (in 3.2), the relationship between fiscal policy and saving (3.3), the role of financial intermediation (3.4), and the role of monetary policy and inflation (3.5).

## 3.1    Policies to Accelerate Economic Growth

At the outset let us examine how the rate of economic growth can be increased by way of government policy. The preceding discussion of growth models gives us a useful starting point to answer this question. The Harrod-Domar model of growth in a closed economy suggests that, focusing on capital accumulation and assuming away any constraints from labour, the growth rate can be predicted by dividing the investment or saving ratio by the incremental capital-output ratio (ICOR). This means that if we know the amount of capital that is available for investment in future periods, we can predict how much additional production and income it will generate.

The Harrod-Domar model, however, is based on assumptions that are unrealistic for the long run, as they exclude the possibility of capital-labour substitution. The neoclassical model, on the other hand, which permits capital-labour substitution, suggests that the rate of steady-state growth depends essentially on the growth rate of labour, which is exogenous in this model. An increased saving propensity translates into a one-time increase of the capital/labour ratio and labour productivity, while the growth rate of capital adjusts to that of labour. Technical change, however, can add to the growth of productivity and income per worker in a continuous fashion. It follows from these considerations that the HD-model may be useful to predict short-run growth, but that to predict longer-run growth it is necessary to introduce also the growth of labour and technical change. Growth-enhancing policies, therefore, must include policies that stimulate education and training, as well as the introduction of new technologies.

In the short-run perspective of the Harrod-Domar model, the second determinant of the growth rate is the ICOR, which informs us how much additional capital is needed to generate a unit of GDP. It must be lowered in order to accelerate growth. A decrease in ICOR can result from two kinds of policy. First, a lower ICOR can be obtained by improving the rate of utilization of the existing capital stock. Unused capacity is a problem in many developing countries. It may result from either cyclical changes in economic activity, such as weakness of demand in the down-swing of the cycle, or from factor price distortions, especially capital use subsidies. The cyclical problem is usually addressed by demand stimulation, but more permanent excess capacities can be reduced by changing the incentive structure. Incentives to invest in excess capacity are often policy-induced, for instance by industry-specific or general investment incentives.

Another way of lowering the ICOR is promoting the use of more labour-intensive production methods. This can be done by labour use subsidies or by eliminating capital use subsidies. Just as in the former case of capital use subsidies, such policies are problematic because the distortion of factor prices always induces a less than optimal allocation of resources. This shows that the encouragement of growth is not an easy matter, especially when it must avoid generating a bias in favour of capital intensity. In addition, the promotion of labour-intensive technologies often runs against the industries' need for more modern technologies to produce modern products of high quality. In the longer run economies are always becoming more capital-intensive with technical change. Therefore, policies focusing on lowering the ICOR may be counter-productive.

## 3.2    Increasing Savings

In his seminal paper on economic development and labour surplus Arthur Lewis claimed that 'the central problem in the theory of economic development is to understand the process by which a community which was previously saving and investing 4 or 5 percent of its national income converts itself into an economy where voluntary saving is running about 12 to 15 percent of the national income or more' (Lewis, 1954). For this purpose, governments may conduct fiscal policies stimulating voluntary savings, or they may impose constraints on the behaviour of economic agents that induce involuntary savings. Forced savings can be generated by inflationary finance discussed in section 3.5, or by direct controls of consumption. The latter strategy was followed by the Indian government in its second development plan. The idea was to strengthen the capacity of the investment goods sector, to the detriment of the consumption goods sector and thereby to raise the savings ratio. The growth model used in the second Indian plan was a two-sector model designed by Mahalanobis.[1]

In a simplified fashion, the process of raising the savings performance by way of shifting resources into the investment goods sector is demonstrated in Table 3.1, which uses the same parameter values as the demonstration of the Harrod-Domar model in Table 2.2. It differs from the earlier model in that it divides total production into consumption and investment goods. The two sectors are assumed to have the same ICOR of 4. We also assume that the capacities in both sectors are being fully used and that the economy is closed. The shares of both sectors in GDP, therefore, correspond to the proportions of consumption and investment in national income.

---

[1]    The numerical exposition of the idea underlying this model is drawn from UN-ECAFE (1960).

**Table 3.1     Macroeconomic growth in a two-sector economy**

| Year | Nat. income and output Y | Allocation of income C | S | Capacity of production C-goods | I-goods | Investment in C-goods | I-goods |
|------|------|------|------|------|------|------|------|
| 1 | 1000 | 800 | 200 | 800 | 200 | 160=4x40 | 40=4x10 |
| 2 | 1050 | 840 | 210 | 840 | 210 | 168=4x42 | 42=4x10.5 |
| 3 | 1102.5 | 882 | 220.5 | 882 | 220.5 | 176.4=4x44.1 | 44.1=4x11 |

Table 3.1 shows how total investment is allocated to the two sectors under balanced growth, that is, equal expansion of all sectors, at a rate of five per cent, compatible with a savings propensity of 20 percent and an ICOR of four. The last two columns show how much investment is needed in each sector in order to permit a capacity expansion of five percent: in the first year 40 additional units of consumption goods require 160 units of additional capital stock, and ten units of investment goods capacity require 40 units of investment in this sector. After two years of balanced growth at five per cent, GDP is at a level of 1102.5, consumption at 882 and investment at 220.5.

Now assume that the government restrains consumption by allowing the consumption goods sector to expand by only two percent for two years, in order to increase more strongly the investment goods sector capacity.

**Table 3.2     Economic growth in a two-sector economy with forced saving**

| Year | Nat.income and output Y | Allocation of income C | S | Capacity of production C-goods | I-goods | Investment in C-goods | I-goods |
|------|------|------|------|------|------|------|------|
| 1 | 1000 | 800 | 200 | 800 | 20 | 64=4x16 | 136 =4x34 |
| 2 | 1050 | 816 | 234 | 816 | 234 | 65.2=4x16.2 | 168.8=4x42.2 |
| 3 | 1108.5 | 832.3 | 276.2 | 832.3 | 276.2 | | |

This policy may be adopted not only to increase savings, but also to make increased investment possible, since investment goods cannot be imported in a closed economy. If more domestic saving was suddenly available, it could not be transformed into increased production capacity unless the investment goods sector expands. At the same time, we see in Table 3.2 that this policy results in 'forced saving', that is, the savings ratio increases from formerly 20 percent to nearly 25 percent in two years.

Table 3.2 demonstrates that, based on such a consumption restraint policy, savings, investment and the production of investment goods would expand by 17 percent (34/200) in the first year and by 18 percent (42.2/234) in the second. The GNP growth rate would rise from five percent in the first year to 5.6 percent in the second and 6.2 percent in the third year. If the economy was then allowed to return to balanced growth, it could continue to grow at a rate of 6.2 percent, since savings and investment have been forced up to a level of nearly 25 percent of GNP in the third year.

In reality, however, this policy would encounter several obstacles. First, it can work only if the government controls all investment decisions. This condition may have been partially fulfilled in India where the Government owned large parts of the industrial sector. Second, the reduction in the supply of consumer goods may lead to price changes in the economy that may prevent the desired outcome from occurring. Third, real economies are never completely closed and in open economies shortages of consumer goods would result in increased imports. Finally, the assumption of a constant ICOR while the economy is undergoing substantial structural changes is somewhat unrealistic. If the investment goods sector is more capital-intensive and has a higher ICOR than the consumption goods sector, the policy would lead to an increase in the total ICOR and thereby to a smaller gain in growth.

This simple two-sector model demonstrates clearly how important the sectoral allocation of investment is for growth, in order to keep demand and supply growing at the same rate. A simple increase in saving, without the capacity to transform it into investments, cannot lead to accelerated growth. The model also shows how potentially fragile the policy of forced saving is. It is possible that the restrained growth in consumption goods could lead to pent-up demand, so that the increased saving ratio could not be maintained in the future. Nevertheless, the policy may be useful in generating an increased capital-goods capacity, if the saving deficiency can be overcome by foreign saving, which we will examine in the next chapter.

Not only India, but also the Soviet Union used this model of starving the consumer goods sector from investments. In this way a larger part of investments could be used to build up its heavy industries and towards its investment-hungry militarization. This was only possible because in this planned economy the government had perfect control over the industrial sector. The price changes could be avoided as prices in this economy were simply set by the central planners. It is worth noting, however, that the predictable shortages of consumer goods resulted in waiting times and queues for consumer goods.


## 3.3      Fiscal Policy and Tax Reform

The discussion of the two-sector growth model of Feldman and Mahalanobis above has introduced the notion of involuntary or forced saving as opposed to voluntary saving. The reduction of consumption through restraint in the growth of the consumption goods sector capacity is only one form of forced saving. Another and more widely known form of forced saving is through inflation, which reduces real consumption. To this subject we come later when dealing with monetary policy and inflation. At this point we focus on voluntary savings and examine how fiscal policies can alter the saving performance of an economy.

We know from international statistics that the low-income developing countries typically save only about 15 percent of their GDP, while middle and upper-middle income developing countries tend to save 20 percent and more. There are, however, numerous exceptions from this tendency; within the group of low-income countries a notable exception is China, which has experienced extremely high saving ratios in recent years, in excess of 25 percent. This means that the group average savings ratio of low-income countries varies substantially, depending on whether China is or is not included. It is also noteworthy that some of the high-income countries, and the U.S. in particular, are among the lowest savers of all countries.

Total domestic saving is the sum of government saving and private saving, where each of them can be further broken down into at least two categories according to the savings agents: government budgetary and public enterprise savings and private household and private enterprise savings. Government saving is the difference between government revenue and current government expenditure. The word current is emphasized here to remind the reader that government saving is not to be confounded with a budget surplus, which is the difference between government revenue and total government expenditure, including investment expenditure. In analogy to total national saving and investment, the recurrent government expenditure corresponds to consumption, whereas government investments must be financed by savings and, if they exceed savings, by borrowing. State-owned enterprises contribute to government saving to the extent that they produce net earnings (after depreciation allowance) and that these are either re-invested or transferred to the treasury.

Private saving comes not only from households but also from corporations in the form of retained earnings. Clearly, fiscal policies have different effects on private saving and on government saving. Whether a tax cut increases total saving depends on the different spending propensities of households, corporations and the government. If a revenue-reducing tax cut is accompanied by a reduction in government's recurrent costs then total saving is likely to increase as households will save part of the increase in income. In the early economic literature a hypothesis has been proposed that consumers, in anticipation of a subsequent tax raise, would increase their saving. This is known as the Ricardian equivalence.[2] In order to see the particular problems of fiscal policy in developing countries we focus first on the government's main revenue source, taxation, and then add some remarks about expenditure.

The levels and sources of tax revenues are shown in Table 3.3 for a sample of low, middle and high-income countries. The first conclusion emerging from this table is that most developing countries collect only a small proportion of their revenues in the form of income taxes, and rely strongly on indirect taxes, especially trade taxes. In the low-income group of countries, trade taxes represent about 37 percent of all tax revenue, domestic commodity taxes about 32 percent, and income taxes only about 26 percent. The remainder is composed of social security and property taxes. In high-income countries, on the other hand, income taxes are the leading source of revenue (35 percent), followed by social security and property taxes (32 percent), domestic commodity taxes (29 percent), and only about two percent are derived from trade taxes. This difference in tax structure is important because trade and commodity taxes tend to be distorting and regressive, while direct taxes, income, property and social taxes tend to be non-distorting and progressive. Where distortions exist, prices in the economy do not reflect the true scarcities of goods and services and thereby lead to a non-optimal allocation of resources. An exhaustive survey of tax structures in developing countries is provided by Tanzi (1987).

---

[2]   A modern version of this argument has been proposed by Barro (1979).

**Table 3.3    Central government revenue in selected low, middle and high-income countries, 1993**

| | GNP p.c.[1] | Revenue[2] | Income tax[3] | Soc. sec[4] | G&S tax[5] | Int'l trade | Other taxes | Non-tax revenue |
|---|---|---|---|---|---|---|---|---|
| | | | | | Percentage of total current revenue | | | |
| **Low income** | | | | | | | | |
| Rwanda | 210 | 13.2 | 15.6 | 2.4 | 34.7 | 31.1 | 4.2 | 12.0 |
| Kenya | 270 | 22.5 | 29.6 | 0.0 | 47.5 | 10.6 | 1.1 | 11.2 |
| India | 300 | 14.4 | 18.7 | 0.0 | 32.1 | 24.9 | 0.4 | 23.9 |
| Nicaragua | 340 | 29.8 | 11.3 | 10.9 | 44.3 | 21.1 | 5.8 | 6.5 |
| Pakistan | 430 | 18.4 | 13.9 | 0.0 | 29.1 | 26.3 | 0.5 | 30.2 |
| Egypt | 660 | 38.7 | 22.0 | 9.8 | 14.2 | 10.9 | 9.5 | 33.6 |
| **Middle Income** | | | | | | | | |
| Indonesia | 740 | 19.4 | 49.3 | 0.0 | 26.4 | 5.2 | 3.2 | 15.9 |
| Peru | 1,490 | 10.8 | 18.3 | 0.0 | 52.3 | 11.0 | 4.6 | 13.8 |
| Botswana | 2,790 | 56.1 | 29.0 | 0.0 | 3.0 | 22.3 | 0.1 | 45.6 |
| Brazil | 2,930 | 26.6 | 16.5 | 28.6 | 17.6 | 1.7 | 5.5 | 30.0 |
| Malaysia | 3,140 | 28.7 | 34.5 | 0.8 | 22.0 | 13.8 | 3.5 | 25.4 |
| Gabon | 4,960 | 32.0 | 27.6 | 0.8 | 23.7 | 17.4 | 1.2 | 29.3 |
| **High Income** | | | | | | | | |
| New Zealand | 12,600 | 34.2 | 59.1 | 0.0 | 27.6 | 2.2 | 2.3 | 8.9 |
| Singapore | 19,850 | 26.6 | 30.0 | 0.0 | 16.7 | 2.0 | 15.1 | 36.1 |
| Canada | 19,970 | 22.1 | 52.7 | 16.7 | 17.7 | 2.9 | 0.0 | 10.0 |
| Netherlands | 20,950 | 50.7 | 30.7 | 36.8 | 21.0 | 0.0 | 3.2 | 8.3 |
| France | 22,490 | 40.7 | 17.3 | 44.5 | 27.0 | 0.0 | 4.1 | 7.1 |
| USA | 24,740 | 19.7 | 50.7 | 34.2 | 3.8 | 1.6 | 1.0 | 8.7 |

(1) G.N.P. per capita in 1993 U.S. dollars.
(2) Total current revenue as a percentage of GNP.
(3) Income, profit, capital gains taxes.
(4) Social security taxes.
(5) Goods and services taxes.
*Source*: World Development Report 1995, Tables 1 and 11.

To increase tax revenue and to make tax regimes more efficient and equitable, governments implement tax reforms. One of the major goals of tax reform is to reduce the importance of trade taxes and to generate more tax revenue from direct sources. The need for this kind of tax reform is particularly obvious under a world-wide tendency of trade liberalization. Whether it occurs multilaterally or within trading block, a move to freer trade will reduce tax revenue. Therefore, even to maintain present revenue levels it is necessary to shift the revenue bases away form external trade towards other revenue sources.

A similar initiative is the replacement of commodity taxes by value-added taxes. Since the rate of household saving in developing countries is typically very low, however, income taxation threatens what little household saving there is, even if it is progressive, that is, the marginal rate rises with income. Yet, excluding or inadequately taxing high-income households means ignoring a major source of transferable surplus. According to Musgrave (1987) the ideal solution would be a progressive expenditure tax; however, severe limits exist to its feasibility. A consumption tax, while being neutral with respect to the resource allocation in production is more favorable to saving and economic growth than the income tax.

Besides shifting taxation towards different revenue sources, the goals of tax reform also include the principles of greater uniformity, neutrality, efficiency and equity. The uniformity of rates is generally thought to enhance neutrality, which means the absence of bias against some or in favour of other activities, as it tends to prevent major distortions. It may, however, clash with the principle of efficiency as uniform rates have a different welfare effect on consumers and producers, depending on the elasticities of demand and supply. The higher these elasticities are the greater is the distorting effect on the resource allocation; therefore lower rates are required by high elasticities. Much emphasis of tax policy and tax reform must be placed on greater efficiency of tax collection. It is well known that tax revenues are often vastly inferior to the taxable capacity of the countries concerned, where the taxable capacity essentially depends on the availability of exportable commodities, especially mineral and oil resources. Rather than introducing new taxes or raising the tax rates, which tends to increase tax evasion (illegal) or avoidance (legal), governments can usually improve significantly their tax collection effort.

The revenue goal is generally recognized as a prime concern in tax reform. It is difficult, however, to conclude in a general way whether efforts to increase tax revenue will result in higher or lower aggregate saving since it will depend on the precise nature of the policy reform. The propensities of current saving and consumption, both on behalf of the government and the taxpayers, will determine whether increased tax revenue will enhance or decrease total saving. Empirical evidence exists of countries that have suffered declines in savings in spite of increased tax rates, because governments were less thrifty than private taxpayers (Please, 1967). Whether public consumption is a complement or substitute for private consumption depends on specific country conditions and has led to opposed empirical findings and conclusions (Agenor and Montiel, 1996, p. 80).

Finally, it must be remembered that the objective of increased saving is increased investment for accelerated growth. Investment ratios tend to be higher than saving ratios, so that the difference, the so-called saving gap, is filled by foreign saving or foreign capital inflows. This raises the question whether fiscal policies should focus on saving or investment. The classical approach to saving and investment is based on the assumption that investment depends upon the availability of savings, implying that saving is a prerequisite for investment. This is known as the prior-savings approach and it contrasts with the Keynesian approach, which is based on the assumption that the encouragement of investment will lead to increased saving. The latter approach focuses more on savings generated by firms than by individuals, as well as on the mobilization of unused resources. The literature abounds with efforts of estimating savings functions, but we shall not survey this literature in the present context. Important references are the surveys by Mikesell and Zinser (1973) and Deaton (1989). If there is any consensus in the findings, it is that saving ratios tend to increase with per capita income and to level off at a middle-income level. Furthermore, Modigliani (1970) hypothesized, and found some empirical evidence to support his theory, that saving does not only fuel growth, but that growth also tends to increase saving, whereby a cumulative process or virtuous circle is generated. For further insights into the problems of fiscal reform the reader is referred to Case Study 5 of the Indonesian tax reform of the 1980s at the end of the present chapter, which has been described by various observers as a success story.

In the area of public expenditure, it is also possible to influence the economy-wide saving performance. Reforms in public expenditure typically focus on shifting expenditures toward more productive or productivity-enhancing expenditures, and on shifting the burden towards the users of services. To some extent, the expenditure shifting toward more productive uses may be equivalent to increased investment and less current expenditure. This would obviously increase government saving. For example, the reduction of government bureaucracy in favour of an improved infrastructure, would be a case in point. The introduction of user fees, on the other hand, tends to diminish private saving, so that an increase in total saving can be expected only if the services covered are supplied and used more efficiently. User fees are typically introduced in higher education, in health services and in agricultural extension services.

A further topic that generated particular interest in the late 1970s and early 1980s is the problem of recurrent costs of investment projects. It refers to the current expenditure that is necessary to maintain and operate recent investments, for instance the material and personnel cost of running a recently built hospital. In the 1970s, extensive droughts in the Sahel region of Africa led to increased aid flows to various countries of the region. Aid flows typically cover only the cost of investment projects, but not the cost of operating and maintaining the newly created facilities, such as roads, irrigation or vaccination programs, hospitals or schools. After project implementation these recurrent costs must be borne by the recipient countries' government budgets. As a consequence of increased aid flows, the recurrent costs of investment projects rose rapidly and came to exceed the governments' budget revenues. This problem was analyzed in an extensive research project by Harvard University and the University of Montreal (Martens and Gray, 1981). The research has led to a greater awareness of the problem and to preventive actions to avoid the potential waste implied by unused or inadequately maintained investments.

## 3.4    Financial Intermediation and Policy Reform

The role of the financial sector consists of financial intermediation, in other words the transformation of savings into investments. This includes the encouragement of savings and the facilitation of investments through the supply of credit to investors. The transformation takes the form of borrowing and lending in various financial markets such as the bond market, the stock market, and savings and loan institutions. While in the goods and services market the price system is assumed to assure an efficient allocation of resources, in the financial markets this role is performed by the interest rate. As in the goods markets, this role can be played efficiently only if the interest rate is allowed to reflect the real scarcity of funds, in other words if it is allowed to react to the demand and supply in the market.

     The first and necessary condition for the efficient functioning of financial markets is the development of financial institutions that form the financial sector. These institutions include a Central Bank, a commercial banking system, other financial institutions like trust and insurance companies, and the stock exchange. In developing countries not all of these institutions exist, and the existing ones are often weakly developed and controlled by governments. This, one could argue, is simply a reflection of the generally less developed state of the economy. But the problem is more complex, because even when different types of financial institutions exist, they may not function to the full advantage of savers and investors. For instance, state-owned companies may hold a monopoly in the credit market, or the government may impose interest rate ceilings that result in artificially low real interest rates. In such cases we talk about financial repression, which means the financial system is inhibited by certain government interventions such as interest rate ceilings or credit control. Several authors have analyzed and described the importance of the financial sector for economic development, in particular Shaw (1973) and McKinnon (1973), and their general argument is that economic development requires financial deepening. This is a long-run process as it involves the growth of economic institutions. In addition, if financial repression exists, it needs to be eliminated by financial liberalization. More recently, it has been shown that financial intermediary development is positively associated with economic growth (cf. Levine et al., 2000).

A financial system is deepened when its institutions and instruments grow and diversify their instruments. Banks extend their branch networks, other financial institutions enter the market, the government borrows on the domestic market and firms offer financial shares in the stock market. The ratio of broadly defined money (M2) to GDP, as shown in Table 3.4, can be used as a proxy indicator of financial depth in a country, although it captures only part of the factors representing financial depth. Other factors are the existence and relative importance of bond and stock markets.

A state of financial repression exists when interest rate ceilings exist and the credit market is not only controlled but also monopolized by the government. Interest rate ceilings can easily result in artificially low real, and often negative, interest rates. The real interest rate is obtained by deducting from the nominal rate the expected rate of inflation. In inflationary circumstances the real interest rate can only reflect the scarcity of capital if it includes a margin for the expected rate of inflation. Under financial repression, interest rates fail to include the inflationary margin, so that the real rate is clearly below the scarcity price of capital and possibly negative. In such a situation firms tend to over-invest, or to invest in excessively capital-intensive methods of production, as capital is cheap. Both consequences lead to an unnecessarily high ICOR and thus a lower growth rate. Excessive capital intensity is also known to cause unemployment. The impact of interest rates on savings, on the other hand, is more ambiguous. Low and possibly negative real interest rates can be expected to discourage savings, at least the financial kind of savings, but the empirical evidence does not fully support this hypothesis (Agenor and Montiel, 1996, p. 80). This may be due to the fact that certain kinds of investments by households are not treated as such by the national accounts. The state of financial repression may be overcome by financial liberalization, for which the reader is referred to Case Study 6 on financial reform in Chile.

**Table 3.4**     Money and interest rates in selected countries

| | GDP growth | | Money/GDP(%) | | Avg. inflation rate | | Nominal interest rate | |
|---|---|---|---|---|---|---|---|---|
| | 1980-1990 | 1990-2001 | 1980 | 2001 | 1980 | 2001 | 1980 | 2001 |
| **Low income** | | | | | | | | |
| Ghana | 3.0 | 4.2 | 16.2 | 18.0 | 51.7 | 34.6 | 19.0 | 25.6 |
| India | 5.7 | 5.9 | 34.7 | 55.0 | 18.6 | 3.5 | 16.5 | 12.3 |
| Kenya | 4.2 | 2.0 | 29.8 | n/a | 10.5 | 11.3 | 10.6 | 22.3 |
| Senegal | 3.1 | 3.9 | 26.6 | 25.4 | 4.9 | 2.6 | 14.5 | 16.8 |
| **Middle income** | | | | | | | | |
| China | 10.3 | 10.0 | 33.2 | 96.0 | 2.1 | 0.1 | 5.0 | 5.9 |
| Brazil | 2.7 | 2.8 | 9.6 | n/a | 91.6 | 7.4 | n/a | 56.8 |
| Chile | 4.2 | 6.3 | 21.0 | n/a | 29.2 | 1.5 | 47.1 | 14.8 |
| Indonesia | 6.1 | 3.8 | 13.2 | 61.0 | 29.2 | 10.8 | n/a | 18.5 |
| Malaysia | 5.3 | 6.5 | 46.1 | 106.0 | 6.8 | -2.6 | 7.8 | 6.8 |
| Mexico | 1.1 | 3.1 | 25.2 | 46.0 | 28.7 | 6.3 | 28.1 | 18.2 |
| **High income** | | | | | | | | |
| Canada | 3.2 | 3.1 | 45.1 | n/a | 10.6 | 1.0 | 14.3 | 7.3 |
| France | 2.4 | 1.9 | 71.7 | 76.3 | 11.4 | 1.4 | 12.5 | 6.7 |
| Japan | 4.1 | 1.3 | 83.4 | 126.0 | 3.8 | -1.4 | 8.3 | 2.1 |
| UK | 3.2 | 2.7 | 29.8 | 91.0 | 19.8 | 2.4 | 16.2 | 6.0 |
| USA | 3.5 | 3.4 | 58.7 | 63.0 | 9.1 | 2.3 | 15.3 | 9.2 |

*Source*: World Bank, International Financial Statistics 1986, World Development Indicators 2003.

Financial liberalization will normally lead to higher interest rates, and this may be seen as an inhibition to growth. Although higher interest rates may be expected to induce more saving, they may also be expected to keep investments low. These relationships are subject to substantial debates in the literature, and empirical studies have supported one or the other view. First, in spite of a few studies suggesting the contrary, it is widely held that saving is mainly determined by income and, in the aggregate, not much by the interest rate. Second, it is easier to show that investments increase when the cost of capital is lowered. But it is also possible to show that misallocation of capital inhibits longer-run growth. Table 3.4 shows nominal rates of interest, inflation rates and the proportion of money in GDP of a sample of developing and high-income countries. The reader may find, by calculating the difference between interest and inflation rates, that in three of the developing countries the real interest rate was negative in 1980, as a consequence of interest rate fixing by government intervention.

## 3.5      Inflation and Monetary Policy

The basic function of monetary policy is to assure monetary stability so that economic development is not hampered by excessive inflation. The role of inflation in economic growth and development, however, is not unambiguous. A modest rate of inflation is often considered to be conducive to growth, as it may stimulate investments. Firms are usually more inclined to invest when the prices of their products are rising, relative to costs, than if they are declining. Rapid inflation, on the other hand, tends to discourage growth since it generates additional uncertainty. In particular, rapid inflation tends to direct economic resources toward short run uses, and to discourage investments with a longer time horizon, such as those in infrastructure and in education. These problems have been examined by various authors, and among the better known studies proposing an optimal level of inflation are the ones by Harberger (1964) and Dorrance (1966). A more recent survey of the literature on inflation and growth is the one by Johnson (1984).

One of the arguments in favour of modest inflation is that there is the possibility of financing development with the help of an inflation tax. The inflation tax is part of the seigniorage that governments extract by circulating money. It refers to the fact that under inflation, borrowers tend to gain and lenders to lose, unless the rate of inflation is correctly predicted and is included in the nominal interest rate. Since money held by the public is a liability to the government but earns interest for the creditors, the holders of money not only forego interest, but also lose through inflation, which erodes the real value of their cash balances. The loss can be expressed as a percentage of money holdings and is known as the inflation tax. It can be computed as follows:

$$(3.1) \quad t = (M - M')/M$$
$$= p/(1 + p)$$

where M is the nominal and real value of the cash balance held with zero inflation, M' is the real value of M after one year of inflation at the rate p, that is, $M' = M/(1 + p)$, and t is the inflation tax expressed as a proportion of the money supply. Governments appropriate this tax when they finance expenditures by issuing money to the public. A simple numerical example demonstrates that the inflation tax can be very substantial when inflation is high. For instance, let the rate of inflation be 50 percent and the money supply represent one third of national income, then the inflation tax represents 33 percent of the money supply and 11 percent of national income, a substantial amount of finance.

Considering the inflation tax as a potential way of financing economic growth, one can calculate what rate of inflation is typically needed to increase the macroeconomic growth rate by 1 percent. Mundell (1965) examined this question by using several simplifying assumptions, and proposed the following model. Assuming first that all investing is done by the government and financed by borrowing from the Central Bank, the yearly increase in capital stock corresponds then to the increase in bank reserves (R) in real terms (all time subscripts omitted):

$$(3.2) \quad dK = dR/P.$$

Since reserves are a fixed proportion (r = the reserve ratio) of the money in circulation, that is, $dR = r \, dM$, and since an increased capital stock leads to increased output via the ICOR (v), assuming full capacity utilization, we obtain after dividing by Y and M:

$$(3.3) \quad g_Y = dY/Y = r/v \; dM/M \; M/PY.$$

Using the quantity theory of money, $Y \, P = M \, V$, with V being the velocity of money, we replace M/PY by 1/V and, remembering its growth rate version, that is, $g_Y + g_P = g_M + g_V$, we can then express the needed rate of inflation as a function of the growth rate of GDP, making the additional assumption that the velocity of money is constant, that is, $g_V = 0$:

$$(3.4) \quad g_P = g_Y \ (V \ v/r - 1).$$

In an economy with $V = 3$, $v = 5$, and $r = .3$, the rate of inflation required to increase the GDP growth rate by 1 percent would be 49 percent. Admittedly, the model is of limited usefulness, due to the number and restrictive nature of the assumptions; but it provides a rough idea of the potential order of magnitude of the inflation/growth rate relationship. One may easily argue that the cost of monetary instability inflicted on the economy by running a 49 percent inflation rate outweighs the benefit of accelerating macroeconomic growth by 1 percent.

Finally, the treatment of inflation in this context would remain incomplete without mention of the monetarist vs. structuralist viewpoints. Structuralists claim that inflation is a structural problem and needs to be addressed by structural policies, such as removing various obstacles to the supply of goods and services. Monetarists, on the other hand, see inflation as purely monetary phenomenon, emphasize more its costs than its benefits, and prescribe policies that are entirely in the monetary realm. We return to inflation and monetary policy in the context of stabilization policies discussed in Chapters 6 and 8.

## References

Agenor, P.R. and P.J. Montiel (1996), *Development Macroeconomics*, Princeton University Press, Princeton, New Jersey.

Barro, R. (1979), 'Are Government Bonds Net Wealth?', *Journal of Political Economy*, November-December.

Deaton, A. (1989), 'Saving in Developing Countries: Theory and Review', Proceedings of the World Bank Annual Conference on Development Economics, Supplement to the *World Bank Economic Review* and *The World Bank Research Observer*.

Dorrance, G. (1966), 'Inflation and Growth: The Statistical Evidence', *IMF Staff Papers*, March.

Harberger, A. (1964), 'Some Notes on Inflation and Monetary Policy in Latin America', in: W. Baer and I. Kerstenetsky, *Inflation and Growth in Latin America*, Irwin, Homewood, Ill.

Johnson, O.E.G. (1984), 'On Growth and Inflation in Developing Countries', *IMF Staff Papers*, December.

Levine, R. et al. (2000), 'Financial intermediation and growth: Causality and causes', *Journal of Monetary Economics*, 46, pp. 31-77.

Lewis, A. (1954), 'Economic Development with Unlimited Supplies of Labour', *Manchester School*, vol.22.

Martens, A. and C. Gray, (1981), "Dépenses récurrentes et développement au Sahel'', *Canadian Journal of Development Studies/Revue canadienne d'études du développement*, II (2), p. 341-365.

McKinnon, R.I. (1973), *Money and Capital in Economic Development*, Brookings Institution, Washington.

Mikesell, R.F., J.E. Zinser (1973), 'The Nature of the Savings Function in Developing Countries: A Survey of the Theoretical and Empirical Literature', *Journal of Economic Literature*, 11.

Modigliani, F. (1970), 'The Life Cycle Hypothesis of Saving and Inter-Country Differences in the Savings Ratio', in W. Eltis et al: *Induction, Growth and Trade: Essays in Honour of Sir Roy Harrod*, Oxford University Press.

Musgrave, R. (1987), 'Tax Reform in Developing Countries', in: D. Newbery and N. Stern, *The Theory of Taxation for Developing Countries*, Oxford University Press.

Please, S. (1967), 'Savings Through Taxation: Reality or Mirage?', *Finance and Development*, 4, 1.

Tanzi, V. (1987), 'Quantitative Characteristics of the Tax Systems of Developing Countries', in: D. Newbery and N. Stern, *The Theory of Taxation for Developing Countries*, Oxford University Press.

UN-ECAFE (1960), *Programming Techniques for Economic Development*, Report of the first group of experts on programming techniques, Bangkok.

World Bank (1995), *World Development Report 1995*, Oxford University Press.

# Case Study 6
# Tax Reform in Indonesia

## Purpose

This case study analyzes the tax reform in Indonesia implemented in 1984. It is recognized by experts as an example of a successful tax reform in a developing country. Here we first examine the general principles of tax reform in developing countries, then focus on the specific case of Indonesia and evaluate the reform's success in terms of the general and country-specific goals of tax reform.

**Background**

The Republic of Indonesia is a multi-ethnic state, the territorial extent of which is defined principally by the boundaries of the former Dutch colonial empire in South East Asia. The nation proclaimed its independence in 1945, but it was not until an armed struggle had ensued with Dutch forces seeking to re-establish control that sovereignty was formally transferred from the Netherlands to Indonesia in 1949.

Government control over the economy is today fairly extensive, and is exercised in a variety of ways. After establishing as its economic objectives stability, growth, and equity, the government proclaimed Repelita I, the first five-year plan to establish developmental priorities and set specific sectoral growth targets. As Repelita I proved a success, Repelitas II-V followed and have been the main blueprints for economic development.

Agriculture (including forestry and fishing) is Indonesia's single largest source of income and employment, and it is a significant earner of foreign exchange. Rice is the most important food crop, and Indonesia is second only to Malaysia worldwide in the production of natural rubber. The mining sector is Indonesia's largest source of export earnings and domestic budgetary revenues. Indonesia is a major producer of oil and a member of Opec. The country has substantial reserves of oil, both explored and unexplored, although many of the country's oil fields are quite small and the maintenance of production levels requires constant exploration and development. The country is also a substantial refiner and marketer of crude oil, and most of the refining of petroleum is carried out by the state oil firm, Pertamina. A corporate income tax on oil along with laws that force foreign contractors and investors to share a substantial portion of their output with Indonesian companies has meant that the oil industry is a huge revenue generator for the state. The manufacturing sector remains fairly inefficient; geared to the production of import-substitutes, it is very protected and uncompetitive. Tourism has also come to be valued recently as a non-oil earner of foreign exchange and a labour intensive service industry that contributes to job creation.

External trade in Indonesia is particularly strong with Japan, the United States, and Singapore, although Germany has recently become a significant importer. Indonesia is by its own definition a relatively open economy, but imports of certain goods are prohibited or restricted through quotas, tariffs and surcharges. When 'adequate domestic production capacity' of an import-substitute has been established, imports are often subject to additional taxes. Different types of export duties are also in place.

The Indonesian government actively encourages foreign investment, although a series of conditions are imposed upon it.

Indonesia is a major recipient of foreign aid from the world community. Billions of dollars of economic and technical assistance have been donated through IGGI, the Inter-Governmental Group on Indonesia, chaired by the Dutch government and originally established to provide loans to finance balance of payments crises. In 1992, following persistent efforts by the Dutch government to attach political conditions to its aid, the Indonesian government decided to reject all further assistance from the Dutch and dissolved IGGI. The Consultative Group for Indonesia, chaired by the World Bank, has replaced IGGI and now administers foreign aid to Indonesia. Most of Indonesia's debt is in the form of medium and long-term loans, mostly publicly guaranteed borrowing. The growth in foreign indebtedness has been accompanied by a sharp rise in the country's external debt service burden. Indonesia has been requesting debt relief since the early 1980s, but as of yet it has not been granted.

Since the 1980s, many important economic reforms have been implemented, including tax reform and an extensive liberalization of the financial sector. The government also lifted subsidies from most parts of the economy, reformed customs, and implemented policy packages intended to increase foreign investment and non-oil exports, and to expand overseas markets. Not only have markets responded well to the opportunities offered by these reforms, but the economy was also able to face up to the severe external shocks experienced in the late 1980s with much greater resilience than would have otherwise been expected.

**Method of Analysis**

After a short review of the principles of tax reform in developing countries (Question 1) we summarize the objectives and planned policy changes in Indonesia (Question 2). Question 3 focuses on the implementation of the reform and in question 4 the impact is analyzed by using the data of Tables 1 and 2, as well as the findings of other authors. The information is found in Musgrave (1987), Gillis (1990), Mansury and Tamsir (1992), as well as the appended tables.

**References**

Economist Intelligence Unit, *Country Profile: Indonesia*, 1986, 1992.

Gillis, M. (1990), 'Tax Reform and the Value-Added Tax: Indonesia', in: M.J. Boskin and C.E. Mclure, Jr., *World Tax Reform*, ICS Press, San Francisco, California.

International Monetary Fund (1993), *International Financial Statistics, Yearbook*.

Mansury, R. and Tamsir, Ismail (1992), 'Tax Reform in Indonesia, 1984', in: Lamb (ed.), *Managing Policy Reform in the Real World: Asian Experiences*, The World Bank.

Musgrave, Richard (1987), 'Tax Reform in Developing Countries', in: D. Newbery and N. Stern (eds.), *The Theory of Taxation for Developing Countries*, Oxford and The World Bank.

**Assigned Questions**

1)      Describe the typical tax structure of a developing country. What are generally the goals of tax reform in developing countries?

2)      What were the goals of the tax reform in Indonesia?

3)      What policy changes were proposed in Indonesia to achieve these goals? How was the reform implemented?

4)      With respect to the stated goals, analyze the overall effects of the tax reform in Indonesia. Use the information provided in the two articles as well as the appended tables to compute the appropriate statistics and answer the following questions:

      i)      What effect did the reform have on government revenue?

      ii)     Following the reform, which taxes declined in importance? Which taxes increased in importance?

      iii)    Did the reform fulfill the stated goals of the Indonesian government? Did the Indonesian reform satisfy the general criteria of tax reform in LDCs as stated under question (1)?

**Table CS6a   Government revenue, GDP and its deflator in Indonesia, 1969-1990**

|       | Revenue | GDP DEFL | GDP      |
|-------|---------|----------|----------|
| 1970  | 360.0   | 9.4      | 35706.0  |
| 71    | 442.0   | 9.6      | 38208.0  |
| 72    | 644.0   | 10.9     | 41808.0  |
| 73    | 1020.0  | 14.5     | 46537.0  |
| 74    | 1832.0  | 21.4     | 50089.0  |
| 75    | 2300.0  | 24.0     | 52583.0  |
| 76    | 2968.0  | 27.5     | 56204.0  |
| 77    | 3634.0  | 31.1     | 61128.0  |
| 78    | 4378.0  | 34.5     | 65921.0  |
| 79    | 7050.0  | 45.7     | 70045.0  |
| 80    | 10406.0 | 59.0     | 76965.0  |
| 81    | 13763.0 | 70.0     | 83066.0  |
| 82    | 12815.0 | 73.6     | 84932.0  |
| 83    | 15511.0 | 87.7     | 88493.0  |
| 84    | 18724.0 | 94.9     | 94666.0  |
| 85    | 20347.0 | 100.0    | 96997.0  |
| 86    | 21324.0 | 100.0    | 102696.0 |
| 87    | 24781.0 | 115.8    | 107754.0 |
| 88    | 24088.0 | 131.2    | 108282.0 |
| 89    | 29093.0 | 136.5    | 122483.0 |
| 90    | 39566.0 | 150.1    | 131230.0 |

*Notes*:    (1) GDP in 1985 prices in Billions of Rupiah.
             (2) Figures from 1968 in Billions of Rupiah; earlier in Millions of Rupiah.
*Source*:   IFS Yearbook 1993.

**Table CS6b    Components of government revenue, Indonesia 1981-1993 (in billions of Rupiah)**

| | 1982-83 | 1983-84 | 1984-85 | 1985-86 | 1986-87 | 1987-88 | 1988-89 | 1989-90 | 1990-91 |
|---|---|---|---|---|---|---|---|---|---|
| DOMESTIC REVENUE (DR) | 12418 | 14433 | 15905 | 19253 | 17833 | 20803 | 23004 | 28740 | 39546 |
| DIRECT TAXES (A) | 9982 | 11584 | 12708 | 13625 | 12903 | 12933 | 13900 | 17330 | 25278 |
| oil/gas company tax (A1) | 8170 | 9520 | 10430 | 11145 | 9738 | 10047 | 9527 | 11252 | 17712 |
| personal income tax (A2) | 289 | 399 | | | | | | | |
| non-oil/gas corp. tax (A2) | 675 | 757 | 2121 | 2313 | 2881 | 2663 | 3949 | 5488 | 6755 |
| land tax | 105 | 132 | 157 | 167 | 284 | 223 | 424 | 590 | 811 |
| INDIRECT TAXES (B) | 1932 | 2265 | 2372 | 3928 | 3857 | 5618 | 7243 | 9072 | 11910 |
| sales taxes & VAT (B1) | 708 | 831 | 878 | 2327 | 2143 | 3390 | 4505 | 5837 | 7463 |
| excise tax | 544 | 620 | 773 | 944 | 1055 | 1106 | 1390 | 1477 | 1917 |
| import duties | 522 | 557 | 530 | 607 | 580 | 938 | 1192 | 1587 | 2486 |
| export taxes | 82 | 104 | 91 | 50 | 79 | 184 | 156 | 171 | 44 |
| OTHER TAXES, DIRECT AND INDIRECT (C) | 69 | 65 | 138 | 208 | 119 | 275 | 292 | 276 | 243 |
| NON-TAX RECEIPTS (D) | 435 | 519 | 687 | 1492 | 954 | 1977 | 1569 | 2062 | 2115 |
| FOREIGN AID RECEIPTS (E) | 1940 | 3882 | 3478 | 3573 | 3589 | 6158 | 9991 | 9429 | 9905 |
| TOTAL (T) | 14358 | 18315 | 19383 | 22826 | 21422 | 26961 | 32995 | 38169 | 49451 |

*Notes:*    (1) 1986-87, 1991-92, and 1992-93 are budgeted years.
          (2) After the 1984 reform, one single income tax replaced all the taxes denoted as A2.

*Source:*    Economist Intelligence Unit Country Profiles 1986 and 1992.

# Case Study 7
# Financial Repression and Liberalization in Chile

## Purpose

In this case study you will analyze the financial liberalization in Chile, following the short-lived regime of Salvador Allende, and its impact on the financial market, aggregate investment and economic growth.

## Background

During a period of relatively stable democracy, 1960-1973, Chile has had governments from the left, right and center of the political spectrum. From 1960-1964, Chile was ruled by a conservative and center-right coalition, whose economic policy was directed at inflation stabilization. In 1964 a Christian democratic administration was elected, whose economic policy emphasized structural changes such as land reform, Chilean participation in copper mines, social expenditure towards low and middle incomes and the indexation of wages. In 1970 a left wing and center-left coalition came to power, headed by Salvador Allende. The objective of Allende's economic policy was to transfer power from capitalists to workers and peasants through nationalization of mines, industrial enterprises and banks, increased wages and an expansion of government expenditure. The effect of that policy was that after three years of Allende's rule the share of public ownership in the nation's productive capital had increased from 14 percent in 1965 to 39 percent in 1973, prices were widely controlled by the government and distortion-ridden, the inflation rate had increased dramatically and economic growth had come to a halt.

In September 1973 the Allende government was ousted by a military coup under the leadership of general Augusto Pinochet. Under this new government Chile, as one of the first Latin American countries, set up a series of ambitious economic reforms with the aim 'to reform a financially repressed and isolated economy into a world-integrated market-oriented economy, by reinstating economic incentives, to restore economic growth, to rationalize the resource allocation and to decrease budget deficit'. Four categories of reforms can be distinguished. External sector reforms were aimed at the reduction of trade tariffs, liberalization of the capital account and an increase in direct foreign investments. Financial reforms entailed lowering reserve requirements, permitting non-bank financial institutions, freeing interest rates and privatizing state-owned banks. Fiscal-sector reforms consisted of cutting government expenditure and rationalizing the tax system. Last but not least, the labor reforms aimed at greater flexibility for employers and the suspension of wage indexation.

The economic reforms started in 1973 and ended in 1983. Three different phases can be identified during this stabilization program. During the first phase (1973-1978) the main objective was macroeconomic stability through the correction of economic distortions of the Allende regime and through orthodox stabilization policies such as fiscal and monetary restraint and devaluation. The following phase was that of the tablita (1978-1981), an active crawling peg exchange rate system (tablita) with the goal of reducing inflation. The last phase of the stabilization program is described as 'the confidence crisis' (1981-1983). The strong overvaluation of peso led to speculation against the currency, interest rates rose, GDP decreased, unemployment increased and Chile found itself in an external debt crisis. By 1984 the Chilean structural reforms were pronounced 'an almost complete failure'. The economy collapsed with negative economic growth, high unemployment, a huge current account deficit and a collapse of the financial sector.

From 1984 on, Chile has known a period of recovery and normalization after it embarked on a major stabilization program backed by IMF, World Bank and Inter-American loans. The country enjoyed substantial growth, reduced unemployment, inflation was kept below 20 percent and the current account deficit was reduced. In addition, Chile reverted to a democratic electoral system in December 1989. The people who had pronounced Chile's structural reforms a failure were now proven wrong.

In this case study, we focus on Chile's financial reforms. Phylaktis (1997) has provided the following description of Chile's financial system: 'The financial system in Chile prior to the reforms was characterized by segmentation. There was a group of specialized entities that allocated resources for specific purposes within the framework of very generalized state regulations, which had a direct or indirect bearing on the determination of the amounts, conditions, and costs of the various lines of credit available in the market. The financial reforms were initiated in early 1974, when reserve requirements, which stood at 100 percent in 1973, were lowered, and new nonbank finance institutions were permitted to operate. These institutions were allowed to freely determine interest rates in short-term financial operations. In 1995, interest rates charged by the commercial banks ... were also decontrolled. ... Along with these reforms the government began a process of privatization of banks, which had been nationalized during the Allende administration'.

## References

Kate Phylaktis (1997), 'Financial liberalization and stabilization policies, the experience of Chile', in: K.L. Gupta (ed.), *Experiences with Financial Liberalization*, Kluwer Academic Publishers, Boston.
J. Cottani and D. Cavallo (1993), 'Financial Reform and Liberalization', in: Dornbusch (ed.), *Policymaking in the Open Economy*, EDI Series in Economic Development, Oxford University Press.

## Assigned Questions

1) Calculate the real interest rate, first on a yearly basis and then compute average rates for the periods 1967-1974, 1975-1981, 1982-1998. What do you conclude from your results?
2) Calculate the ratios of M1 and M2 to national income. Has financial deepening occurred in Chile and in which periods? Relate the observed changes to policy changes.
3) Compute the inflation tax as a share of GDP (hint: use M1). What do you conclude?
4) Calculate investments as a proportion of GDP. Has financial liberalization stimulated investment? Can you explain the negative shocks in I/GDP?
5) Compute annual rates (discrete) of real growth of the economy during the study period. What were the average growth rates before and after the economic reforms? Has financial liberalization contributed to economic growth?
6) What conclusions have been drawn in the literature regarding financial reforms in the framework of broader economic reforms? Is the Chilean experience typical for this type of policy reform?

**Table CS7   Money, interest rate and inflation in Chile, 1967-1998**

| Year | Infla-tion (%) | Deposit rate (%) | M1 | M2 | GDP | Real GDP | Invest-ment |
|---|---|---|---|---|---|---|---|
| 1967 | 21.1 | 3.06 | 3.24 | 4.823 | 34.124 | 1866.2 | 5.492 |
| 1968 | 26.1 | 3.02 | 4.471 | 6.873 | 47.288 | 1933.0 | 7.714 |
| 1969 | 29.3 | 3.05 | 6.058 | 9.499 | 68.601 | 2004.9 | 10.36 |
| 1970 | 33.3 | 3.04 | 10.027 | 15.003 | 98.417 | 2046.1 | 16.175 |
| 1971 | 19.0 | 3.05 | 21.273 | 30.3 | 126.979 | 2229.3 | 18.404 |
| 1972 | 77.3 | 3.01 | 54.1 | 74.1 | 234.5 | 2202.3 | 28.9 |
| 1973 | 354.5 | 1.63 | 228.6 | 321.6 | 1146.8 | 2079.7 | 91 |
| 1974 | 504.5 | 117.62 | 836.7 | 1277.7 | 9198.9 | 2100.0 | 1945 |
| 1975 | 374.7 | n.a. | 2978.7 | 5196.7 | 35446.6 | 1828.9 | 4645 |
| 1976 | 211.9 | n.a. | 11502 | 26775 | 128676.1 | 1893.2 | 16447 |
| 1977 | 91.9 | 94.92 | 19800 | 53400 | 287800 | 2079.9 | 41000 |
| 1978 | 40.1 | 63.53 | 39400 | 103600 | 487500 | 2250.8 | 87000 |
| 1979 | 33.4 | 45.19 | 66800 | 172400 | 772200 | 2437.2 | 137000 |
| 1980 | 35.1 | 37.72 | 101000 | 279500 | 1075300 | 2626.8 | 226000 |
| 1981 | 19.7 | 40.90 | 110600 | 359400 | 1273100 | 2772.2 | 289000 |
| 1982 | 9.9 | 48.68 | 113700 | 484600 | 1239100 | 2381.5 | 139000 |
| 1983 | 27.3 | 28.01 | 131500 | 588600 | 1557700 | 2364.1 | 153000 |
| 1984 | 19.9 | 27.63 | 161400 | 720400 | 1893400 | 2514.5 | 258000 |
| 1985 | 30.7 | 31.97 | 200500 | 1061200 | 2651900 | 2576.6 | 456000 |
| 1986 | 19.5 | 18.99 | 287200 | 1329400 | 3419200 | 2721.9 | 646000 |
| 1987 | 19.9 | 25.22 | 346500 | 1794800 | 4540600 | 2878.0 | 1010000 |
| 1988 | 14.7 | 15.11 | 509100 | 2281800 | 5917900 | 3090.1 | 1348000 |
| 1989 | 17.0 | 27.72 | 5960 | 2993100 | 7353700 | 3398.4 | 1850000 |
| 1990 | 26.0 | 40.27 | 735400 | 3697500 | 9245500 | 3471.4 | 2322000 |
| 1991 | 21.8 | 22.32 | 1064500 | 4735800 | 12100500 | 3680.3 | 2729000 |
| 1992 | 15.4 | 18.26 | 1344000 | 5839800 | 15185400 | 4064.1 | 3615000 |
| 1993 | 12.7 | 18.24 | 1628900 | 7205300 | 17974900 | 4347.9 | 4765000 |
| 1994 | 11.4 | 15.08 | 1892300 | 8022800 | 21395300 | 4596.2 | 5155000 |
| 1995 | 8.2 | 13.73 | 2312900 | 10096600 | 25875700 | 5084.7 | 6674000 |
| 1996 | 7.4 | 13.46 | 2686700 | 12071600 | 28268400 | 5461.6 | 7599000 |
| 1997 | 6.1 | 12.02 | 3228100 | 14040400 | 31774000 | 5875.3 | 8524000 |
| 1998 | 5.1 | 14.91 | 2799400 | 15386900 | 33577700 | 6075.7 | 8913000 |

*Notes:*   All values in million Chilean pesos. M1 includes demand deposits and currency outside banks. M2 includes also time and savings deposits. Real GDP at 1985-prices.

## Case Study 7: Solution

1)      The real interest rate is obtained by subtracting the rate of inflation from the nominal interest rate and the dividing the difference by one plus the rate of inflation. As the inflation and deposit rates are given as percentages they must be entered into the real interest formula as decimals.

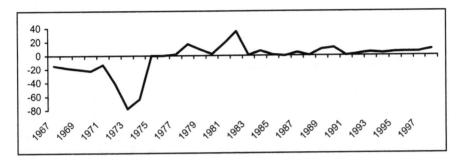

**Figure CS7a     The real interest rate in Chile**

In the period 1967-1974, the average real interest rate was −34 percent. In the periods 1975-1981 and 1982-1998, the average real interest rate was nine percent and six percent, respectively. Thus, we find strongly negative real interest rates in Chile from 1967 to 1974 (before the financial liberalization), even as low as −77 percent in 1973. This is an indication that the financial system was repressed during that period. After the financial liberalization, we find positive real interest rates, indicating that the financial reforms have succeeded in eliminating the financial repression.
        The information provided by Phylaktis can explain the cause of financial repression: (a) High reserve requirements before the liberalization. They stood at 100 percent in 1973. In 1979 the reserve requirements were 42 percent, and by the late 1980 a mere 10 percent. (b) Banks were state-owned. (c) Interest rate ceilings applied.

2)      Referring to the graph below, we can see that M1/GDP has remained relatively constant over time, except for the period 1971-1973. M2/GDP has increased substantially after the financial liberalization period in Chile. This indicates that there has been a deepening of the financial system. The difference between M2/GDP and M1/GDP, that is, the share of savings deposits, has increased. This means that Chileans have allocated a larger proportion of money M2 to savings deposits.

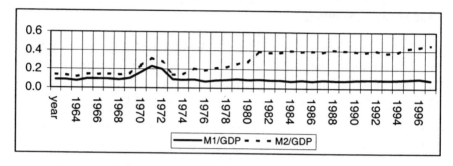

**Figure CS7b    Financial deepening in Chile**

3)      The inflation tax is computed as $[\pi/(1+\pi)]*M1$, where $\pi$ is the rate of inflation. To express the inflation tax as a proportion of GDP, we simply divide it by GDP. Referring to the graph below, it becomes clear that the inflation tax increased sharply during the years of the Allende regime. After the economic reforms in the late 70s, its importance decreased gradually. In question 2, we saw that the share of M1 to GDP remained relatively constant. It is therefore clear that the inflation tax is mainly due to the high rates of inflation rather than an increasing stock of money in circulation.

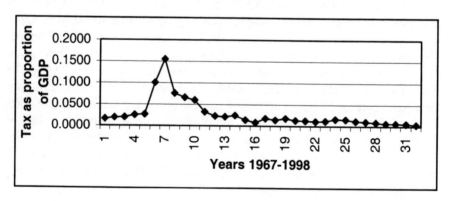

**Figure CS7c    The inflation tax in Chile**

4)      Investments are obtained by adding up gross Fixed Capital Formation and the change in stocks. The ratio of investments to GDP is plotted over time in the following diagram:

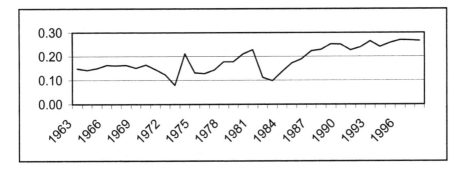

**Figure CS7d     Investments per GDP in Chile**

The average share of investments in GDP before the financial liberalization was 14.5 percent. For the period 1975-1998, this ratio was 20.4 percent. We could say that the liberalization of the financial system coincided with increased levels of investment.

The increase of investments as a share of GDP has not been a steady one. In the graph we can see several negative shocks in I/GDP. A first serious dip in I/GDP occurred in the period 1970-1973. The objective of the Allende government was to transfer power from capitalists to workers and peasants through nationalization (of mines, industrial enterprises, banks), higher wages and an expansion of government expenditure. During the Allende years there was a dramatic increase in inflation and economic growth fell from eight percent to minus five percent. This was obviously not a climate stimulating investments. The second substantial decline of investments occurred in 1982-1983, a period that Phylaktis describes as 'the confidence crisis'. A deep recession occurred in those years (see question 5), unemployment increased to 22 percent, and Chile was in a debt crisis. Again, this was not a climate stimulating investment. These observations may explain why the financial liberalization was not accompanied by a continuous increase in investments.

5)      The following diagram shows Chile's economic growth rates during the period 1964-1998.

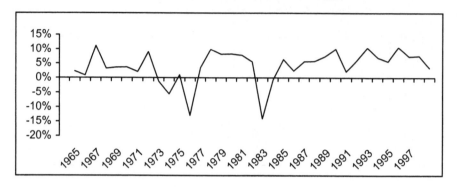

**Figure CS7e    Economic growth in Chile**

The average growth rate during the period 1964-1974, before the financial liberalization, was 2.7 percent. The average growth rate after the liberalization, during the period 1975-1998 was 4.7 percent. In a more sophisticated analysis one would compare the actual growth performance with a counterfactual scenario, that is, if financial liberalization had not occurred. In the present and simpler analysis we conclude that economic growth was positively affected by the financial liberalization.

6)       The literature on financial reforms emphasizes two aspects, the importance of reforms when financial repression prevails and the order in which various reforms should be undertaken.

High inflation and the reliance of the government on inflationary finance, which are symptoms of financial repression, need to be addressed first before capital account restrictions can be removed. High inflation is a major obstacle to healthy economic growth and an equitable distribution of incomes. Thus, stabilization is a precondition of financial opening.

# Chapter 4

# Financing Economic Growth from External Sources

In an open economy investments are financed not only from domestic saving but also from external sources. The principal foreign sources of investment capital are external borrowing, foreign investment and official transfers in the form of development assistance. In spite of the different nature of these sources, we often lump them together and refer to them as foreign saving or capital inflows. Their relative importance in the recipient countries can be seen from data shown in Table 4.1. In this table, the main net capital flows to all developing countries are shown for 1990 and 1995. It suggests that the sources of foreign savings have changed in relative importance during this time period. Official development finance declined from over 50 percent of total resource flows in 1990 to less than 30 percent in 1995, while private flows increased from less than 50 percent to more than 70 percent. Foreign direct (39 percent) and portfolio investment (24 percent) are now the main sources of foreign capital inflows, while both official grants (14 percent) and loans (13 percent) have declined to roughly half of the relative share they occupied in 1990. Official foreign borrowing is further broken down into concessionary and non-concessionary borrowing. Concessionary loans involve lower than market interest rates and longer payback terms and, together with official grants, sum up to Official Development Assistance (ODA). Non-concessionary loans are made on commercial terms, just like private borrowing. The relative importance of the different sources of foreign saving varies, however, from country to country. Before discussing their specific characteristics, let us see what role foreign saving plays with respect to the growth of an economy.

## 4.1    The Dual Role of Foreign Saving and the Two-gap Model

Foreign capital inflows have two different functions in the economy: they supplement domestic savings, and they provide foreign exchange. The first function, supplementing domestic saving, is easily understood to enhance

economic growth. The second function, supplementing foreign exchange
earnings, is equally important for growth. It allows investment goods to be
imported, which the country, at its present stage of development, may not
be able to produce. Also, in the short run, a developing economy may be
unable to reallocate domestic resources from the production of domestic
goods to exports, in order to generate the foreign exchange needed for
importing the required investment goods. Neither can consumption goods
be converted into investment goods.

**Table 4.1    Net resource flows to developing countries, 1991-2000**

| | 1991 | | 1995 | | 2000 | |
|---|---|---|---|---|---|---|
| | **Billion $** | **% of total** | **Billion $** | **% of total** | **Billion $** | **% of total** |
| **Total** | **123.0** | **100.0** | **261.2** | **100.0** | **295.8** | **100.0** |
| Official dev. finance | 60.9 | 49.5 | 55.1 | 21.1 | 38.6 | 13.0 |
| Official dev. assistance | 49.5 | 40.2 | 46.2 | 17.7 | 41.6 | 14.1 |
| Grants | 35.1 | 28.5 | 32.7 | 12.5 | 29.6 | 10.0 |
| Bilateral | 29.5 | 24.0 | 26.1 | 10.0 | 22.6 | 7.6 |
| Multilateral | 5.6 | 4.6 | 6.6 | 2.5 | 7.0 | 2.4 |
| Concessionary Loans | 14.4 | 11.7 | 13.5 | 5.2 | 11.7 | 4.0 |
| Bilateral | 6.3 | 5.1 | 4.9 | 1.9 | 5.1 | 1.7 |
| Multilateral | 8.1 | 6.6 | 8.6 | 3.3 | 6.6 | 2.2 |
| Non concessionary Loans | 11.4 | 9.3 | 8.9 | 3.4 | -3.0 | -1.0 |
| Bilateral | 3.9 | 3.2 | 5.2 | 2.0 | 7.3 | 2.5 |
| Multilateral | 7.5 | 6.1 | 3.7 | 1.4 | 4.3 | 1.5 |
| Private flows | 62.1 | 50.5 | 206.1 | 78.9 | 257.2 | 87.0 |
| Capital markets | 23.3 | 18.9 | 99.1 | 37.9 | 79.2 | 26.8 |
| Debt flows | 18.8 | 15.3 | 63.0 | 24.1 | 31.3 | 10.6 |
| Bank lending | 5.0 | 4.1 | 30.5 | 11.7 | 0.7 | 0.2 |
| Bond financing | 10.9 | 8.9 | 30.8 | 11.8 | 30.3 | 10.2 |
| Other | 2.8 | 2.3 | 1.7 | 0.7 | 0.3 | 0.1 |
| Equity flows | 7.6 | 6.2 | 36.1 | 13.8 | 47.9 | 16.2 |
| Foreign Direct Investment | 35.7 | 29.0 | 107.0 | 41.0 | 178.0 | 60.2 |

*Source*: OECD DAC; World Bank, Global Development Finance 2001.

The dual role played by foreign capital inflows implies that economic growth may be affected differently, depending on which role is more constraining. In other words, the capital productivity in generating GDP (equal to the inverse of ICOR) may be different for domestic and for imported capital goods. If, for instance, the ICOR of imported capital goods is higher, implying a lower growth rate than the one based on domestic capital goods, then the lower growth rate will prevail. In this case some amount of saving, domestic plus foreign, remains unused for growth. The distinction between the two functions of foreign capital inflows is crucial for the analysis of various constraints to growth. It has led to the design of various two-gap models, pioneered by Chenery and his collaborators (cf. Chenery and Bruno, 1962) and McKinnon (1964).

The two-gap model is essentially a Harrod-Domar model, but which is open to trade and factor flows. To see the structure of a simplified two-gap model, let us start with the condition of macroeconomic equilibrium in the open economy:

(4.1)    $I - S = M - X$

We remember that this equation is an ex-post identity, because, according to national accounting definitions, consumption (C), investment (I) and net exports (X - M) add up to national income (Y), which in turn is spent on consumption (C) and saving (S). In fact, it is common practice for national statistics bureaus to compute S as a residual by deducting foreign capital inflows from investments. In an ex-ante perspective, however, the equation is an equilibrium condition because it states that the difference between planned investments and planned savings equals the difference between planned imports and planned exports. The value of the difference between I and S is the investment-savings gap, and the one between M and X is the trade or foreign exchange gap. Both gaps are filled by the inflow of foreign capital (F). When the two gaps are simultaneously filled, based on planned savings, investments, imports and exports, then aggregate demand and supply are in equilibrium. Usually, however, the two gaps are not identical, so that economic growth is then constrained by the larger of the two gaps, and some resources of the non-binding constraint remain unused. Based on these concepts, we can now assemble the building blocks of a simple two-gap model. The first component is the familiar assumption about the behavior of domestic savers written as:

(4.2)    $S = s\,Y$

that is, savings are assumed to equal a fixed proportion of national income. The second component specifies the behavior of investors, who generate output capacity according to a fixed capital coefficient or ICOR (v), just like in the Harrod-Domar growth model of a closed economy:

$$(4.3) \quad I = v \, \Delta Y$$

The third component is the condition of internal equilibrium in an open economy:

$$(4.4) \quad F = I - S$$

where F is foreign saving, equal to net capital inflows. If we ignore for a moment the existence of imports, exports and their relationship with national income, assuming that the capital inflow will simply fill the savings gap, we can compute the growth rate based on internal equilibrium. Combining the equations 4.2 to 4.4, by substituting 4.4 and 4.2 into 4.3 and dividing by Y, we solve for the GDP growth rate $g_Y = \Delta Y/Y$:

$$(4.5) \quad g_Y = s/v + (1/v) \, f$$

where $f = F/Y$ is the capital inflow expressed as a proportion of national income or GDP. We shall call this rate the savings-constrained growth rate $(g_s)$, replacing the subscript Y by the subscript s. This growth rate is identical to the Harrod-Domar growth rate, with the only exception that the proportion of foreign capital inflow adds to the savings ratio.

The fourth component of the model is a very simple export function according to which exports are entirely endogenous or supply-determined:

$$(4.6) \quad X = e \, Y$$

where e is the average ratio of exports to GDP, which is assumed to be fixed. Imports consist of consumption goods, assumed to be a fixed proportion $(m_c)$ of GDP, and of a proportion $(m_i)$ of all investment goods:

$$(4.7) \quad M = m_c \, Y + m_i \, I$$

and, substituting (4.3) into (4.7),

$$(4.7a) \quad M = m_c \, Y + m_i \, v \, \Delta Y$$

where $1/(m_i v)$ is the marginal productivity of imported capital in generating GDP. This composite parameter determines the impact of imported capital on growth, which may differ from the productivity of domestic capital on growth.

The final component of our model is the external side of the condition for full macroeconomic equilibrium, based on the balance of payments. External equilibrium exists when the trade deficit is exactly offset by the capital inflow:

$$(4.8) \quad F = M - X.$$

In the real world, capital inflows balance the total current account balance and not only the trade balance, but equation 4.8 may be taken as a simplified expression of the balance of payments. The foreign-exchange constrained (or trade-constrained) growth rate $(g_f)$ can then be computed by combining equations 4.3, 4.6, 4.7 and 4.8, and solving for $g = \Delta Y/Y$:

$$(4.9) \quad g_f = (e - m_c)/(m_i v) + (1/m_i v) f.$$

This expression says that the growth rate depends on the foreign exchange available from exports minus consumption spending plus capital inflows, and on the ICOR modified by the parameter $m_i$. Both growth rates are, according to equations 4.5 and 4.9, linear functions of the rate of capital inflows (f) and are shown in Figure 4.1, measuring f on the horizontal and the GDP growth rate on the vertical axis. To draw this diagram we have arbitrarily assumed parameter values, so that the slope of $g_f$ is steeper than that of $g_s$. The parameter values used in Figure 4.1 are: s=0.16, v = 4, e = 0.20, and $m_i$ = 0.75 and $m_c$ = 0.14. The vertical intercept of the $g_s$ function is s/v, the Harrod-Domar growth rate, and the corresponding slope of the $g_f$ function is $1/(m_i v)$.

Based on the assumptions of the model and the numerical parameter values chosen, it follows that for 0< f <0.24 the binding constraint is the trade constraint, since in this region $g_f < g_s$, and the foreign exchange gap is the larger of the two gaps. When capital inflows represent 24 percent of GDP, both constraints are simultaneously binding. Above f = 0.24, the savings constraint is binding since $g_s$ is the lower of the two growth rates.

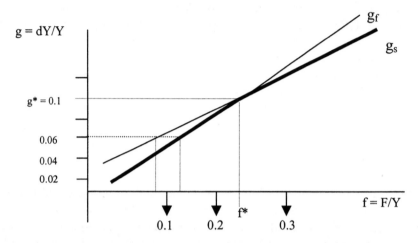

**Figure 4.1   The savings- and trade-constrained growth rates as functions of foreign capital inflows (the binding constraint is emphasized)**

The position of the two constraint lines, which depends on the functional form and parameter values, may be quite different from the one shown in Figure 4.1. For instance, for smaller values of $m_i$ than 3/4, the slope of $g_f$ would be steeper, and its intercept larger, so that the constraint lines would possibly intersect in the negative range of f. This would indicate that both constraints are binding when capital flows outward, and that in the positive range of f, the savings constraint is always binding.

What can we learn from this model, and what policy conclusions can be derived? The model is useful to predict:

a.   which constraint is binding at given levels of f;
b.   what level of capital inflow is necessary to achieve specific target growth rates; and
c.   what growth rate is achievable with given levels of capital inflow.

Referring to the diagram, a target growth rate of 6 percent requires capital inflows of 8 percent according to the savings constraint, and 12 percent according to the trade constraint. Therefore, the target can be reached only if foreign exchange representing 12 percent of GDP are available. In this case some amount of saving will remain unused for the purpose of capacity expansion. If foreign exchange in the order of only eight percent of GDP are available, the policy maker must concentrate on easing the trade constraint, which means shifting the $g_f$ function upwards so that it intersects the $g_s$ function at $f = 0.08$. This could be achieved by either promoting exports, which raises e, or by lowering $m_c$, the propensity to import for consumption, or by lowering $m_i$, the proportion of investment goods that are imported. Alternatively, the policy maker may also try to reach the 6 percent growth target with the given constraints by increasing the foreign capital inflow to 12 percent. This may be possible by attracting more foreign investment or aid flows, or by borrowing on the international capital market.

## 4.2    Empirical Evidence and Testing of the Two-gap Model

The two-gap model has been applied in numerous studies analysing the constraints to economic growth in both single-country and multi-country analyzes. One of the pioneering studies by Chenery and Bruno (1962) found that countries tend to face a dominant savings constraint in earlier stages and a dominant foreign exchange constraint at later stages of development. Landau's study of saving functions in Latin America (1971) found that in a sample of 18 countries eight of them experienced a binding trade constraint, in four countries the saving constraint was binding, and the remaining six countries seemed to have experienced alternating constraints from savings and foreign exchange.

The existing tests of the model are of a great variety and, in some cases, considerable intricacy. Therefore, we will limit the discussion to the description of only one of these test methods, the one used by Landau. But prior to that, let us first suggest a simple inspection of how the data match with the hypotheses of constrained growth. For this purpose we plot the observed combinations of annual GDP growth (g) and capital inflow as a proportion of GDP (f) in the diagram and identify the constraint that is more strongly supported by the data. This can be done by testing equations 4.5 and 4.9 in linear regression analysis, such that the equation with the better fit is then considered as the binding constraint. If a sufficient number of observations is available, the whole set of data may also be partitioned according to lower and higher levels of f, as the binding constraint may not be the same for different levels of capital inflows. Alternatively, the equations of the model may be estimated separately and the resulting parameter values may then be introduced into the constraint functions. Comparing the latter with the best fitting constraint lines then shows how well the model fits the observed data of growth and capital inflows.

The Landau test is less ambitious in that it does not test the entire growth model. Instead, it focuses on the question which of the two constraints may be binding, savings or foreign exchange availability. This depends on which of the two gaps is larger. Since both gaps are equal ex post, and the larger ex-ante gap represents the binding constraint, the smaller gap must adjust in order to achieve ex-post equality of the gaps. The following two equations were estimated by Landau:

$$(4.10) \quad S = S' + \alpha_1 F = a_1 + b_1 Y + \alpha_1 F \qquad \text{for } S \leq S'$$

$$(4.11) \quad M = M' + \alpha_2 F = a_2 + b_2 Y + \alpha_2 F \qquad \text{for } M \geq M'$$

where $S' = a_1 + b_1 Y$ is ex-ante saving and 4.10 defines ex-post savings, and $M' = a_2 + b_2 Y$ is ex-ante imports and 4.11 defines ex-post imports. Landau assumes that for I and X the ex-post values are always equal to the ex-ante values, so that S and M alone bear the burden of adjustment. For instance, if $S < S'$, that is, actual savings fall short of planned savings, then $\alpha_1 < 0$. This may happen if the capital inflow does not lead to higher investments, so that saving is lower than planned saving. Instead of supplementing saving, capital inflow acts as a substitute for domestic saving.

Suppose the trade gap is binding, that is, $(M'-X') > (I'-S')$ and $M = M'$, then it follows that $\alpha_2 = 0$ and, since it is assumed that $X = X'$ and $I = I'$, that the ex-post equality between the two gaps can only be reached by S falling short of S', implying $\alpha_1 < 0$. Therefore, we conclude that the trade gap is binding if $\alpha_1 < 0$ and $\alpha_2 = 0$.

Alternatively, if the savings gap is binding, that is, $(I'-S') > (M'-X')$ and $S = S'$, it follows that $\alpha_1 = 0$. Ex-post equality between the gaps is then reached if $M > M'$, implying $\alpha_2 > 0$. We conclude that the saving gap is binding if $\alpha_1 = 0$ and $\alpha_2 > 0$.

Finally, Landau has argued that when $\alpha_1$ is significantly negative, but with an absolute value of less than unity, and when $\alpha_2$ is significantly positive, we have a case of alternating binding constraints, and neither gap clearly dominates.

This test, however, has its limitations. First, the assumption that X and I are always in line with their planned values is convenient, but not entirely plausible. Second, the simultaneous estimation of equations 4.10 and 4.11 using the ordinary least squares method leads to biased and inconsistent estimates. Third, the estimated coefficients $\alpha_1$ and $\alpha_2$ are not true parameters reflecting the behavior of economic agents; they are simply ratios, $\alpha_1 = (S-S')/F$ and $\alpha_2 = (M-M')/F$, and there is no reason for these ratios to be constant over time.

Tests of the full two-gap model of growth are problematic because the model relies on a number of hypotheses, which need to be tested each at a time. While the Landau test focuses on the question of which constraint may be binding, other tests focus on the relationship between the gaps and the growth rate of GDP. The test is further complicated by the fact that the model deals with situations of disequilibrium, which are more difficult to analyze than situations of full equilibrium.

A modified version of the two-gap model [1] has been used extensively by the World Bank for calculating investment requirements to achieve target growth rates in developing countries. Recently, this model has come under attack after it became clear that many World Bank projects had failed to generate economic growth. Some of the critical voices came out of the Bank's own ranks.

W. Easterly, a World Bank economist, has criticized the financing-gap model for its lack of empirical support (Easterly, 1999). The assumption that the investments required to obtain a target growth are a linear function of the targeted growth ($I = v \ \Delta Y$), and the policy recommendation that the savings gap should be filled by capital inflows (F) in order to obtain the target growth rate, imply two propositions that Easterly tested and strongly rejected: 1) aid will go into investment one-for-one and 2) there will be a fixed linear relationship between growth and investment in the short run.

First, Easterly tested the proposition that aid will go to investment one-for-one by regressing the ratio of Gross Domestic Investments (GDI) to GDP against Official Development Assistance (ODA) as a share of GDP. He covered the period 1965-1995, a period in which he considered the U.S.$ 1 trillion in aid as one of the largest policy experiments ever tried of an economic model. The results of this test indicate an extremely weak support for the model. Only seven percent of the sample countries show a positive and significant one-for-one relationship between aid and investments, and only 19 percent show a positive and significant relationship. Most worrying is the finding that 60 percent of the countries even show a negative relationship. However, ODA is only one component of total capital inflows (F) and it is widely known to encourage governments' consumption expenditure. A more precise test of the financing gap model would have been the regression of GDI/GDP over F/GDP.

Easterly also tested the relationship between growth and investments by regressing GDP growth over GDI/GDP. Although he

[1]    The Revised Minimum Standard Model (RMSM) is also known as financing-gap model.

acknowledged that this relationship is most valid in the long run, he tested it in the short run. Only eight percent of the sample countries showed a positive and significant coefficient of growth. Easterly also criticized the financing-gap model in the short run by examining how often high growth episodes have been accompanied by the investment rates that had been indicated as 'necessary' by the model. With an ICOR of 3.5 this necessary investment condition was only fulfilled in 11 percent of the cases and even with an ICOR of 2 only in 49 percent of high growth occurrences. These findings put in question the short-run relationship[2] between investment and growth. It must be stressed, however, that the short-run link between investment and growth is well known to be weak. It is normal that investments, such as those in infrastructure, education, health care, and so on, do not generate a higher growth rate in one year. It would be more valid to look at the intermediate-run or long-run relationship that has been found to be stronger by Levine and Renelt (1991).

Finally, it is not clear why Easterly rejected the two-gap model, while attacking the relationships between aid flows and investments and between investments and growth. The very essence of the two-gap and similar gap models is the possibility that growth may be constrained by other factors than finance, such as the shortage of foreign exchange.

## 4.3     Official Development Assistance (ODA)

Among the three main forms of capital inflows that we briefly review here, official development aid, external borrowing and foreign investment, aid flows are the most problematic. Development aid has many interesting institutional characteristics, which are not discussed in detail here. The reader may consult more extensive treatments of the subject, such as Gillis et al. (1996, Chapter 15), or Eaton (1989) for this purpose. We shall focus here only on their importance in terms of relative size, as well as their role in accelerating economic growth and development.

Development aid is disbursed either directly by donor countries (bilateral aid) or indirectly by international institutions (multilateral aid). It is also known as Official Development Assistance (ODA) and consists of grants, which require no reimbursement, and concessionary loans, which involve lower than market interest rates and favourable repayment conditions. As Table 4.1 shows, until recently it represented the most important category of resource flows to developing countries, but had

---

[2]     Easterly used a lag of 1 year.

declined to only 20 percent of total capital inflows by 1995. In many countries that do not attract much foreign investment, however, it still accounts for a large part of capital inflows.

**Table 4.2    Official Development Assistance, by donor country, 1970, 1995 and 2002**

|  | 1970 | | 1995 | | 2002 | |
|---|---|---|---|---|---|---|
|  | Million $ | % of GDP | Million $ | % of GDP | Million $ | % of GDP |
| Australia | 212 | 0.59 | 1 136 | 0.34 | 989 | 0.26 |
| Austria | 11 | 0.07 | 747 | 0.32 | 520 | 0.26 |
| Belgium | 121 | 0.46 | 1 034 | 0.38 | 1 072 | 0.43 |
| Canada | 337 | 0.41 | 2 153 | 0.39 | 2 006 | 0.28 |
| Denmark | 59 | 0.38 | 1 623 | 0.96 | 1 643 | 0.96 |
| Finland | 7 | 0.06 | 388 | 0.32 | 462 | 0.35 |
| France | 971 | 0.66 | 8 443 | 0.55 | 5 486 | 0.38 |
| Germany | 599 | 0.32 | 7 481 | 0.31 | 5 324 | 0.27 |
| Ireland | n/a | n/a | 143 | 0.27 | 398 | 0.40 |
| Italy | 0.1 | 0.16 | 162 | 0.15 | 2 332 | 0.20 |
| Japan | 458 | 0.23 | 14 484 | 0.28 | 9 283 | 0.23 |
| Luxembourg | n/a | n/a | 68 | 0.38 | 147 | 0.77 |
| Netherlands | 196 | 0.61 | 3 226 | 0.78 | 3 338 | 0.81 |
| New Zealand | 15 | 0.23 | 123 | 0.20 | 122 | 0.22 |
| Norway | 37 | 0.32 | 1 244 | 0.87 | 1 696 | 0.89 |
| Portugal | n/a | n/a | 271 | 0.27 | 323 | 0.27 |
| Spain | n/a | n/a | 1 348 | 0.24 | 1 712 | 0.26 |
| Sweden | 424 | 0.38 | 1 704 | 0.77 | 1 991 | 0.83 |
| Switzerland | 30 | 0.15 | 1 084 | 0.34 | 939 | 0.32 |
| United Kingdom | 499 | 0.41 | 3 185 | 0.29 | 4 924 | 0.31 |
| United States | 3153 | 0.32 | 7 367 | 0.10 | 13 290 | 0.13 |

*Source*:   OECD, ODA flows; International Financial Statistics, World Development Report 1995; Statistics Norway 2000, Official Development Assistance 1995.

In terms of donor country GNPs, aid flows represent only very small proportions. The one percent target recommended by the Pearson Commission in 1969 (Commission on International Development, 1969) is presently met only by a few European countries, such as Denmark, Norway and Sweden, who have increased their contributions substantially within the last 20 years. Table 4.2 shows the international aid effort for the main donor countries in 1970 and 1993, both in absolute terms and as percentage of their GNP. It is noteworthy that for the donor countries as a whole the percentage given as aid has declined since the 1970s and reached a low point of less than a quarter of one percent of their combined GNP by the end of the 20th century. The decline is particularly evident for the U.S., although the absolute size of American aid is still very substantial.

**Table 4.3      Net official development assistance to developing countries, by recipient country, 2001**

|  | GDP p.c. (U.S. $) | ODA received (Million $) | ODA Received p.c. (U.S. $) | ODA received (% of GDP) |
|---|---|---|---|---|
| **Low Income** | | | | |
| Burkina Faso | 215 | 389 | 31.7 | 15.6 |
| Bangladesh | 350 | 1024 | 7.3 | 2.2 |
| Kenya | 371 | 453 | 14.6 | 4.0 |
| Pakistan | 415 | 1938 | 13.2 | 3.3 |
| India | 462 | 1705 | 1.7 | 0.4 |
| Senegal | 476 | 419 | 43.5 | 9.0 |
| **Lower Middle Income** | | | | |
| China | 911 | 1460 | 1.1 | 0.1 |
| Philippines | 912 | 577 | 7.5 | 0.8 |
| Morocco | 1173 | 516 | 17.5 | 1.5 |
| Thailand | 1874 | 281 | 4.6 | 0.2 |
| Russian Federation | 2141 | 1110 | 7.7 | 0.4 |
| **Upper Middle Income** | | | | |
| Chile | 4314 | 58 | 3.7 | 0.1 |
| Poland | 4561 | 966 | 25.0 | 0.5 |
| Czech Republic | 5554 | 314 | 30.6 | 0.6 |
| Uruguay | 5554 | 15 | 4.6 | 0.1 |
| Argentina | 7166 | 51 | 4.0 | 0.1 |
| **Aggregates** | | | | |
| East Asia and Pacific | 1267 | 5934 | 3.9 | 0.4 |
| Latin America/Carribean | 3752 | 13019 | 11.4 | 0.2 |
| South Asia | 508 | 6032 | 4.2 | 0.8 |
| Sub-Saharan Africa | 475 | 5050 | 20.6 | - |

*Source*: United Nations Development Program, Human Development Report 2003.

From the point of view of the recipient countries, ODA can represent a substantial proportion of their GNP. For instance, as Table 4.3 shows, in Sub-Saharan Africa it represented $35.7 per capita, or 11.5 percent of GNP in the early 1990s. The proportion is particularly high in small countries like Rwanda (24.1 percent), Ghana (10.4 percent) and Senegal (8.8 percent), whereas it represents only 0.6 percent in India and 1.4 percent in Indonesia.

Another characteristic of foreign aid is the fact that much of it is tied to specific projects and donor country suppliers. The equipment and technologies provided by such suppliers are not always optimally suited for the needs of the recipient countries. Furthermore, the tying of aid to donor country suppliers reduces its value, whenever the implicit prices of goods and services exceed the prices of alternative suppliers. One form of aid that is potentially most useful, but in reality often unproductive, is technical assistance focusing on the transfer of know-how and technologies. In such projects the transfer of know-how often does not take place, because the transfer mechanism is ill understood and not well planned. For instance, governments could benefit from technical assistance in economic policy making, but they may be, and often are, unprepared for the transfer of analytical skills, because such transfers require the recipients to possess the required background and to have the necessary motivation linked to an incentive structure at their work place. Often recipient governments accept such projects while being opposed to technical assistance because they may see it as a threat to their sovereignty.

## 4.4    Foreign Investment

While Official Development Assistance consists of funds that are committed by foreign governments and invested by the recipient country governments, foreign investments are normally private and remain the property of the foreign investors. Two kinds of foreign investment can be distinguished, portfolio and foreign direct investment (FDI). The former involves arms-length and minority foreign ownership, whereas the latter consists of direct and often majority ownership and control of domestic enterprises. Since foreign investment does not generate debt, it could be seen as unequivocally favorable to economic development. This is not always the case, however. It is often controversial and even unwelcome in some countries. Let us examine therefore its importance, benefits and costs to recipient countries. Table 4.4 shows the relative importance of foreign direct investment in selected low, middle and high-income countries. The data shown in this table suggest that with exception of China the flow of FDI is generally small as a proportion of the recipient countries' GDP, that is, less than one percent in the low-income group and one to two percent in the middle-income group.

**Table 4.4     Net inward foreign direct investment in developing countries, 1990 and 2001**

|  | GDP p.c. (U.S. $) 2001 | FDI as a % of GDP 1990 | FDI as a % of GDP 2001 | FDI 2001 (Billions $) |
|---|---|---|---|---|
| **Low Income** | | | | |
| Nigeria | 319 | 2.1 | 2.7 | 1.1 |
| Vietnam | 411 | 0.2 | 4.0 | 1.3 |
| Pakistan | 415 | 0.6 | 0.7 | 0.4 |
| India | 462 | 0.1 | 0.7 | 3.4 |
| Angola | 701 | -3.3 | 11.8 | 1.1 |
| **Lower Middle Income** | | | | |
| China | 911 | 1.0 | 3.8 | 44.2 |
| Morocco | 1173 | 0.6 | 7.8 | 2.7 |
| Egypt | 1511 | 1.7 | 0.5 | 0.5 |
| Algeria | 1773 | - | 2.2 | 1.2 |
| Thailand | 1874 | 2.9 | 3.3 | 3.8 |
| Russian Federation | 2141 | 0.0 | 0.8 | 2.5 |
| South Africa | 2620 | - | 6.3 | 7.2 |
| Brazil | 2915 | 0.2 | 4.5 | 22.6 |
| **Upper Middle Income** | | | | |
| Malaysia | 3699 | 5.3 | 0.6 | 0.6 |
| Slovak Republik | 3786 | 0.0 | 7.2 | 1.5 |
| Poland | 4561 | 0.2 | 3.2 | 5.7 |
| Venezuela | 5073 | 0.9 | 2.8 | 3.4 |
| Hungary | 5097 | 0.9 | 4.7 | 2.4 |
| Czech Republic | 5554 | 0.2 | 8.7 | 4.9 |
| Mexico | 6214 | 1.0 | 4.0 | 24.7 |
| Argentina | 7166 | 1.3 | 1.2 | 3.2 |

*Source*:   UN Development Program, Human Development Report 2003; World Bank, Global Development Finance 2003, Statistical Appendix.

The basic rationale for foreign investors to transfer their funds into foreign countries is the opportunity for higher returns than are available in the home country. These higher returns can be earned in developing countries mainly because the costs of labour tend to be lower than in the home countries of the investors. Additional incentives to invest abroad may exist, such as the existence of natural resources, or the availability of fiscal incentives provided by host country governments. From the viewpoint of the recipient countries, foreign direct investments generate three kinds of benefits: employment and income, tax revenue for the government, and privileged access to technologies and know-how.

While additional employment and income are always welcome, they can also be problematic. Foreign firms, which are often branch plants of multinational corporations (MNCs), tend to pay higher incomes and offer better working conditions than local enterprises. By functioning in so-called high-income 'enclaves' they are likely to contribute to inequality. The tax revenue they potentially generate, while clearly beneficial, is often foregone by recipient governments, who offer generous tax breaks in order to attract foreign investors. The objects of greatest interest to recipient countries are technologies that are more easily transferred by the owners through FDI than through other channels of technology transfer. Proprietary technologies are typically protected by secrecy and strict control by the owners and can be accessed only through direct investment. But even non-proprietary technologies are more easily transferred through direct investments because the profit motive of foreign owners creates an incentive to transfer skills and to 'indigenize' technical know-how.

The main disadvantages or costs of FDI, besides the enclave effect mentioned earlier, are related to the size and nature of the investing firms. Most foreign direct investments are undertaken by multinational corporations whose size, in terms of the value of production or the value of assets, is often larger than that of the recipient economy. The host country governments and the investing firms are then unequal partners, and the outcome of their negotiations may be biased in favor of the MNCs and to the disadvantage of the host countries. In addition, extensive foreign ownership of the productive means of a country also implies that there is a steady outflow of dividends in foreign exchange. The long-run balance of payments situation is therefore aggravated by the presence of foreign investments. This problem is diminished if the foreign-owned firms produce mainly for export, but many MNC branch plants are set up to produce essentially for the domestic market, often importing most of the intermediate inputs. In addition, multinationals tend to employ expatriate managers and technicians to whom they guarantee the transfer of a substantial proportion of their salaries in foreign currency.

Indirect or portfolio investments do not pose the same problems of foreign control as FDI, but their benefits may be reduced by their volatility. Short-term capital inflows can quickly turn into outflows, when the international investors change their evaluation of country-specific risks. Strong fluctuations in the recipient countries' capital account are often the cause of financial crises, economic instability and decline.

Whether a specific foreign investment is beneficial to the recipient country depends on various conditions, which can, to a certain extent, be influenced by host country governments. Incentives to attract foreign investors imply costs that may exceed the benefits of such investments. On the whole, however, developing countries can derive important benefits from foreign investments in the form of internationally competitive producers, access to new technologies, incomes, foreign exchange earnings and tax revenues.

## 4.5    Foreign Borrowing and the Debt Problem

As we have seen earlier, foreign borrowing includes both official and private borrowing, where the former is typically contracted on concessionary terms. Here we focus on the more general conditions under which foreign borrowing is beneficial to developing countries. We shall ignore the grant element of official borrowing and concentrate on both official and private non-concessionary borrowing.

The first question concerns the rationale of borrowing, and it can be answered by comparing the behavior of governments with that of individuals and firms. Both individuals and firms derive net benefits from borrowing if the rate of return from the investment financed by the loan exceeds the rate of interest to be paid for the loan. The same principle applies to countries that borrow from abroad, but the rate of return must consider social rather than only private benefits and costs. The method of calculating the net socio-economic benefits of an investment is discussed in Chapter 9. An additional problem exists in that foreign loans must be repaid in foreign exchange, and there is no guarantee that even an investment with a high return will generate enough foreign exchange to repay both the interest and the principal.

The accumulation of loans leads to foreign debt, which can be unsustainable and lead to default of debt service. For monitoring external debt it is useful to observe the debt-service ratio. It divides the annual debt service, consisting of interest and repayment of principal, by the foreign exchange earnings, and is an important indicator of a country's ability to service its debt. A ratio of 25 percent or higher is usually considered as a warning of difficulties, since a debt service obligation of this size represents a serious burden to the economy. In addition to the financial burden of the debt service for government budgets, the use of scarce foreign exchange limits the country's capacity to import, and import shortages are frequently a constraint to economic growth. The debt-service ratio is not easily calculated, however, since this requires the knowledge of the structure of total debt in terms of the due dates of different loans. It is easier to observe the debt-exports ratio, which we shall use in a simple model of debt projection. Another significant indicator is the ratio of total debt to GDP or GNP.

What level of debt is sustainable in a particular country depends on the structure of the debt in terms of the repayment dates of loans, the interest rates and the country's export capacity. A simple computation based on the debt service threshold of 25 percent can help in answering the question. Let the annual increase in debt, $\Delta D$, be determined by the trade deficit and the debt service:

$$(4.12) \quad \Delta D = (M - X) + i D + \pi D$$

where D is the total accumulated debt, i is the average interest rate on outstanding loans and $\pi$ is the proportion of loans maturing in the present year. If the debt service, $D(i + \pi)$, must not exceed 25 percent of exports, then:

$$(4.13) \quad D/X < 1/(i + \pi)4.$$

For an interest rate of five percent and a proportion of 7.5 percent of the debt maturing, the critical debt/export ratio is then $D/X = 2$. This ratio is close to the observed average in developing countries in the 1980s. For a country exporting 30 percent of GDP, the corresponding critical level of debt is 60 percent of GDP. This ratio is being used as debt ceiling allowed under the stability pact by the European Union. Based on these considerations it can be easily seen that a country with a higher proportion of maturing loans than 7.5 percent and/or an average interest rate on outstanding debt higher than five percent the debt service exceeds 25 percent of exports and the level of debt exceeds its critical ratios of D/X and D/Y.

Governments usually try to avoid defaulting on debt service payments, since it limits their ability to borrow in the future. Recent history, especially the debt crisis of the early 1980s, shows that countries can default and reschedule their debt burdens in many, and some quite innovative, fashions. This, contrary to the situation of individuals, is possible because sovereign debt, which official country debt is referred to as, is rarely seen as the sole responsibility of the debtor country, but also involves the policies and interests of international lenders and the international community at large. Even third countries not involved in lending to a particular debtor can be partially responsible for its problems because they may have contributed to a rise in the international interest rate. Therefore, all countries that will derive benefits from settling the debt problem of a particular country can be expected to contribute to finding a solution. This argument is the rationale behind several innovative methods of solving the debt problems of particular debtor nations applied in recent years. Among such methods there are rescheduling agreements, debt buy-backs and debt-equity swaps. For the functioning of such arrangements the interested reader may be referred to the discussion of the 1980s debt crisis in Perkins et al., (2001, Chapter 15), or in Husain and Diwan (1989). One of the more recent solutions to the debt problem of developing countries is the one proposed by Anne Krueger, presently chief economist of the IMF, known as Sovereign Debt Restructuring Mechanism (SDRM). It is a legal mechanism comparable to the bankruptcy procedures in the private sector, permitting countries to obtain payments standstills, restructuring and, if necessary, write-downs of debt.

A further method of predicting future debt burdens, in order to avoid default, is the following growth model of debt proposed by Fishlow (1988). Assuming that the debt repayment is added to the trade balance, the annual change in total debt is the sum of the annual external deficit (net of debt repayment) and the interest to be paid on the existing debt:

(4.14)   $dD/dt = M - X + i\,D$

where D is the accumulated level of debt, $dD/dt$ is its annual change, and i is the average rate of interest to be paid on the total debt. This equation describes a process of growth, which, under certain assumptions, converges towards a fixed ratio of D/X. The necessary assumptions are that (a) the interest rate remains fixed, and (b) imports and exports grow at the same rate, implying that the deficit/export ratio, $a = (M-X)/X$, remains fixed. Based on these assumptions we compute the D/X ratio, towards which the process converges, by setting $dD/Ddt = dX/Xdt = g_x$ and solving for D/X:

(4.15)   $D/X = a/(g_x - i)$.

Suppose the external deficit ratio is six percent, trade flows grow at five percent and the interest rate is four percent, then the debt/exports ratio converges towards a level of six. If the present debt is twice the annual value of exports, the average ratio observed in developing countries in the 1980s, this means that the country is facing a rapidly growing debt/export ratio. It also means that the debt burden is likely to be unsustainable. The model can easily be simulated in order to see how the problem varies with parameter changes. A lower interest rate would obviously lower the long-term ratio of D/X and, thereby, slow down the growth of the debt burden.

Alternatively, more rapid growth of exports would have a similar effect. When exports grow faster than imports, the ratio 'a' diminishes and there is no convergence towards a fixed D/X ratio. The country can grow out of its debt problem and even become a creditor. The opposite case, when imports grow faster than exports, is the worst possible scenario, because it leads to the growth of debt beyond any limit, which is clearly an unsustainable situation. The discussion permits us to conclude that the promotion of exports is likely to be the most effective policy for solving a national debt problem. The model is to be applied in Case Study 8, which deals with the Brazilian debt problem of the 1980s.

## References

Chenery, Hollis and M. Bruno (1962), 'Development Alternatives in an Open Economy: The Case of Israel', *Economic Journal*, 72, March, pp. 79-103.

Commission on International Development (1969), *Partners in Development*, L.B. Pearson (chair), Praeger, New York.

Easterly, W. (1999), 'The ghost of the financing gap', *Journal of Development Economics*, vol.60, pp. 423-438.

Eaton, Jonathan (1989), 'Foreign Public Capital Flows', in: Chenery and Srinavasan (eds.), *Handbook of Development Economics*, vol.II, Chapter 26, North Holland.

Fishlow, Albert (1988), 'External Borrowing and Debt Management', in: Dornbusch and Helmers (eds.), *The Open Economy: Tools for Policymakers in Developing Countries*, Oxford University Press.

Husain, Ishrat and I. Diwan (eds.) (1989), *Dealing with the Debt Crisis*, The World Bank, Washington.

Landau, Luis (1971), 'Saving Functions for Latin America', in: Chenery (ed.), *Studies in Development Planning*, Harvard University Press, Cambridge, Massachusets.

McKinnon, R.I. (1964), 'Foreign exchange constraints in economic development and efficient aid allocation', *Economic Journal*, 74, pp. 388-409.

Perkins, Dwight H. et al. (2001), *Economics of Development*, 5th edition, Norton, New York.

# Case Study 8
# The Brazilian Debt Crisis

Prior to the 1980s there seems to have been a consensus in the developed and developing countries that the development of poor countries could/should be financed from external sources. This was done via official, concessional and non-concessional, and private borrowing to less developed countries, a strategy called growth-cum-debt (or debt-led-growth). In August 1992, Mexico announced that it was unable to pay back the interests and principal of its foreign debt. This was the beginning of what is known as the international debt crisis. In this case study, we examine the case of the Brazilian debt crisis.

## Historical Background

Brazil's external debt problem of the 1980s was not something new to the country. The accumulation of external debt started already after Brazil's declaration of independence and continued throughout the 19th century. Brazil experienced a debt crisis when it stopped servicing its foreign debt in 1931, which was also a period of international debt problems in Latin America.

During the 1950s, Brazil's ambitious industrialization plans required large amounts of capital. These were found in the form of direct foreign investments and loans. The result was that the level of external debt in 1960 was already double that of 1955. The economic problems of that period (debt and inflation) coincided with considerable political turmoil. After president Quadros's resignation in August 1961, president Goulart did not execute the stabilization program designed by the IMF, but embarked on an own reform program. Foreign governments and international financial institutions did not support Goulart's reform efforts, which were perceived as leftist. Capital inflows from important lending capitalist countries such as the U.S. ceased and the World Bank did not concede any new loans to Brazil. In April 1964, the military ousted the leftist government of Goulart. The new government was perceived much more favorable by the international community and by international financial institutions. Brazil's debt was rescheduled and new loans were conceded by the IMF and the Agency for International Development.

In the late 1960s and especially after the first oil crisis in 1973 the oil producing countries placed their oil revenues in foreign banks, which actively looked for borrowers of these Eurodollar funds. Loans to developing countries became abundantly available from commercial banks and carried relatively low interest rates. Brazil was one of the first countries to respond to the flood of easy money as it implemented its debt-based growth policy for development.

The oil shock of 1973 affected Brazil strongly as it was the largest oil importing developing country. First, its terms of trade worsened, but a higher coffee price helped reverse the declining terms-of-trade. But Brazil's foreign debt kept increasing as economic growth requirements determined the need for debt. On the eve of the second oil shock in 1979, the Brazilian debt was the largest in the world. Already in the late 1970s, before the sudden surge in interest rates, the reverse flow of service payments was beginning to cancel the new inflows. The second oil shock put an end to the period of abundant funds and interest rates soared. The tight monetary policy of the Reagan Administration in the U.S. contributed to the increase in interest rates. As Brazil had taken on many loans at flexible interest rates, the world's largest debtor was bound to face problems of debt service. While earlier debt accumulation amounted to a large transfer of real resources, more and more borrowing was now needed simply to cover interest obligations on earlier loans.

## Reference

E.A. Cardoso and A. Fishlow (1990), 'The Macroeconomics of the Brazilian External Debt', in: J.D. Sachs (ed.), *Developing Country Debt and Economic Performance, volume 2: Country studies*, University of Chicago Press.

## Assigned Questions

1)     The process of debt accumulation can be described as $dD^*_t = M_t - X_t + iD^*_{t-1}$, where $D_t$ and $dD_t$ are total debt and its annual increase, respectively, and starred variables are projected values. Using the initial stock of gross foreign debt in 1970 ($5295.2 million) and this model of accumulation, project Brazil's foreign debt during the period 1971-1985 (hint: compute $D^*_t = dD^*_t + D^*_{t-1}$ for the whole period ). Compare the projected debt ($D^*_t$) with actual debt ($D_t$). How accurate is your projection and what factors may be responsible for the deviations?

The data provided in the table below show that Brazil's gross foreign debt has increased from $4,403 million in 1969 to no less than $101,759 million in 1986. On February 20 1987, the Brazilian government announced that it would stop servicing its external debt. With the following questions we will try to determine what could have been the causes of Brazil's debt crisis.

2)      The interest rate is one of the factors that affect the process of debt accumulation. How did the nominal interest rate evolve over the periods before 1973, 1973-1979 and 1979-1985? What were the causes of this evolution?

3)      The second factor in the accumulation of debt is the country's current account. Use the trade data provided in the table above to describe the evolution of Brazil's current account. Also calculate export price inflation, import price inflation and terms-of-trade. What were the main reasons for Brazil's current account deficits? Was the current account the major factor leading to the debt crisis?

So far, we have looked into the factors that could have affected Brazil's debt and that are also described in our model of debt accumulation. We can investigate if these factors indeed have had the expected effect on Brazil's debt accumulation using simple regression analysis.

4)      Run the following regression: $dD_t = \alpha + \beta (M_t - X_t) + \gamma iD_{t-1}$ and interpret the parameter values. Then use this equation to project the debt for the whole period. How does this projection compare with the earlier one and with the actual debt? What do you conclude from this exercise regarding the determinants of the accumulation of debt in Brazil?

For further insights, we shall examine some widely used debt indicators, such as the debt/export ratio and the debt service ratio.

5)      Calculate Brazil's debt/export ratio and the debt service ratio and comment on their evolution. What can you conclude out of these debt indicators with respect to the accumulation of debt?

6)      On February 20 1987, the Brazilian government announced that it would stop servicing its external debt. Using the reference articles as well as your answers to questions 1-5 to describe briefly (1/2 page) what were the main events leading to the Brazilian debt moratorium of 1987?

## Table CS8    The current account and foreign debt in Brazil

| Year | Interest rate paid[3] | Exports[4] | Imports[5] | Gross foreign debt[6] | Export price index | Import price index | Debt service[7] |
|------|-----------|---------|---------|---------------|--------|--------|----------|
| 1969 | n.a.  | 2311  | 1993  | 4403.0   | 33.3  | 41.6  | n.a.     |
| 1970 | n.a.  | 2739  | 2507  | 5295.2   | 37.6  | 42.4  | 906.61   |
| 1971 | 7.4   | 2904  | 3245  | 6621.6   | 36.3  | 44.1  | 1152.89  |
| 1972 | 7.3   | 3991  | 4235  | 9521.0   | 41.0  | 47.0  | 1560.48  |
| 1973 | 9.6   | 6199  | 6192  | 12571.5  | 56.4  | 58.9  | 2188.25  |
| 1974 | 10.6  | 7951  | 12641 | 17165.7  | 71.1  | 90.7  | 2560.22  |
| 1975 | 12.6  | 8670  | 12210 | 21171.4  | 71.1  | 93.6  | 3684.75  |
| 1976 | 10.6  | 10128 | 12347 | 25985.4  | 82.0  | 96.2  | 4820.93  |
| 1977 | 10.8  | 12120 | 12023 | 32037.2  | 100.0 | 100.0 | 6241.80  |
| 1978 | 10.9  | 12659 | 13683 | 43510.7  | 89.7  | 102.5 | 8139.74  |
| 1979 | 13.2  | 15244 | 18084 | 49904.2  | 101.0 | 128.0 | 10731.80 |
| 1980 | 15.7  | 20132 | 22955 | 53847.5  | 107.0 | 163.9 | 13025.40 |
| 1981 | 19.5  | 23293 | 22091 | 61410.8  | 100.7 | 182.1 | 16677.80 |
| 1982 | 21.1  | 20213 | 19395 | 70197.5  | 94.6  | 176.1 | 18616.20 |
| 1983 | 14.5  | 21899 | 15429 | 81319.2  | 89.5  | 166.8 | 19621.50 |
| 1984 | 13.3  | 27005 | 13937 | 91091.0  | 91.3  | 158.4 | n.a.     |
| 1985 | 12.2  | 25639 | 13153 | 95856.7  | 86.1  | 149.2 | n.a.     |
| 1986 | n.a.  | 22393 | 14044 | 101759.0 | n.a.  | n.a.  | n.a.     |

*Source*: Debt and adjustment policies in Brazil, J.C. Batista, 1992.

---

[3]   Average of actual interest rates paid (Source: Batista, op. cit.).
[4]   In $U.S. millions.
[5]   In $U.S. millions.
[6]   In $U.S. millions.
[7]   In $U.S. millions. Obtained from the debt service ratio provided by Batista (op. cit.).

# Case Study 9
# Constraints to Economic Growth in Kenya:
# The Two-gap Model

## Purpose

Building on the Harrod-Domar growth model, we now apply the two-gap model of growth, which introduces an additional constraint, the availability of foreign exchange. The idea, which is central to this model, is that a country with a limited capacity to produce the capital goods necessary for investments, is therefore dependent on imports for growth. The feasible growth rate is then either the saving-determined rate, or the foreign-exchange-determined rate, whichever is lower. The lower of these two growth rates indicates the binding constraint. If a certain rate is targeted, the model shows us the amounts of either savings or foreign exchange required by the target, depending on whether the saving or the trade constraint is binding. Alternatively, if the inflow of foreign capital is given, the model shows us which growth rate is attainable, which again depends on the binding constraint. For example assume that the targeted growth rate is 6 percent. If the growth rate allowed by saving is 5 percent, while the growth rate allowed by foreign exchange is 6 percent, the saving constraint is binding and the total foreign exchange-based growth potential cannot be realized. The targeted growth rate may be reached nevertheless if it is possible to shift the saving constraint upward.

Knowledge of the growth constraints allows us to predict potential growth, given the amount of foreign saving that the country can attract. The model proposed here is very simplified. There are of course many other factors that affect growth, for instance the availability of skills. To capture such additional constraints, the model could be extended to a multi-gap model. The two-gap model focuses on the double function of foreign saving: it acts as saving supplement and as foreign-exchange supplement.

## Background

Kenya is a small country with an average GDP per capita of only about $350 and an estimated population of 24 million (1990). During the early 1970s, the country experienced strong economic growth; real GDP grew at 8.3 percent per annum between 1969 and 1973, while average prices rose by only 4-5 percent per annum. Since then the economy has performed less well, registering an average real growth rate of about 4.5 percent while prices rose by about 10 percent. Since the break-up of the East African Community (1977), exports have declined from 29 percent of GDP to around 15 percent in 1992. Another factor which has affected Kenya's trade balance is the decline in the terms of trade.

Given its high population growth (above 3 percent) Kenya needs to achieve rapid growth of GDP in order to experience rising living standards. The government in its yearly budget and longer-term planning effort (the Development Plan is a 5-year exercise) needs to know what growth target is feasible and what policies need to be adopted in order to enhance economic growth. Given the recently poor performance of exports, it is likely that foreign exchange represents a constraint to growth.

**Method of Analysis**

In stage 1 of this case study the parameters of the two-gap model are estimated and the model is then written down in the form of its two constraints, which are also drawn in a diagram with f = F/Y an the horizontal and g on the vertical axis. On the basis of these equations and the diagram you will be able to conclude which constraint has been binding under different levels of capital inflows (f).

In stage 2 we assume that the two-gap model estimated in stage 1 is well supported by the data. You use the model then for predictions of (a) the attainable growth rate for given levels of capital inflow, and (b) of the required levels of capital inflow for given target growth rates. You also check whether the model is actually well supported by the Kenyan data. A very simple answer to this question is obtained by checking whether the observed growth rate and capital inflow combinations (that is, the dots g, f) are lying close to the constraint lines.

In stage 3, after having examined the question of model validity, you try to modify your policy conclusions from stage 2, by taking another look at the data and avoiding model-based conclusions. For this exercise it is useful to graph the variables I, F and S over time.

**Assigned Questions**

*The model and its parameter values*

1) Using the data provided below and on diskette, estimate the parameters s, v, mc and mi by submitting the chapter equations 4.2, 4.3, 4.6 and 4.7 to simple regression analysis (OLS).

2) Interpret and explain the values of the parameters focusing on key characteristics of the economy. In particular, comment on the saving ratio (s), the export propensity (e), the ICOR (v) and the two import ratios mc and mi.

3) Using the parameter values, compute the saving-constrained and the trade-constrained growth rates (gs and gf) as a function of f. Draw a diagram with f on the horizontal axis and g on the vertical axis showing these constraint lines.

4) Plot the observed growth rates with the corresponding f values in the same diagram. Do the observed growth points fit the model well? Explain why or why not?

*Policy conclusions based on the model*

5) If the Kenyan government wishes to achieve a growth rate of 5 percent, what rate of foreign capital inflows (f) would be required assuming that the estimated growth model fits the data well?

6) Now assume that the government believes that foreign capital inflows will be available at the rate of at 10 percent of GDP. It wishes, nevertheless, to achieve the growth target of 5 percent. What policies can the government use to achieve this goal? Show how these policies may affect the model through changes in parameter values.

*Policy conclusions not based on the model*

7) Should the model appear to you as over-simplified and not robust enough for policy conclusions, what would you conclude from the data analysis about the possibilities of increasing the growth rate? What policies should the government pursue to enhance the growth performance?

**Table CS9   National accounts data of Kenya**

| Year | Income (Y) | Imports (M) | Exports (X) | Net imp. (M – X) | Investment (I) |
|---|---|---|---|---|---|
| 1972 | 1,901.2 | 566.8 | 366.2 | 200.6 | 676.9 |
| 1973 | 1,981.5 | 599.7 | 458.0 | 141.7 | 667.2 |
| 1974 | 2,041.6 | 870.5 | 518.8 | 351.7 | 590.5 |
| 1975 | 2,100.0 | 700.0 | 444.8 | 255.2 | 605.2 |
| 1976 | 2,189.3 | 678.3 | 559.0 | 119.3 | 598.2 |
| 1977 | 2,368.2 | 747.4 | 675.5 | 71.9 | 723.0 |
| 1978 | 2,550.0 | 919.5 | 514.6 | 404.9 | 852.2 |
| 1979 | 2,675.3 | 816.1 | 507.2 | 308.8 | 787.5 |
| 1980 | 2,782.6 | 1,161.0 | 590.3 | 570.7 | 807.3 |
| 1981 | 2,948.4 | 1,033.7 | 569.7 | 464.0 | 850.6 |
| 1982 | 3,049.3 | 900.3 | 545.7 | 354.6 | 668.2 |
| 1983 | 3,140.7 | 818.8 | 572.4 | 246.4 | 576.0 |
| 1984 | 3,153.9 | 892.8 | 614.2 | 278.6 | 593.4 |
| 1985 | 3,313.7 | 895.9 | 588.1 | 307.8 | 597.2 |
| 1986 | 3,498.6 | 915.1 | 655.3 | 259.8 | 668.1 |
| 1987 | 3,667.7 | 929.2 | 489.2 | 439.9 | 707.9 |
| 1988 | 3,857.5 | 1,050.7 | 546.3 | 504.4 | 766.7 |
| 1989 | 4,052.6 | 1,228.0 | 548.4 | 679.5 | 760.3 |
| 1990 | 4,222.7 | 1,283.1 | 621.2 | 661.9 | 786.7 |
| 1991 | 4,312.2 | 1,198.3 | 694.7 | 503.7 | 762.3 |
| 1992 | 4,328.0 | 1,153.4 | 666.7 | 486.7 | 691.3 |

**Case Study 9: Solution**

1) The model and its parameter values

i) The parameters were estimated by ordinary least squares regression. Their values are as follows:

$s = 0.097$ (average savings ratio)
$v = 4.9$ (ICOR)
$e = 0.176$ (export coefficient)
$m_c = 0.173$ (marginal propensity to import for consumption)
$m_i = 0.575$ (proportion of imported capital goods to total investment)

ii) In the regression analysis it is important to set the constant term equal to zero in order to obtain the very simplified equations of the model. The importance of this is obvious in the case of the savings function. If one chooses for regression a savings function with constant term one would obtain a negative marginal savings rate and a large positive intercept. Constraining the savings function to go through the origin, however leads to an average savings ratio of $s = 0.097$ (9.7 percent).

The ICOR of 4.9 implies that it takes nearly five Kenya shillings of capital to generate one shilling of GDP. The export coefficient means that on average 17.6 percent of GDP have been exported in the study period. The import coefficients inform us that 17.3 percent of GDP were needed for imports of consumption goods and that 57.5 percent of investments had to be imported.

iii)    $g_s = 0.02 + 0.2$ f(savings-constrained growth rate)
$g_f = 0.001 + 0.35$ (foreign exchange-constrained growth rate)
The intersection of the two constraint lines occurs at $f = 0.127$ and $g = 0.045$. That means that for capital inflows of 12.7 percent and a growth rate of 4.5 percent both constraints are binding. At lower rates of capital inflow ($< 12.7$ percent) the trade constraint is binding and at higher rates the savings constraint is binding.

iv)    The diagram reveals that the observed points, that is, growth rates achieved at different levels of f in various years, do not follow closely the constraint lines. This is not surprising because the model is extremely simplified, as we saw above in the discussion of the savings parameter.

2)    Policy conclusions based on the model

i)    A growth target of five percent requires 15 percent capital inflows. This follows from inserting the growth target of five percent into the binding savings constraint. Based on the trade constraint, only 14 percent of capital inflows would be needed for the five percent growth target.

ii)    If only ten percent foreign savings are available, both constraints need to be eased in order to meet the five percent growth target.

Geometrically speaking this means that both constraint lines need to be shifted upwards, in particular the trade constraint. This can be done by (a) increasing exports, (b) by lowering the imports for consumption, (c) by lowering the proportion of imports needed for investments, and (d) by lowering the ICOR. While the first three policy goals (a, b and c) are unambiguously beneficial, the lowering of ICOR may be problematic. It may imply going backwards in terms of capital intensity of the economy, unless a lower ICOR can be obtained by increasing the rate of capacity utilization. Exports can be raised by introducing export incentives and imports of consumption goods may be lowered by raising excise taxes. The policy target (c) can be approached by creating incentives to use domestic resources for investments as much as possible. Finally, the savings constraint can be raised by increasing the savings propensity by appropriate fiscal policy. The most effective way of achieving this goal in the short run is likely to be reduced government consumption in favour of more investment.

3)      Policy conclusions not based on the model

Since we know that the model contains extremely simplified functions and that it is not supported by the data (that is, the observed g, f – combinations are not close to the constraint lines) it may be hazardous to draw policy conclusions which are based on the model used in the analysis. Another approach is to go back to the raw data, plot them over time and observe the trend lines of investments, capital inflows and domestic saving.

While the investment trend line is more or less flat, capital inflows increased significantly during the study period. This happened because Kenya increased its trade deficit over time and could do that because capital inflows allowed it to remain in external balance. A substantial part of the capital inflows come from official development assistance in form of investment projects in roads, hospitals and other parts of the infrastructure. This seems to have led the Kenya government to lower its own investments in favour of recurrent costs, much of it in a growing bureaucracy. This explains why foreign savings have not played the role they are supposed to play, that is, to supplement domestic investments. Rather, they have substituted for domestic investment and failed to boost economic growth.

In order to make optimal use of capital inflows, the government should use the flows that it controls to make additional investments instead of curtailing its own investments.

# Chapter 5

# International Trade and Development

International trade theory is one of the corner stones of economic thought and has grown to an extensive body of literature. The purpose of this chapter is not to survey the theory of international trade, but to address a few topics that are most relevant to analysis of trade policies in developing countries. While most of the theoretical literature deals with the determinants of trade, here we focus on the consequences of trade and alternative trade policies for developing countries. The explanations of trade include productivity differences as postulated in the classical (Ricardian) model, differences in factor abundance (Heckscher-Ohlin), advantages arising from the product life cycle (Vernon), product differentiation and economies of scale (Krugman) and various other contributions. The most general and most fundamental principle explaining trade and its benefits, however, is the one of comparative advantage.

The importance of trade for economic development is often measured by its share of GDP. While in large countries trade tends to play a relatively minor role, possibly less than ten percent of GDP, small countries depend more strongly on imports and need to export proportionately more. This relationship between the proportion of trade and country size reflects the availability of resources and the size of markets. Large countries are more likely to possess most of the natural resources they require, and their markets are sufficiently large to produce industrial goods benefiting from economies of scale. Small countries, require export markets in order to produce economically at large scale. They are also likely to import many goods at prices that are lower than their own potential costs of production. In the rest of the chapter we shall focus first on the main rationale for trade and the gains from trade, and then examine the arguments against free trade. Next, we discuss the instruments and consequences of inward-oriented trade regimes, as well as trade policy reforms and outward orientation.

## 5.1     Comparative Advantage and the Gains from Trade

International trade is known to be beneficial to countries that specialize in activities, in which they have comparative advantage. The principle of comparative advantage, which was first rigorously analyzed by Ricardo, is one of the most fundamental ones in economics. It states that even if a country is less productive in all activities than other countries, it can nevertheless gain from trading with these countries, provided that it specializes in those activities in which it is relatively more productive. The greater relative productivity is measurable as opportunity cost, which poses no conceptual problems as long as we analyze the simple case of two activities, two countries and a single factor of production, as Ricardo did in his famous demonstration of comparative advantage. To recall, let the two goods, food (F) and clothing (C), be produced in both, the Home country (H) and a foreign country (F). We assume for simplicity that only one factor of production, labour, is used and that the following amounts of labour per unit of output ($L_F$ and $L_C$) are required:

|          | Home | Foreign |
|----------|------|---------|
| Food     | 5    | 6       |
| Clothing | 10   | 18      |

The opportunity cost of clothing in terms of food equals the factor input ratio, $L_C/L_F$, which is two in Home and three in Foreign. Therefore, producers in Home have comparative advantage in clothing and producers in Foreign have comparative advantage in Food. This is true in spite of Home's absolute advantage in both products as its workers are more productive (lower labour requirements) in both products than the workers in Foreign.

How comparative advantage leads to gains from trade is demonstrated in the following diagrams (Figure 5.1), where the two countries, Home and Foreign, produce food and clothing at constant cost, using their endowment of labour. The diagrams correspond to the foregoing numerical example and assume similar endowments of labour in both countries. The constant cost assumption is reflected by the linear production possibilities frontiers (PPFs). Under autarchy, that is, before trade takes place, both countries produce and consume both goods at point A and A*, respectively, where their PPFs are tangent to their highest possible indifference curve. Since their opportunity costs of production differs, that is, their PPFs have different slopes, they can trade the two goods at an intermediate price ratio to mutual advantage. In the left-hand diagram, Home's opportunity cost of clothing in terms of food is shown as the slope of $F°C°$ and it is lower than Foreign's, that is, the slope of its PPF is flatter than that in Foreign. This is the geometrical presentation of comparative advantage in this simple framework of two goods and two countries. In order to realize gains from trade, both countries must shift resources into the activities, in which they have comparative advantage, and export the excess over their own consumption, that is, Home exports C and Foreign exports F, importing the goods in which they are relatively less productive. The shifting of resources from a relatively balanced mix of production under autarchy (points A and A*, respectively) to the production of more export goods, is called specialization. It will be complete under the assumption of constant cost (straight-line PPFs) and profit maximization, so that nothing of the importable will be produced (points $C°$ and $F°$, respectively).

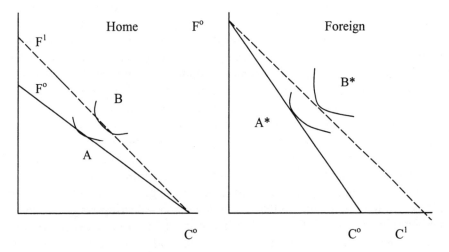

**Figure 5.1   Gains from trade under constant costs**

When the two countries trade at the price ratio shown as $C°F^1$ (or $C^1F°$ in Foreign) production takes place at $C°$ in Home and at $F°$ in Foreign, and consumption at B and B* instead of A and A*. The movement from a lower indifference curve at A to a higher one at B is a measure of Home's gains from trade. Home may be less productive in both activities than Foreign and gain, nevertheless, because only relative costs of production, that is, opportunity costs in terms of the other good, are important to establish comparative advantage.[1]

---

[1]   The diagrams also show the quantities exported by Home ($C°-C^1$) and Foreign ($F°-F^1$).

In the real world, where there are more than two activities (products), it is technically more difficult to measure comparative advantage. This follows from the ambiguity of opportunity costs for more than two goods. As demonstrated by Dornbusch, Fischer and Samuelson (1977), comparative advantage measurement for a continuum of goods requires the introduction of money wages. In addition, in the presence of several productive factors and intermediate inputs, the measurement of comparative advantage in a multi-product context requires consideration of full costs. This, however, leads to the problem of deciding which prices of factors and products to use. Clearly, arbitrarily distorted prices cannot be used. When market prices are used, which are possibly distorted, unit costs determine competitive, but not comparative advantage. Competitive advantage, which is the ability to export, may be based on subsidies or exchange rate misalignment, or other kinds of distortions. For comparative advantage, on the other hand, unit costs must be based on market-clearing prices.

Let us examine this proposition by referring to the previous numerical example. If the wage rate equals one dollar in both countries then Food would cost five dollars and clothing ten dollars in Home, and six and eighteen dollars respectively in Foreign. At these prices and with free trade Foreign would want to import both food and clothing from Home, but could not export anything. In other words, Foreign is not competitive in either product, although it still has comparative advantage in food. In order to be able to export food to Home, Foreign needs to lower its wage rate to less than 5/6 dollars, say $0.8. If Foreign's wage rate was only $0.5, this would make Home non-competitive in both goods. Therefore, given Home's wage rate of one dollar, Foreign's market-clearing wage rate must lie between $5/6 and $10/18. Only if the wage differential between Foreign and Home remains within this range, can both countries realize their respective comparative advantage and trade to mutual benefit.

If the two countries use different currencies, a misaligned exchange rate may lead to the same situation as under a non-market-clearing wage rate. It is therefore necessary in the analysis of comparative advantage that only market clearing prices and exchange rates be used, both for factors and products. A country has then comparative advantage in an activity if its unit cost at equilibrium prices is lower than that of a competing country. Applying this rule to the single-factor, two-product case means that for comparative advantage unit labour cost at equilibrium wages must be inferior to unit labour cost abroad. This is equivalent to stating that a country's relative productivity *vis-à-vis* her competitors must exceed their relative wage rate at market-clearing wages. Given the great importance of these conclusions, the discussion is continued later in the context of measuring competitiveness and comparative advantage in Chapter 9.

The gains from trade described above are static as they refer to given endowments of resources, given production functions and given preferences. Obviously, all of these conditions are in constant change. Over time, some natural resources become scarce or depleted, others are newly discovered, human resources grow and improve through education and training, and capital accumulates. These changes do not affect all activities in the same way, and so comparative advantage changes over time; it can grow in some activities and get lost in others. The structure of trade is therefore expected to change over time. Trade is known to contribute positively to the formation of comparative advantage. By shifting resources into activities with potential comparative advantage, say for the purpose of exporting, the cost of production declines and a comparative cost advantage is likely to result. This may happen simply by exploiting economies of scale. Equally important, the experience of production may lead to learning, which results in cost decline. These dynamic gains from trade are perhaps less well understood, but they are potentially even more important than the static gains from trade.

The discussion of comparative advantage so far has been limited to the classical trade model with fixed coefficients, but was extended to n goods and more than one factor. It was also left unclear whether comparative advantage results from differences in technology or differences in factor prices. The neoclassical trade model with substitution between factors and the Heckscher-Ohlin assumptions of differences in factor abundance adds an important aspect to the theory of comparative advantage. It explains factor abundance as a source of comparative advantage. Can that also be said for the more recent trade models such as the product cycle (Vernon) and intra-industry trade (Krugman) models? Here opinions diverge. Many authors consider that intra-industry trade based on product differentiation and economies of scale is non-comparative advantage trade. In our opinion, this corresponds to an overly narrow interpretation of the principle of comparative advantage. A firm producing a differentiated (e.g. brand name) product with economies of scale in one country and exports it to others can also be said to have comparative advantage. It derives from the cost advantage of producing at large scale, combined with the market power derived from the differentiated product, which keeps other potential competitors out of the market.

## 5.2     Arguments in Favour of Trade Restrictions

In theory, the restriction of trade can lead to static welfare benefits if the restricting country is large enough to influence the world prices of its imports or exports. For instance, the restriction of imports through a tariff, which reduces domestic demand and raises domestic supply, may contribute to a price decline of the imported goods. An export tax may have the opposite effect on the international price of the exported commodity. The resulting increase in the terms of trade (Px/Pm) raises the welfare level in the restricting country. The optimal tariff is then the level of import duty at which further terms of trade gains are balanced by the welfare losses caused by the reduction in trade. The argument loses its appeal, however, if the trading partner retaliates with its own tariff and both countries engage in a trade war. Also, most developing countries are price takers in their respective import markets. In practice, the optimal tariff argument has therefore limited relevance for trade policies in less developed countries.

Although the argument in favour of free trade is based on a strong rationale, that is, the combined principles of comparative advantage and gains from trade, trade restrictions are widespread, especially in developing countries, but for other reasons than the optimal tariff. First, there is the need to collect taxes for government revenue, and trade taxes are more easily collected than income taxes. The main arguments in favour of trade restrictions, however, are based on historical experience of developing countries with their terms of trade, excessive specialization and the need for infant industry protection. When a country specializes and exports only a few primary products, in which it has comparative advantage, it is strongly affected by fluctuations in world prices of its exports. When export prices fluctuate, specialization and trade dependence can translate into domestic instability. Export instability can be diminished by diversification and, to a certain extent, through certain kinds of trade agreements, which we discuss later. First we examine the terms of trade and infant industry arguments.

The terms of trade of a country, by which we normally mean an index of export prices divided by an index of import prices, Px/Pm, may either rise or fall, depending on the particular mix of exported and imported goods and on the world market conditions of the goods concerned. Rising terms of trade imply welfare gains, and falling terms of trade imply welfare losses. This is easily seen in Figure 5.1 when we increase or decrease the relative price of C in terms of F. For the Home country, which specializes in and exports clothing, a clockwise rotation means a rise of the relative price of clothing and therefore an improvement of the terms of trade. A flatter slope of the line F'C°, on the other hand, corresponds to a deterioration of Home's and an improvement of Foreign's terms of trade. It is clear that an increased price ratio $P_C/P_F$ enables Home to consume at a higher level of welfare than before.

The possibility of longer-term deteriorating terms of trade in developing countries is one of the arguments in favour of restricted trade. It is based on the empirical observation of declining terms of trade, which in turn is related to the particular composition of LDC exports. Traditionally, those exports consist mainly of raw materials from agriculture, forests and mining. Countries whose exports are prone to terms of trade losses, may find it beneficial to restrict trade in order to direct their resources into other activities with less present comparative advantage. This argument was expressed powerfully by the economists Raoul Prebish (1950) and Hans Singer (1950), and became known in the literature as the Prebish-Singer thesis. Based on empirical evidence from a study of British and South-American data, the authors argued that the terms of trade of developing countries tend to decline over longer periods of time. The prediction is based on observations about the typical structure of exports and imports of developing countries. Food exports typically face a low income-elasticity, since consumers tend to spend more on other than food items at higher income levels. The demand for raw materials suffers when, due to technical change, synthetic materials are substituted for natural raw materials, such as synthetic fibres for cotton and jute, synthetic rubber for natural rubber, and fibre optics for copper in electrical circuits. Manufactured goods, and especially investment goods, on the other hand, which are widely imported by less developed countries, tend to experience longer-term price increases, due to their higher income elasticity. The empirical evidence of longer-run terms of trade deterioration, however, is not unambiguous. All depends on the specific country, its product mix of exports and imports, and on the particular time period considered. Oil exporting countries, for instance, realized important gains in the 1970s, but losses in the 1980s.

The Prebish-Singer thesis provides an argument for trade restrictions and protection of the developing countries' domestic manufacturing sector. Such policies were adopted not only by individual governments but also advocated by the United Nations Conference for Trade and Development (UNCTAD). It ultimately led to more than two decades of inward-oriented trade policies in a large number of countries. Since the 1970s, however, several important and critical studies have pointed to the negative effects of such policies for longer-run development.

Even without the concern with terms of trade deterioration and export instability, a further argument in favour of trade restrictions is based on the fundamental objective of industrialization, combined with the need for protection of infant industries. The goal of industrialization relies on the promise of higher productivity levels and growth, higher incomes and urban living standards, which are known to accompany industrialization. Since industries are not easily developing in an environment of fierce international competition, industrialization requires infant industry protection. The theory is that by temporarily increasing the price of competing imports of manufactured goods through import taxes, new and existing domestic firms are enticed to invest, to 'learn by doing' and to produce at larger scale, until they are efficient enough to face international competition. Since in this strategy former imports are replaced by domestic production, the process is called import substitution or import-substituting industrialization (ISI).

The argument in favour of infant industry protection is based on the assumptions of cost-lowering learning effects and of economies of large-scale production and of positive external effects related to learning. External benefits exist, if the whole economy benefits above and beyond the benefits accruing to the protected firms, such as improved skills of the labour force. If the protection of industries always led to efficient domestic competitors, the strategy of import substitution would not have attracted so much criticism; but industrial protection tends to become permanent and to spiral into a vicious circle of rewards for non-competitiveness. To see how this happens, we shall examine the policy instruments of inward-oriented trade regimes and their effects on producers and consumers.

Finally, it can also be argued that even without long-run terms of trade decline and export instability, free trade offers no guarantees for gains, because international prices tend to be distorted as a consequence of other countries' policies or of market imperfections. For instance, the international price of various agricultural commodities such as sugar, are known to be artificially low as a consequence of protection and/or subsidization by the rich countries. This prevents countries whose natural comparative advantage may lie, for instance, in sugar production, to realize gains from exporting sugar, or even from producing it for their own markets. The existence of such distortions and various protective policies on behalf of trading partners has led developing country governments to a more protective attitude than they would have adopted otherwise.

## 5.3    Inward-oriented Trade Regimes

Based on the concerns for terms-of-trade losses, industrialization and infant industry protection, many less developed countries established inward-oriented trade regimes in the second half of the twentieth century. Such regimes consist, essentially, of high and differentiated import duties for industrial products, combined with various quantitative restrictions like quotas and import licensing regimes, exchange controls and taxes on exports. Examining these policy instruments with respect to their effectiveness and cost, we show that even under the accepted objectives of accelerated industrialization and reduced trade dependency, the incentives generated by these policies lead to major distortions and welfare costs.

Viewed from a welfare standpoint, the major tool of industry protection should be the tariff or, alternatively, production subsidies. The tariff has the advantage of generating tax revenue, while subsidies are expenses to the government and require tax revenue from other sources. The differentiation of duty rates permits the protection of various industries at different rates. This, however, is a source of potential problems. When tariff rates vary substantially, the resulting structure of protection can result in strongly distorted incentive structures and policy biases. This is examined in more detail in section 5.5.

In addition to tariffs, governments often use quantitative restrictions of various kinds to protect industries. Quota and import licensing regimes tend to restrict imports more than tariffs, thereby pushing the domestic prices even higher than with only a tariff. Further incentives to producers are usually added in form of tax exemptions, privileged access to credit, and artificially low interest rates from state-owned development banks. When such incentive regimes have become firmly established, producers become dependent on them, and the pressure to raise productivity is eliminated. Entrepreneurs have been found spending much of their resources lobbying the government for additional protection, which, in the words of Anne Krueger (1974), leads to a 'rent-seeking societies'. Furthermore, the existing protection combined with a usually fixed exchange rate and some degree of inflation, tend to result in currency overvaluation, which in itself is a powerful disincentive for domestic producers. Exchange rate over-valuation, in turn, leads to pressure for even more protection.

The cost of protection to the whole economy is the efficiency or deadweight loss caused by driving the price up beyond its potential level as given by the world price. Consumers consume less at the tariff-ridden price, and producers produce more than under free trade. This is seen in the standard partial equilibrium welfare analysis of Figure 5.2, where domestic demand (D) and supply (S) are shown, foreign supply is assumed to be infinitely elastic at the world price (Pw) and an ad-valorem tariff (t) raises the domestic import price from Pw to Pd. The domestic price (Pd) is then given as Pw $(1 + t)$.

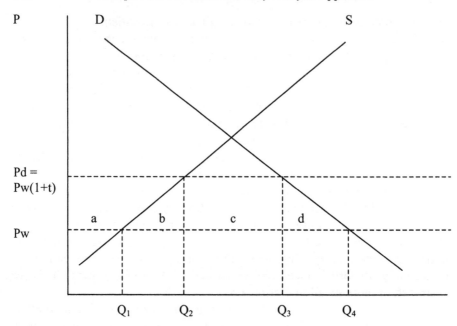

**Figure 5.2    The cost of protection**

The static welfare gains and losses in the form of consumers' surplus, producers' surplus and tax revenue are shown as surfaces a to d. In comparison with the free trade situation, the imposition of the tariff (t) makes consumers lose consumers' surplus (area a + b + c + d), producers gain surplus (area a), and the government gains tax revenue (area c), so that the total effect amounts to a loss (areas b and d). In order to estimate the numerical cost of protection, one needs to compute the value of the two welfare triangles a and d. This can be done by estimating the elasticities of demand and supply, as well as the changes in quantity of production and consumption following the price change. It can also be seen from the diagram that if the tariff is replaced by an equivalent quantitative restriction, say a quota of $Q_3$-$Q_2$, the cost of protection is higher because the tariff revenue is not captured by the government and most likely lost for the importing economy, unless the quota is auctioned off by the government. Numerous empirical studies have estimated the cost of protection in various countries. As a proportion of GDP, the cost varies substantially, depending on the level of protection and the elasticity involved. For countries with low trade barriers the cost is typically no more than one or two percent of GDP, but in developing countries with highly protected industries the cost may easily amount to five or ten percent of GDP.

When inward-oriented trade regimes are established, they usually lead to accelerated industry growth for a while, but this easy phase of import substitution is eventually followed by stagnation. The first stages of import substitution are typically easy to achieve: they include the expansion of production of light consumer goods, mainly non-durables. Later stages of import substitution, including the production of intermediate goods, consumer durables and capital goods, are more difficult and may require more protection, especially when domestic production is hampered by the smallness of the domestic market, while international producers use large-scale production. Due to the existing protection, domestic firms tend to become inefficient high-cost producers, and the country's resources are increasingly drawn into activities that have neither a present comparative advantage, nor a likelihood of developing one in the future.

As to the macroeconomic effects, one might expect import substitution to lead to an improved balance of payments since import purchases are replaced by domestic value added. In reality, it has been observed, however, that imports tend to rise faster than exports in such regimes. This happens because the high protection encourages inefficient use of inputs and discourages the use of domestically available resources. Automobile and appliance assembly plants are typical in this respect. Producers in this industry often import total kits of parts, which had been already assembled but were 'knocked down' for export, and then re-assemble them in their branch plants in developing countries. The value of these parts at international prices is close to the value of the final product. Adding domestic value therefore increases the price substantially above its international level, so protection is needed. In the end, the operation may require more foreign exchange than simply importing the cars.

Another problem resulting from such import substitution regimes is the reinforcement of the dualistic nature of economies. Since highly protected firms can afford to pay relatively high wages, salaries and profits, which are substantially above those in the rest of the economy, they reinforce income inequality and rural-urban migration. To the extent that they use inappropriately capital-intensive technologies, they may further contribute to unemployment.

The arguments presented above seem to suggest that import substitution policies always lead to high social costs with few benefits. This, however, will depend on how the policies are implemented and, in particular, for how long they are perpetuated. If, after a reasonable period of industrial 'infancy' leading to increased competitive strength, protection is lowered, such industries can even be turned into export industries, as countries like Korea, Taiwan, Hong Kong, Brazil, and Mexico have shown.

An appropriate industrial strategy determines the right moment to 'open up' the economy and to promote outward orientation.

## 5.4     Trade Liberalization and Outward Orientation

The objective of trade liberalization in developing countries is to reduce the usually high level of protection and to make the remaining protection more uniform. Reduction to a zero level of protection is for many countries unrealistic for reasons such as the pursuit of industrialization, and avoidance of extreme specialization in primary commodities. Since the tariff implies a lower cost of protection than quantitative restrictions, trade liberalization usually begins with the elimination of quotas and the reduction of the coverage by import licensing, followed by a simplification and lowering of tariff rates and eventually adoption a low and uniform tariff rate. Import licensing usually consists of granting import licences to importers according to a scheme of priorities. In very protective regimes the coverage of products is nearly complete; in more liberal regimes only few product categories are subject to import licensing.

In inward-oriented trade regimes the incentive structure is biased in favour of import substitutes and against exportables, which are often agricultural products. The bias can be measured as explained in section 5.5. Outward orientation does not mean a reversal of the bias in favour of exportables or agriculture. This would not be consistent with the logic of a market-based economy. For outward orientation it is sufficient to establish neutrality of incentives, or absence of any significant bias. This means that existing biases, which may be caused by the protection of certain activities, must be neutralized. In addition to the trade liberalization measures mentioned above, there are further measures destined to counterbalance the existing biases. One example of such countervailing measures is the duty drawback regime, in which the exporter of manufactured products is being reimbursed for the duties paid on imported intermediate inputs used in the exported goods. The same goal can be reached by manufacturing in bonded warehouses, where the imported inputs remain extra-territorial from the customs point of view, or in export processing zones, where the whole production unit is treated as extra-territorial. Alternatively, exporters may receive an incentive to export in form of an export subsidy.

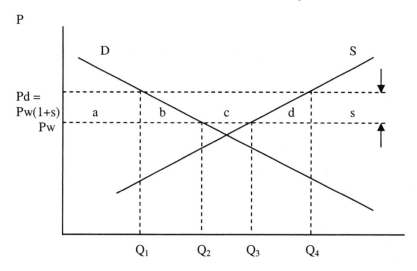

**Figure 5.3    Welfare cost of an export subsidy**

Figure 5.3 demonstrates that export subsidies impose a similar static welfare cost on the economy as import duties. In this diagram Pw is the world price at which exporters sell their products, and s is the ad-valorem subsidy received by them, on top of the export price. In comparison with the situation without the subsidy, the total value of the subsidy paid by the government is equal to the combined area (b+c+d), domestic consumers lose (a+b) by paying the increased price, and producers gain additional surplus of (a+b+c). On the whole, the subsidy causes a welfare loss of the areas b and d, but in addition, the government needs to generate revenue otherwise to pay the subsidy. While export subsidies may neutralize the existing bias against exports, for instance in form of import taxes on tradable inputs, it adds to the welfare cost of the existing bias. Duty draw-back, bonded warehouse and processing zones do not share this disadvantage and are therefore preferable from a welfare point of view.

Outward orientation, by opening the frontiers to lower-priced imports and balancing the remaining protection with subsidies, is expected to have two major consequences. First, resources are re-directed towards activities of comparative advantage, due to the neutralization of existing biases. Second, the promotion of exports through the various methods described above should help to eliminate the trade and balance of payments deficit that is typical for inward-oriented regimes. A third possible benefit is the reduction of the total welfare burden of such policies, but that depends on the extent to which subsidies are being used as opposed to the simple reduction of trade barriers.

## 5.5     Analysis of Trade Policy Reforms

In order to analyze the impact of a trade policy reform on a particular sector or the whole economy, one must first establish, which of the typical measures of such reforms have actually been implemented, to what extent and at what moment. On this account, some earlier studies of reforms have been deficient, as they simply compare reforming countries with non-reforming ones, or the pre-reform situation of a country with its post-reform situation. Often reforms remain ineffective, not because the reform measures are inappropriate, but because they are poorly or incompletely implemented. The impact of policy changes on the incentive structure facing the producers, importers and exporters is measured by indicators of protection, such as the nominal and effective rates of protection. The second study goal should be to examine the bias in favour or against specific sectors or against exports resulting from the trade regime, and to show how the bias has changed through the trade reform. Finally, it is also of great interest to policy makers to analyze the impact of trade policy reform on government revenue.

### 5.5.1    The level of protection and sector biases

The level of protection is measured by calculating the nominal and the effective rates of protection. The nominal rate of protection (NRP) is defined as the excess of the domestic (ex-factory or farm gate) price (Pd) over the international or world price (Pw),[2] expressed as a proportion of the world price:

$$(5.1) \quad NRP \quad = Pd/Pw - 1.$$

When the NRP is computed in this fashion, that is, by comparing the observed domestic with the international price, it is sometimes referred to as implicit nominal rate of protection (cf. ten Kate et al., 1980), in order to distinguish it from the hypothetical NRP, which equals the tariff. The NRP as defined above reflects not only the import duty (tariff), but also the influence of various factors that may apply, such as quotas, exonerations, duty evasion (smuggling), and price controls of domestic products. All of these secondary factors can make the tariff redundant upwards or downwards. The tariff is upward redundant if the NRP exceeds the tariff,

---

[2]   It is customary to refer to the international price also as world or border price. It is usually measured as the price of the lowest international supplier including shipping and insurance cost (cif) to the port of entry.

and downward redundant if it falls short of the tariff. Upward redundancy is usually the result of quantitative restrictions, whereas downward redundancy can result from duty exemptions, as well as from customs duty evasion through smuggling or under-invoicing.

The NRP may also be negative, when Pd < Pw, indicating that, in spite of the tariff, the domestic product costs less than its imported equivalent. Normally this is a sign of strong domestic competitiveness and the product may then be regarded as an exportable rather than an importable. But even products that are exported under free trade would normally fetch the international price (fob).[3] If the price received by the exporter is less than the world price, this is usually a consequence of an export tax or of marketing boards that charge the producer fees similar to taxes. If negative NRPs are observed in many industries or sectors, it may also signal an undervalued exchange rate, especially if they result from recent currency devaluation.

More important, however, than the NRP as a measure of protection is the effective rate of protection (ERP), because it indicates the strength of protection taking into account not only the protection of output but also that of intermediate inputs. Remembering that value added is the difference between the value of output, VO or P (price) and the value of intermediate inputs (VI), the ERP is defined as:

$$(5.2) \quad ERP = VAd / VAw - 1$$

where VAd is value added at domestic prices (= Pd - VId) and VAw is value added at world prices (= Pw - VIw). If we designate $t_i$ as the NRP on output, and $t_j$ as the average NRP on the value of intermediate inputs, then we can write:

$$(5.3) \quad VId = VIw (1 + t_j) \text{ and}$$

$$(5.4) \quad VAd = Pd - VId$$
$$= Pw(1 + t_i) - VIw(1 + t_j).$$

Defining further the intermediate input coefficient $a_{ij} = VIw/Pw$, we can then rewrite the ERP as a function of $t_i$, $t_j$ and $a_{ij}$, substituting 5.3 and 5.4 into 5.2:

$$(5.5) \quad ERP = (t_i - a_{ij} t_j)/(1 - a_{ij}).$$

---

[3] The export price under free trade is generally taken to include the transport cost to the carrier (fob or free on board).

It is clear from this expression that:

if      $t_i > t_j$ then ERP > NRP and

if      $t_i = t_j$ then ERP = NRP and

if      $t_i < t_j$ then ERP < NRP.

While a negative NRP is unambiguous, although having different potential causes as we saw, a negative ERP can be ambiguous. It is unambiguous if VAw exceeds VAd and both are positive. This means that, due to input and output prices and different rates of protection, producers are negatively protected, or we can say, they are implicitly taxed. If, on the other hand, ERP < 0 results from VAW < 0, then it is referred to as a case of super protection and we have ERP < -1. To see this, let us examine how value added at world prices can become negative. Value added at domestic prices is normally positive, otherwise firms would make continuous losses and go out of business. When VAw is calculated from VAd, by replacing the domestic by world prices, it can easily become negative, provided the output is strongly protected (high $t_i$) and intermediate inputs are little or not protected (small or zero $t_j$). In such circumstances the value of intermediate inputs at world prices may exceed the value of output at world prices. This case, whenever it occurs, is evidence of wasteful production, since the inputs are worth more than the output.

How can this case arise in reality? It arises as a consequence of excessive protection. When firms are highly protected on the output side they can afford to be inefficient in input use, such that the international input value exceeds the value of output. In this situation they can generate profits due to the distorted domestic prices, although the economy is losing foreign exchange, in comparison to simply importing the products in question.

The protection of an activity or sector leads to a resource pull in favour of this sector, to which we have referred as bias. Inversely, we can say that a sector that is negatively protected or implicitly taxed experiences a negative bias. The total bias against a sector includes the direct bias, that is, the negative incentive at the output price level, and the effect of a positive bias in favour of the rest of the economy. Take, for instance, the typical bias against products of the agricultural sector in LDCs. Its negative direct bias stems from the fact that agricultural export products typically fetch farm gate prices that are lower than world prices, due to export taxes and other factors. Industrial sector products, on the other hand, are typically protected through the tariff. This adds an indirect effect to the direct bias against these products.

The same reasoning applies to the anti-export bias, which incorporates the negative nominal protection of export products as well as the positive protection of import substitutes. The total bias against exports *vis-à-vis* import substitutes is then calculated as:

$$(5.6) \quad B_X = (1 + NRP_x)/(1 + NRP_{IS}) - 1$$

where the subscripts X and IS refer to export products or sub-sectors and import substitutes, respectively. It is noteworthy that the bias measure is based on a similar idea as the one underlying the ERP, because it incorporates the price incentives or disincentives on the output side as well as those in other industries or sectors. While the ERP applies most easily to single industries with well-defined input coefficients, the bias measure applies more to whole sub-sectors and attributes the same weight to the NRP in both sectors that are being compared.

The measurement of protection, nominal and effective, is based on the comparison between the (distorted) domestic and the international ('world') prices of identical or equivalent products. This approach encounters several problems that deserve a discussion. First, price comparisons are always somewhat difficult, especially when we deal with heterogeneous products. One difficulty is to assure that the domestic product and its imported equivalent are of the same quality. If this is not the case, price adjustments must be made by estimating the value of the quality difference, and to take account of it in the computation of the rate of protection. Second, if price comparison is not possible, one may use the tariff instead of the implicit rate of protection; but it is important then to interpret the results accordingly. If neither quantitative restrictions are in place, nor any other factor that could cause tariff redundancy, then the tariff should be a correct measure of nominal protection. Third, one may ask what exactly is meant by the international price. The idea of the implicit NRP is to compare the 'protected' price with the free-trade price. The border price, that is, cost, insurance, freight (cif) before customs duty, is usually taken to correspond to the free-trade price.

The free-trade standard of comparison, which is so important in the theory of protection, is problematic in a further sense, regarding the valuation of intermediate inputs for the computation of effective protection. Since their quantities and prices are known only in the tariff- or distortion-ridden form, one has to adjust the input coefficients to their free-trade level as follows:

$$(5.7) \quad a_{ij} = \hat{a}_{ij} (1+t_i)/(1+t_j)$$

where $a_{ij}^{*}$ is the observed and distorted input coefficient, and $t_i$ and $t_j$ are defined as before. This procedure frees the coefficients from their price distortions, but not from the consequences of the trade restriction on input use. In other words, $a_{ij}$ as computed above is not a true free-trade coefficient. To obtain true free-trade coefficients, one would need an appropriate general equilibrium model. There are modern approaches to estimate rates of protection under general equilibrium conditions, but their discussion would go beyond the limits of the present framework.

### 5.5.2    Trade liberalization and the sources of growth

Trade liberalization is expected to re-direct resources from import-substituting activities towards exports, or more generally, from activities with positive price distortions towards those activities that are either undistorted or negatively distorted. As a consequence, exports should become more important as a source of growth, and import substitution less. The following analysis, pioneered by Chenery (1960) and Lewis and Soligo (1965) permits us to examine quantitatively, to what extent such changes in the sources of growth have occurred.

The relationship between output growth and its sources is based on the ex-post equality between demand and supply. In any activity, the sum of domestic demand (D) and export demand (X) equals the sum of domestic supply (Q) and imports (M). This equation holds at the level of quantities as well as of values. When import substitution occurs, the import coefficient, that is, the ratio of imports to total supply, $M/(Q+M)$, declines. The intensity of import substitution can therefore be measured by the change in the import coefficient. The other contributions to growth are domestic demand expansion and export expansion, which are measured by keeping the domestic production coefficient, $u = Q/(Q+M)$, constant. The total increase in output is then imputed to three components:

$$(5.8) \quad \Delta Q = u_1 \Delta D + u_1 \Delta X + S_2(u_2 - u_1)$$
$$\quad\quad\quad (a) \quad\quad (b) \quad\quad\quad (c)$$

where term (a) is the domestic demand component, term (b) is the export demand component, and term (c) is the import substitution component, and where $\Delta Q$ is the change in output from period 1 to period 2, the subscripts refer to periods 1 and 2, S is total supply, equal to domestic output plus imports, and $\Delta D$ and $\Delta X$ are the change in domestic demand and exports between periods 1 and 2. Equation (5.8) can be re-written either in growth rate form as:

(5.9)     $\Delta Q/Q = u_1\Delta D/Q + u_1\Delta X/Q + S_2(u_2 - u_1)/Q$

or, dividing by $\Delta Q$ (instead of Q), so that the components add up to one. In the latter form, the equation shows the relative importance of the three demand sources of output growth. In periods of trade liberalization it is expected that the import substitution component is small or negative and that the export component is of relatively great importance.

Other important issues related to trade liberalization are those of timing and sequencing, and of the transition cost. Appropriate timing is important because the effectiveness of a trade policy reform depends crucially on whether it is undertaken in the right moment and whether the policy changes follow an optimal sequence. Transition costs arise from the fact that trade policy reform always generates winners and losers, and the compensation of losers can be seen as a transition cost. Both these issues will be addressed in the context of more complete reform programs known as structural adjustment programs, which are discussed in Chapter 8.

To evaluate the success and failure of trade reform in developing countries is a difficult task, especially when one tries to make judgements about larger regions and to generalize. The difficulty comes from the fact that comparable data on tariff and non-tariff barriers, on effective protection and sector biases are rarely available for many countries and for the same time periods. Even in single countries the recent history of trade policy consists, typically, of various liberalization episodes combined with various other reform measures.

Table 5.1 shows, in a summary fashion, recent changes in trade policy in eleven developing countries. Three aspects are being measured, average tariff rates, the tariff range (max over min) and the incidence of quantitative restrictions, always before and after recent reforms. The impression this table conveys is that, in spite of significant progress, there is still much room for further trade liberalization.

**Table 5.1     Indicators of trade reform in selected developing countries**

| | Average Tariff Rates (%) | | Tariff Range (%, High/Low) | | Quantity Restrictions | |
|---|---|---|---|---|---|---|
| | Before | After | Before | After | Before | After |
| **South Asia** | | | | | | |
| Bangladesh (1989, 1993) | 94[a] | 50[a] | 508.5/2.5 | 100/7.5 | 39.5[d] | 10[d] |
| India (1987, 1992) | 77[b] | 64[b] | >300/0 | 110/0 | | |
| (1990, 1993) | 87[b] | 47[b] | | | 93[f] | <50[f] |
| **Africa** | | | | | | |
| Ghana (1983, 1991) | 30[a] | 17[a] | 30/10 | 25/0 | | |
| Kenya (1987, 1991) | 40[a] | 34[a] | 170/ | 70/ | 71[d] | .2[d] |
| Nigeria (1984, 1988) | 33[b] | 28[b] | | 300/0 | all[g] | 17[g] |
| Senegal (1986, 1991) | 98[a,h] | 90[a,h] | | | | |
| **Latin America** | | | | | | |
| Brazil (1987, 1992) | 51[a] | 21[a] | 105/0 | 65/0 | 39[d] | 1[d] |
| Colombia (1984, 1992) | 61[a] | 12[a] | 220/0 | 20/5 | 99[d] | 1[d] |
| Mexico (1985,1990) | 23. 5[c] | 12.5[c] | 100/0 | 20/10 | 92.2[f] | 19.9[f] |
| **East Asia** | | | | | | |
| China  (1986, 1992) | 38.1[a] | 43[a] | | 143/0 | | 70[e] |
| Indonesia (1985, 1991) | 19[c] | 15[c] | | | 41[f] | 22[f] |

*Notes*:
[a]unweighted
[b]weighted by imports
[c]weighted by domestic production
[d]percent tariff lines covered by licensing requirements
[e]percent imports covered by licensing or quantitative restraints
[f]percent domestic production covered by licensing or quantitative restraints
[g]number of goods categories
[h]includes surcharges

*Source*:    J. Dean, S. Desai and J. Riedel, 'Trade Policy Reform in Developing Countries since 1985', World Bank Discussion Paper 267.


## 5.6     International Trade Agreements

Unilateral trade liberalization may be welfare-maximizing on purely theoretical grounds, but in the context of underdevelopment and existing (world-wide) trade restrictions, countries may be better off with a mild degree of trade policy intervention. Among such interventions, we shall focus here on international commodity agreements and buffer stocks, whereas preferential trade agreements receive only short attention here and will be dealt with in more detail in Chapter 7 on regional integration.

### 5.6.1   Commodity agreements and buffer stocks

The problems of export instability, due to the volatility of international commodity prices, and of declining terms of trade have led the developing countries to seek arrangements for greater income stability and more advantageous prices. International commodity agreements, which have been concluded for commodities such as sugar, tin, rubber, cocoa and coffee, are meant to stabilize prices by restricting output when prices decline and by encouraging output when prices are rising. For such agreements to work, there must be not only initial agreement among the producing and consuming nations, but also the willingness to enforce the agreement. Most of the agreements have failed to assure long-term stability because the producing nations have been unable to enforce the quota they had agreed to. One particular form of such agreements is the export cartel, which aims also at higher export prices, by imposing export quotas on their members. Its success depends on the willingness of its members to resist the temptation of cheating and to respect the quota. One well-known example of such a cartel is the Organization of Petroleum Exporting Countries (OPEC). In spite of its original success in raising the international oil price, it suffers from periodic crises stemming from the problem of discipline inherent in cartels, as well as from the fact that not all international exporters are members of the organization.

Buffer stocks are also supposed to achieve the goal of price stabilization, but by means of a reserve fund to finance the buying and stockpiling of excess supply in specific markets. When the price declines below a set target price (or price band), the buffer stock must buy the excess supply, and it must sell to absorb the excess demand. It is clear, however, that buffer stocks are not necessarily useful for the interests of the participating members. Although buffer stocks can stabilize prices they may not be able to stabilize export revenues. This depends on whether the fluctuation is caused by a supply shortfall on behalf of the members, or whether it results from fluctuating demand. If the members' supply is temporarily reduced, the resulting price increase would stabilize their revenue. A buffer stock, by keeping the price down at the target level, would then contribute to a revenue shortfall for the members. The main problem of buffer stocks, however, is that they are very costly to operate, as the stockpiling of commodities requires considerable funds.

## 5.6.2    *Preferential trade agreements*

There are various forms of preferential trade agreements, ranging from the simple free trade agreement and the customs union to the common market and the full economic union. They are, in that order, agreements with an increasing degree of integration. In free trade agreements the members do not share common external tariff towards non-member countries. The common external tariff is the distinguishing feature of the customs union. In common markets, the factors of production are also free to move, and in the economic union, economic policies are widely coordinated. The highest degree of integration is reached in an economic union with a common currency. Economic integration holds considerable promise for developing countries because their potential to gain from trade is limited by several factors, such as the traditional structure of their exports towards the developed countries, that is, being mainly exports of raw materials, and the protection of developed country markets against certain imports from developing countries. In practice, however, economic integration in the South has not had the success it deserves. Due to the importance and problems of this subject, the discussion is continued in Chapter 7, after having examined the external account and the exchange rate.

## References

Chenery, Hollis (1960), 'Patterns of Industrial Growth', *American Economic Review*, vol.50, September.

Krueger, Anne O. (1974), 'The Political Economy of Rent-Seeking', *American Economic Review*, 64, 3.

Lewis, Stephen R. Jr. and R. Soligo (1965), 'Growth and Structural Change in Pakistan's Manufacturing Industry, 1954-64', *Pakistan Development Review*, Spring.

Prebisch, Raoul (1950), *The Economic Development of Latin America and its Principal Problems*, United Nations.

Singer, Hans W. (1950), 'The Distribution of Trade between Investing and Borrowing Countries', *American Economic Review*, vol.40, May, pp. 470-85.

ten Kate, Adriaan (1992), 'Liberalization and Economic Stabilization in Mexico: Lessons of Experience', *World Development*, 20, no. 5, May.

# Case Study 10
# Trade Policy Reform in Senegal: 1986-1990

## Purpose

The purpose of this case study is to analyze the nature and effects of the recent trade policy reform in Senegal. The 'Nouvelle politique industrielle' (NPI) was introduced in 1986 in an attempt to create an economic environment that would stimulate the industrial sector. The main goal of this case study is to examine how successful Senegal was in implementing the NPI and also to examine the adverse factors.

This case study also aims at familiarizing students with the arithmetic of protection. Nominal rates of protection (NRP) and effective rates of protection (ERP) will be examined and computed for different industrial sectors.

The following readings are required to answer the assignment questions. They provide background information as well as other valuable information that help you in answering the questions.

## References

Siggel, E. (1994), 'Trade and Industrial Policy in Senegal: 1986-1990', in: Bacha (ed.), *Economics in a Changing World: Vol.4: Development, Trade and the Environment*, St. Martin's Press.
Chambas, G. and Geourjon, A.M. (1992), 'The new industrial policy in Senegal: a highly controversial reform', Adhikari, Kirkpatrick, Weiss, *Industrial and Trade Policy Reform in Developing Countries*, Manchester University Press.

They provided data on protection are from a different study DPS (1992)[4] than the two references above. There may be contradictions between these data and the findings of the two studies. In the assignment, students are expected to base their quantitative reasoning on the provided. Background information from the two readings may be used to either, back-up the findings from the quantitative analysis, or to point out contradictory findings.

---

[4] DPS (1992), *L'industrie sénégalaise et la Nouvelle Politique Industrielle (NPI)*, Direction de la Prévision et de la Statistique, Ministère de l'Économie, Finance et du Plan, République du Sénégal, (miméo).

## Background

Senegal's 'Nouvelle politique industrielle' (NPI) is essentially a trade and industrial policy reform, but it was designed as part of a broader program of structural adjustment advised by the World Bank and IMF. The trade regime which had determined the conditions in Senegal's industrial sector up to 1986 was inward-oriented and consisted of three main elements. First, trade was restricted by a system of tariffs and non-tariff barriers. Second, the Government had signed a number of conventions with industrial, primary and service sector enterprises that included guaranteed prices of essential inputs, such as electricity, fuel oil, sugar and cement. Third, Senegal's currency, the FCFA, had become substantially overvalued by the mid-1980s, which contributed to the country's weak international competitiveness in many industries. The NPI was meant to reduce the existing price distortions and, with the exception of some competitive weakness attributable to the exchange rate, to make the sector more competitive.

## Method of Analysis

The main analytical tools in this case study are the nominal (NRP) and effective (ERP) rates of protection. They are defined in the chapter equations 5.1 to 5.5, and the input coefficients given in the data table are already the ones at international prices (aij).

When aij at world prices is computed from aij', ti and tj, it is possible that aij is found to be larger than 1. This indicates that, measured at world prices, the value of intermediate inputs exceeds that of output. By implication, value added and its ratio to output at world prices are negative. It is very important to detect such cases of negative value added, as they produce incorrect values of ERP. Formally, dividing by a negative value added ratio (1-aij), leads to a negative ERP. This however is incorrect since aij>1 results from high output protection relative to input protection, that is, ti>>tj. Therefore, cases of negative value added at world prices must be interpreted as super-protection, implying that the ERP is infinitely large. This is particularly important, when average ERPs are computed, since the super-protection cases would enter with values of <-1, although their true value is infinity.

**Assigned Questions**

1) Compute the ERPs for 1986 and 1990 using the provided data for NRPs (ti, tj) and intermediate input coefficients (aij).

2) Has the level of protection and dispersion in the industrial sector generally changed according to the expectations of a trade liberalization? Explain. Hint: To answer the question you may compute the simple average ERP for the 23 industries and compute a dispersion index, such as the standard deviation.

3) Which factors can you identify as responsible for the change in effective protection. Include in your answer both tariff changes and NTBs, as well as other factors such as customs fraud (smuggling). Be specific providing industry-specific information whenever possible, drawing also on the assigned readings.

4) Has the trade policy reform led to the expected results in terms of output and employment growth? Explain.

5) Based on your findings under 2, 3 and 4, how would you evaluate the success of the NPI? Have the goals been reached? Why or why not?

**Table CS10  Nominal rates of protection in a sample of manufacturing industries in Senegal**

| | Products | VAd | 1986 ti | tj | aij | 1990 ti | tj | aij |
|---|---|---|---|---|---|---|---|---|
| 1 | Tinned fish | 0.143 | 0.130 | 0.020 | 0.949 | 0.070 | 0.050 | 0.873 |
| 2 | Frozen fish | 0.410 | 0.000 | 0.000 | 0.590 | 0.000 | 0.000 | 0.590 |
| 3 | Milk products | 0.417 | 0.590 | 0.250 | 0.742 | 0.350 | 0.160 | 0.678 |
| 4 | Tomatoes | 0.380 | 0.430 | 0.330 | 0.667 | 0.670 | 0.370 | 0.756 |
| 5 | Confectioneries | 0.391 | 0.230 | 1.970 | 0.252 | 0.500 | 0.200 | 0.761 |
| 6 | Biscuits | 0.330 | 0.200 | 0.300 | 0.618 | 0.250 | 0.250 | 0.670 |
| 7 | Animal feed | 0.390 | 0.250 | 0.380 | 0.553 | 0.150 | 0.100 | 0.638 |
| 8 | Drinks | 0.500 | 0.690 | 0.690 | 0.500 | 0.850 | 0.430 | 0.647 |
| 9 | Tobacco | 0.331 | 0.550 | 0.420 | 0.730 | 0.630 | 0.350 | 0.808 |
| 10 | Cotton yarn | 0.394 | 0.190 | 0.320 | 0.546 | 0.140 | -0.040 | 0.720 |
| 11 | Petroleum prod. | 0.535 | 0.120 | 0.000 | 0.520 | 0.460 | 0.100 | 0.620 |
| 12 | Pharmaceut. | 0.259 | 0.030 | 0.100 | 0.694 | 0.000 | 0.050 | 0.706 |
| 13 | Soap | 0.260 | 0.950 | 0.250 | 1.154 | 0.540 | 0.680 | 0.678 |
| 14 | Phytosanit. prod. | 0.250 | 0.060 | 0.050 | 0.757 | 0.260 | 0.050 | 0.900 |
| 15 | Cosmetics | 0.200 | 0.000 | 0.390 | 0.576 | 0.650 | 0.250 | 1.056 |
| 16 | Cement | 0.468 | 0.750 | 0.110 | 0.839 | 1.750 | 1.200 | 0.665 |
| 17 | Fibro Cement | 0.563 | 0.550 | 0.460 | 0.464 | 0.440 | 0.650 | 0.381 |
| 18 | Plaster | 0.020 | 0.190 | 0.190 | 0.980 | 0.150 | 0.340 | 0.841 |
| 19 | Metal drums | 0.380 | 0.270 | 0.040 | 0.757 | 0.180 | 0.120 | 0.653 |
| 20 | Metallic | 0.373 | 0.270 | 0.040 | 0.766 | 0.060 | 0.060 | 0.627 |
| 21 | Metals works | 0.434 | 0.100 | 0.430 | 0.435 | 0.450 | 0.200 | 0.684 |
| 22 | Bicycles | 0.210 | 0.500 | 0.220 | 0.971 | 0.450 | 0.200 | 0.955 |
| 23 | Electric batteries | 0.218 | 0.140 | 0.020 | 0.874 | 0.410 | 0.200 | 0.919 |

*Source*: DPS (1992).

# Case Study 11
# Changing Sources of Growth in the Mexican Manufacturing Sector

## Purpose

The purpose of this case study is to analyze the changes in the sources of growth of demand in the Mexican manufacturing sector following Mexico's 1986 trade reform. We will examine three demand sources of growth:

i)      Domestic demand
ii)     Exports
iii)    Import substitution

Domestic demand represents the part of total supply of manufacturing goods that is purchased domestically. Exports represent the foreign demand for Mexican goods. Import substitution occurs when the proportion of imports in total supply declines and the domestic supply increases.

## Background

The Mexican economy has experienced, for the greater part of the study period (1960-91), an inward-oriented trade regime. In spite of some attempts to liberalize in the 1970s, the trade policy regime remained dominated by significant, although modest (in comparison with other developing countries) trade restrictions. At the same time, the exchange rate indicated varying levels of overvaluation, which is common in such regimes. In the early 1980s the trade restrictions were reinforced in order to cope with deteriorating balance of payments and international debt problems. A structural adjustment program was implemented in the 1980s which transformed Mexico into a more open economy. The measures most relevant to the industry structure of the economy were adjustments of the exchange rate, the reduction of quantitative restrictions and the reduction and simplification of the tariff. The various sets of policies applied over the 30-year study period have provided incentives to different patterns of growth, such as growth driven by domestic demand, by import substitution, or by foreign demand. The present study of the demand sources of growth in the manufacturing sector demonstrates how the changes in trade regime have influenced the determinants of manufacturing growth.

## Method

The method of imputing the change in domestic production to various demand sources was pioneered by Chenery, Lewis and others. It is based on the fundamental balance equation between supply and demand in every sector:

$$(1) \qquad O + M = D + X$$

where O is domestic output, M is imports, D is domestic demand and X is exports. This market clearing condition is an ex-post identity, where D is obtained as a residual. An increase in domestic production in any period can than be broken down into the contributions of domestic demand, exports and import substitution. This is done using the equations 5.8 and 5.9 in the chapter section 5.5.2. Equation 5.9, when dividing by $\Delta O$ instead of O, becomes:

$$(2) \qquad 1 = u_1 \, \Delta D/\Delta O + u_1 \, \Delta X/\Delta O + S_2(u_2 - u_1)/\Delta O$$

which shows the percentage contribution of each component out of 100 percent. For example we might have domestic demand representing 80 percent of the output growth, exports representing 12 percent and import substitution representing eight percent.

## Calculation of the Average Annual Growth Rate of Output

The average annual growth rate of output is to be computed using the continuous growth rate formula:

$$(3) \qquad g = 1/t \, \ln (O_2/O_1)$$

where g is the average annualized output growth rate, t is the number of years, and $O_2$ and $O_1$ represent the output level at the beginning and end years of each sub-period. The same applies to the variables D, M and X.

The sub-periods, for which the sources of growth are to be calculated are:

| | |
|---|---|
| i) | 1960-1970 |
| ii) | 1970-1980 |
| iii) | 1980-1985 |
| iv) | 1985-1991. |

The values for the first three time periods are expressed in 1970 prices and the values for the fourth period are expressed in 1980 prices. Since we are interested in growth rates and the relative contributions of each component, the different price levels do not affect the results.

## Assigned Questions

1) Calculate the average annual growth rates of output, domestic demand, imports and exports for each of the four time periods using the continuous (compound) growth rate formula.
2) Calculate the demand sources of growth in the Mexican manufacturing sector by breaking the output growth rates down into components attributable to its demand sources. Express the sources of growth in percentage form. Do this for the four periods, using the methodology described above and present the results in a table.
3) Analyze and interpret your results in view of the expected changes in the sources of growth, given the policy changes. Explain which component was accountable for most of output growth in each period and whether the results are what was to be expected.

4) What was the fate of Mexico's trade policy reforms in the 1990s? Consult documents such as the WTO Trade Policy Review of 1997 and 2002.

## References

Siggel, E. (1996), "Trade policy reform and industrial sector growth in Mexico: 1960-1991", *Canadian Journal of Economics*, April, pp. S417-S422.
WTO-Trade Policy Review-Mexico, 1997 and 2002.

## Table CS11 **Manufacturing output and trade in Mexico**

| YEAR | Output (O) | Imports (M) | Exports(X) |
|------|------------|-------------|------------|
| **1960-1985 in 1970 prices** | | | |
| 1960 | 175,132 | 31,269 | 6,708 |
| 1961 | 184,072 | 28,669 | 7,470 |
| 1962 | 191,650 | 28,443 | 8,312 |
| 1963 | 209,559 | 29,677 | 8,698 |
| 1964 | 239,456 | 38,623 | 8,914 |
| 1965 | 259,349 | 40,376 | 9,039 |
| 1966 | 278,369 | 37,854 | 10,222 |
| 1967 | 296,953 | 43,119 | 8,482 |
| 1968 | 324,021 | 45,318 | 10,006 |
| 1969 | 345,429 | 44,754 | 11,905 |
| 1970 | 372,600 | 42,083 | 11,370 |
| 1971 | 389,166 | 39,627 | 11,014 |
| 1972 | 427,327 | 42,870 | 12,734 |
| 1973 | 468,194 | 50,669 | 14,515 |
| 1974 | 496,606 | 60,974 | 14,469 |
| 1975 | 522,441 | 60,194 | 12,291 |
| 1976 | 547,738 | 54,515 | 13,588 |
| 1977 | 566,481 | 46,934 | 14,738 |
| 1978 | 617,183 | 60,222 | 19,088 |
| 1979 | 680,777 | 83,680 | 20,146 |
| 1980 | 729,050 | 110,338 | 19,593 |
| 1981 | 784,558 | 127,829 | 18,801 |
| 1982 | 768,641 | 81,585 | 20,890 |
| 1983 | 726,859 | 37,512 | 27,966 |
| 1984 | 750,505 | 48,053 | 33,464 |
| 1985 | 785,430 | 59,020 | 33,155 |
| **1985-1991 in 1980 prices** | | | |
| 1985 | 3,570,091 | 338,124 | 199,370 |
| 1986 | 3,398,448 | 300,444 | 238,695 |
| 1987 | 3,455,140 | 311,638 | 293,508 |
| 1988 | 3,502,796 | 515,394 | 365,851 |
| 1989 | 3,684,461 | 650,354 | 382,816 |
| 1990 | 3,885,652 | 792,822 | 413,065 |
| 1991 | 4,007,277 | 967,211 | 441,820 |

**Case Study 11: Solution**

1)      The average annual growth rates are computed, for simplicity, by considering only the base and end years of each of the four sub-periods,

example, for 1960-70:   $g = \ln(y^{1970} / y^{1960})/10$

The growth rates are shown in percent.

**Table CS11a  Growth rates of output, imports, exports and domestic demand in Mexican manufacturing**

| Sub-period | Output | Imports | Exports | Domestic demand |
|---|---|---|---|---|
| 1960-70 | 7.6 | 3.0 | 5.3 | 7.0 |
| 1970-80 | 6.7 | 9.6 | 5.4 | 7.1 |
| 1980-85 | 1.5 | -12.5 | 10.5 | -0.2 |
| 1985-91 | 1.9 | 17.5 | 13.3 | 3.3 |

2)      The demand sources of output growth are shown as proportions (in percent) of output growth, such that they add up to 100 percent. Therefore, when individual entries exceed 100 percent their joint complements must be negative.

**Table CS11b  Contributions to output growth of domestic demand, exports and import substitution**

| Sub-period | Dom. demand growth | Export growth | Import substitution |
|---|---|---|---|
| 1960-70 | 87.5 | 2.0 | 10.5 |
| 1970-80 | 105.0 | 2.1 | -7.1 |
| 1980-85 | -13.1 | 20.9 | 92.2 |
| 1985-91 | 172.1 | 50.7 | -122.8 |

3)      While the sub-periods of 1960-70 and 1970-80 were essentially characterized by the traditional inward-oriented trade regime, with only a short attempt of trade liberalization in the late 1970s, the early 1980s (1980-85) were dominated first by trade restrictions to cope with an external balance and external debt problem, culminating in the 1982 debt crisis, and by heavy devaluation of the peso, the late 1980s (1985-91) were characterized by trade liberalization. The numerical results in the table above can be interpreted in the following way:

*1960-70*  The average growth of domestic output of annually 7.6 percent is mainly accounted for by the expansion of domestic demand, at a rate of 87.5 percent. Import substitution accounted for 10.5 percent and export growth for only 2 percent. This shows that in the 1960s Mexican manufacturing was substantially oriented towards the domestic market. Mexican products dominated domestic consumption, which is shown by the high ratio of domestic production to total supply (u), which was above 85 percent all the time and rose to 90 percent in 1970. This increase reflects the ongoing import substitution resulting from the inward-oriented trade policy regime.

*1970-80*  The average output growth is again mainly accounted for by domestic demand expansion (105 percent), but due to an episode of trade liberalization, import substitution is turned into import penetration, that is, the contribution of import substitution is negative (-7.1 percent). Exports still play a marginal role in output growth (2.1 percent).

*1980-85*  Since average output growth was very slow in this period and domestic demand declined, reflecting a major recession in 1982 and 1983, the domestic demand contribution is negative (-13.1 percent). The import substitution component is of greatest importance (92.2 percent), due to the trade restrictions imposed by the government to remedy the external imbalance and external debt problems. Exports, on the other hand have become an important source of growth (20.9 percent), reflecting the increase competitiveness of industries after the depreciation of the peso in 1982 and 1983.

*1985-91*  This is the period of trade liberalization, which took place mainly in 1986. The growth of production of annually 1.9 percent is mainly driven by domestic demand expansion (172 percent), while import substitution contributes negatively (-123.8 percent) as imports expand rapidly. Export, however, have become a major source of output growth, contributing to it at a rate of 50.7 percent, as one would expect after strong currency depreciation and trade liberalization.

On the whole, we can say that the sources of growth have shifted in the way we would expect them to shift, as a consequence of currency depreciation and trade liberalization, that is, from import substitution to export expansion. The domestic demand has played a substantial role all along, first because the economy was strongly inward-oriented in the 1960s, and later because the recession and subsequent recovery have had a strong influence on output growth. The events of the 1980s prepared the country for the strong export expansion in manufacturing that happened in the 1990s, when Mexico entered the North American Free Trade Area (NAFTA).

4)      The trade reforms of the 1980s were only a preliminary episode. Mexico broadened and deepened the reforms in the 1990s pursuing several specific goals, such as participation in the Uruguay round, membership in the WTO, entry into the OECD, membership in NAFTA and other regional free trade agreements. The country experienced a major recession in 1994/95, which was brought about by an increasing external deficit, capital outflows and a strong devaluation of the currency. Contrary to its experience in the early 1980s, however, Mexico managed to overcome these problems within two years, not by restricting trade but by adjustment and further integration into the world economy.

Import duties were lowered further so that the simple average (MFN) rate declined to about 13 percent by 1997, and the rate within NAFTA declined to about four percent. The weighted average tariff was less than three percent by 1997. Quantitative restrictions were reduced, but new anti-dumping measures were introduced and export incentives were used to counter the anti-export bias resulting from the remaining level of protection.

In addition to trade liberalization, Mexico opened up to foreign investments and became the second largest recipient of foreign direct investment (FDI), following China. In the years between 1994 and 1997 Mexico's inflow of FDI totaled about $40 billion. Capital inflow was a major source of economic growth and modernization in the private sector. The manufacturing sector was thereby transformed from an entirely inward-oriented to an export-oriented sector. The in-bond (maquiladora) industries located near the US border accounted for 40 percent of Mexico's total exports and nearly half of its manufactured exports in 1996. In spite of its generally open trade regime, Mexico has maintained and strengthened, in the 1990s, some special regimes of relatively high protection, such as those of the automobile and parts industry, as well as the textile, clothing and footwear industries.

Trade and foreign investment have been the main engines of growth in the Mexican economy. Between 1997 and 2000 the Mexican GDP grew at an annual average rate of 5.2 percent and private investment grew at 10.6 percent. Close to one third of this growth was accounted for by exports. While in the early 1980s Mexico's exports consisted mainly of petroleum products (70 percent), in 2001 close to 90 percent of exports were manufactured products. Mexico's entry into NAFTA was a major incentive for much of the transformation. More than ¾ of Mexico's trade is with the U.S., but the country has also concluded free-trade agreements with Columbia, Venezuela, Bolivia and Costa Rica, and since 1997 with the European Free Trade Association, the European Union, Israel, Nicaragua, Salvador, Guatemala and Honduras.

# Chapter 6

# External Balance and the Exchange Rate

In earlier chapters the problem of external balance was briefly mentioned; in particular, we discussed in Chapter 4 how the aggregate growth rate may depend either on the savings or on the foreign exchange constraint, and in Chapter 5, external balance was taken as one of the policy goals determining trade policies. In this chapter we review the external account in some more detail and examine the objective of external balance, as well as the policy tools to achieve it. In this context, the exchange rate and its variation are of central importance. The exchange rate is an important link between the macroeconomic goals of stability, growth and external balance on the one hand, and the microeconomic concerns of efficiency, protection and relative prices on the other. The discussion will be further extended to stabilization and structural adjustment programmes in Chapter 8.

## 6.1    Review of the External Account

The external account or balance of payments consists of two parts, the current account and the capital account. The current account includes all those operations that are confined to the accounting period: usually a fiscal year. The capital account, on the other hand, includes those transactions that have financial consequences beyond the accounting period, such as foreign borrowing or lending, which lead to foreign debt or credit, and foreign investment, which results in foreign ownership of domestic capital, and domestic ownership of foreign capital.

The current account captures several types of transactions, such as merchandise trade, trade in services, factor service payments, and unilateral transfers. The merchandise trade balance is the most important part of the current account and is, for simplification, often taken as representative of the entire current account. This was the case in our earlier discussion of foreign saving, where we simply equated the foreign capital inflow with the trade balance. We can now be more precise and review further components of the current account. Trade in services, such as tourism, international transport, international financial services and insurance are becoming increasingly important to those developing countries that have a competitive advantage in these labour-intensive activities. One of the major contributions of the Uruguay Round of trade negotiations at the level of the GATT was the inclusion of trade in services. For countries like Kenya, for instance, the foreign revenue from tourism is as important as the revenue from the traditional cash crops, coffee and tea. Factor services are an important expenditure for countries that host much foreign investment and/or employ many foreign workers, since both lead to a continuous outflow of foreign exchange. Unilateral transfers, like grants of official development assistance, and private transfers from individuals working abroad, can be important sources of foreign exchange inflows.

The current account balance of the developing countries typically registers a deficit for several reasons. First, imports tend to exceed exports because the low level of development of industries means that lots of products need to be imported; and exports require international competitiveness, which is not easily achieved. Second, even if a developing country is able to generate a surplus in merchandise and service trade, it is likely to use foreign capital and labour to overcome its capital and skill shortage. Hence, it faces continuous outflows of factor service payments. Third, a current account deficit requires capital inflows for external balance. It is rational for developing countries to borrow capital in order to grow faster in the present and repay the debt later, provided that the borrowed funds are well invested and yield a return that exceeds the cost of borrowing.

The capital account includes, in addition to foreign borrowing or lending and foreign investment, the foreign reserve account. This is the balancing account showing whether the total balance of payments registers a surplus or deficit. Foreign exchange reserves are needed to finance imports and interest payments, or any other outflow denominated in foreign currency. If, for instance, the current account is in deficit and the deficit exceeds the net capital inflow, then the country will lose foreign exchange reserves. The foreign reserve position is also important for monetary policy, as we will see later. Whether a country accumulates reserves of foreign exchange or faces dwindling reserves depends on the exchange rate regime that it has chosen, as well as on the level of the exchange rate. In a flexible exchange rate regime, deficits or surpluses in the balance of payments lead to automatic adjustments in the exchange rate, so that foreign reserves undergo only short run fluctuations. In a fixed rate regime, however, the foreign reserve position acts like the red light signalling danger whenever it shrinks below a critical level, or even when it keeps growing continuously. Some kind of intervention is then needed to return to external balance. If the signal is one of declining foreign reserves and chronic external deficit, the required intervention is devaluation of the currency, or stated popularly, of the exchange rate.[1] Before discussing the policy option of devaluation, let us briefly review the main exchange rate regimes, as well as the determinants of the exchange rate.

## 6.2    Exchange Rate Regimes and Policies

While in macroeconomic theory we distinguish simply between fixed and flexible rates, in practice there are numerous degrees of flexibility. Furthermore, in segmented regimes there are dual or multiple rates, for instance an official rate for imports and exports and a parallel rate for all other, mainly financial, transactions. Dual or multiple rates are considered sub-optimal, but in sub-optimal policy environments they can serve specific purposes. A dual rate regime may be indicated when violent financial shocks would lead to strong fluctuations of the exchange rate. A dual rate regime may protect the trade flows from such fluctuations.

In terms of flexibility, one can distinguish between the strictly fixed and the freely floating rate, as well as several intermediate kinds of regime. Starting from the rigidly fixed rate regimes, such as currency boards[2] or the adoption of a foreign currency as domestic currency (e.g. dollarization) we observe, in increasing order of flexibility, the adjustable peg, the crawling peg, wider-band systems and the managed float. While the adjustable peg allows adjustments when necessary, the crawling peg implies planned adjustments based on predicted price increases. Wider bands imply limited flexibility within the limits of the band, for instance a target rate plus/minus 15 percent. Managed floats involve interventions by the Central Bank with the intention to maintain a rate that is either above or below the level likely to be attained in a completely free market.

According to the IMF's exchange rate classification, there are five rate categories: Fixing to a single currency, fixing to a currency basket, limited flexibility (e.g. the ERM[3]), managed flexibility and independent

---

[1]   It is quite common to read about 'devaluation of the exchange rate'. Strictly speaking, this is an incorrect use of the term and should be replaced by 'devaluation of the currency'.

[2]   The currency board is a regime, in which the Central Bank is committed to exchanging any amount of local currency against the reserve currency, on which it is pegged. This implies that there is no room for monetary policy, as the money supply depends strictly on the size of the reserve.

[3]   The currencies of the European Exchange Rate Mechanism (ERM) were fixed against each other within margins of 2.25 to 6.5 percent, but float against all other currencies. Some other currencies are pegged against individual member currencies, for instance the franc CFA against the French franc.

floating. There is of course a continuum of degrees of fixedness since even a country that pegs its currency firmly towards a lead currency will have a limited degree of flexibility *vis-à-vis* currencies that are flexible *vis-à-vis* the same lead currency.

The main advantage of maintaining a fixed rate is to avoid rate fluctuations and the uncertainty they entail for traders. Fixed rates are also used as an anchor to keep inflation rates low. An international monetary regime based on fixed rates was advocated by the Bretton Woods conference in 1944 and became the rule after the Second World War. This regime was a gold-exchange standard, which relied on the stability of and the confidence in the main reserve currency, the U.S.$. In the late 1960s and early 1970s it came increasingly under fire, due to increasing budget and external deficits of the U.S., as well as rapidly increasing international needs for reserve currency, but limited gold stocks. Many authors then considered flexible regimes to be more in line with modern growth and liberal trade policy. Between 1971 and 1973 the regime was abandoned by the main trading nations and replaced by a flexible rate regime. Today we find cases of both fixed and flexible rates, with most currencies in intermediate positions, that is, of limited degrees of flexibility. In some countries fixed and semi-fixed rates are pegged either against a major international currencies like the U.S. dollar, or against baskets of currencies reflecting the particular trade relationships of a country, or against the Special Drawing Rights (SDR), regarded as the currency of the International Monetary Fund (IMF). A particularly interesting case is the currency of the European Union, the Euro, the case of a monetary union, which is equivalent of a rigidly fixed exchange rate. *Vis-à-vis* the U.S.$ and other currencies, however, the Euro is flexible. Even before the introduction of the Euro in 1999, the currencies of the European Union members were in a fixed relationship known as the European Monetary System (EMS).

The exchange rate is a price and it is usually expressed as the domestic price of foreign currency, with the dimension of domestic currency units (dcu) per foreign currency unit (fcu). A second way of expressing it is as the foreign currency price of the domestic currency (fcu/dcu). The former definition is more widely used by economists than the latter, because it makes it convenient to treat the exchange rate as the price of a productive factor, foreign exchange. It is probably the single most important price in the economy, due to its pervasive influence on most sectors of the economy. While a perfectly flexible rate can be expected to be an equilibrium rate, pegged rates are more likely to be misaligned. What exactly is meant by misalignment depends on the perspective. Generally, we say that an exchange rate is well aligned if it leads to external equilibrium. In a long-run perspective it should also reflect the true purchasing power of the currency. There are various ways of calculating the degree of misalignment of an exchange rate. The more traditional way is to estimate a shadow or general equilibrium rate and to compare it with the going rate. If the going rate is clearly inferior to the equilibrium rate (defined as the price of foreign currency), we say that the domestic currency is over-valued. A more modern approach is to compute the real exchange rate and to use it for inference about over- or under-valuation. This is demonstrated in more detail in the later section 6.4.

## 6.3    Policies for External Balance

External balance is an important policy objective under a fixed exchange rate. It means that there are no major changes in the external reserve position. The central bank tries to maintain a sufficient amount of foreign reserves to meet its obligations in terms of payments in foreign exchange. Such payments obligations arise from imports of goods and services, factor service payments and transfers, as well as from capital outflows. Under a fully flexible exchange rate regime the foreign currency in and outflows tend to be balanced, although fluctuations in foreign reserves can occur, due to shocks that require more time for the economy to adjust. Under a fixed exchange rate regime, however, external imbalances frequently arise and need to be corrected by policy interventions.

Since under a fixed exchange rate monetary policy tends to be ineffective, governments rely heavily on fiscal policies. But this may be insufficient for assuring simultaneously internal and external balance. An external deficit would require fiscal restraint, which may, however, be unwelcome if the economy is also below full employment. In this case, the government needs to devalue the currency by setting a new exchange rate. Under the Bretton Woods regime such devaluations required the sanction of the IMF, but under the present more flexible international regime, devaluations can be implemented without such approval. The well-known Swan diagram (Swan, 1963) in Figure 1 can be used to demonstrate the appropriate choice of policies to overcome external imbalances in the presence of alternative scenarios of internal balance.

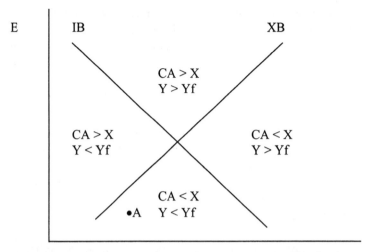

Fiscal ease

**Figure 6.1    The Swan diagram**

The axes in the Swan diagram are used to measure the direction and strength of the two available policy tools, fiscal ease (i.e. increased spending or decreased taxation) on the horizontal axis, and currency devaluation (an increase of the exchange rate) on the vertical axis. The two lines in the diagram are equilibrium loci showing the policy combinations for which external (XX) and internal (II) balance are achieved. All policy combinations that are not on one of these lines are disequilibrium situations in internal and external markets. The four areas created by the two equilibrium loci are areas of economic discomfort. On the right-hand side of XB-line (under it) the economy experiences external deficit (CA < X), because increased fiscal ease would increase imports and deteriorate the current account. To the left and above the XB-line, lower fiscal spending, or a higher exchange rate would imply a current account surplus (CA > X), because devaluation or fiscal restraint would lead to that outcome. Similarly, on the right-hand side of the IB-line (above it) greater fiscal ease would create inflationary pressure (Y > Yf), and the same result would be expected from currency devaluation. The area to the left of the IB-line is one of unemployment (Y < Yf). Yf is the full-employment level of national income (Y) and X is the target rate of the current account (CA).

A situation of external deficit and massive unemployment shown in the diagram by the point A requires a combination of currency devaluation and greater fiscal ease rather than a single policy change, in order to achieve simultaneously external and internal balance. More generally, most situations of disequilibrium require more than one policy measure in order to achieve more than one policy goal. A combination of expenditure-changing (fiscal ease) and expenditure-switching (currency de-or revaluation) is needed to achieve internal and external balance. The Swan diagram also invites a discussion of the assignment problem, that is, which authority is responsible for which policy target, as well as the timing of policy interventions. Since the central bank deals with the exchange rate it naturally bears the responsibility for the external balance target, and the finance minister for internal balance. Exchange rate interventions have a much shorter, even immediate, implementation lag than fiscal policy changes. They may over-shoot the target, however, and need to be coordinated with changes in fiscal ease.

Often governments try to avoid devaluation out of fear of increased inflationary pressure and political instability, and then resort to alternative policies, such as import restrictions. In the short run, such policies can help to achieve external balance, but they come at a cost of efficiency losses due to the introduction or increase of price distortions, as we have seen in the previous chapter.

## 6.4    The Real Exchange Rate as a Tool of Analysis

The real exchange rate is an important tool for the analysis of currency misalignment. It has been defined in various ways by different authors. The first, and perhaps most common, definition is that of the nominal rate adjusted for price levels:

$$(6.1) \quad RER = E\, P_f/P_d$$

where $E$ is the nominal rate (i.e. the domestic price of foreign currency), and $P_d$ and $P_f$ are the domestic and foreign price indices, respectively. This definition of the real exchange rate implies that it appreciates[4] if domestic prices rise faster than international prices, while the nominal rate remains constant. Alternatively, real appreciation also occurs when the nominal rate declines, relative to the price ratio $P_f/P_d$. Dornbusch uses the inverse

---

[4]    In the case of the real exchange rate, it is more valid to talk about appreciation and depreciation of the real rate, because of the following potential contradiction. When domestic prices rise, while foreign prices and the nominal exchange rate remain constant, the real rate appreciates (RER falls), but the currency actually loses real value. What appreciates is the official value of the currency as expressed by the nominal rate relative to the intrinsic value of the currency as expressed by its purchasing power, which declines.

definition (c.f. Dornbusch and Kuenzler, 1993), which is also used by the IMF in exchange rate indices:

$$(6.2) \quad RER^* = P_d/(E \, P_f)$$

This inverse of RER has the advantage over the former that it expresses the value of the domestic currency in terms of foreign currency. Therefore, an increase means appreciation and a decrease means depreciation.

A third definition is the one advocated by Edwards (1988) and others:

$$(6.3) \quad RER^{**} = \text{Price of tradable goods/Price of non-tradable goods}$$

This definition is more ad hoc and will not be used in the present context. In a theoretical sense, this price ratio captures the essence of the real exchange rate as traded goods reflect foreign prices, and non-traded goods reflect domestic prices, but it is empirically not very operational since it is extremely difficult to obtain representative price indices of tradable and non-tradable goods in any economy.

In order to investigate potential misalignment by help of the real exchange rate, using the IMF definition, one computes first RER* for the whole study period. The value, although different from 1/E, has still the dimension of foreign currency units per domestic currency unit. Then one transforms the whole time sequence of RER* into a real exchange rate index (RERI) equal to 100 in the base year. The two price indices, Pd and Pf, are normally computed for the same base year, unless they come from different statistical sources. It is then practical to use the same year as base year for RERI, at least as an intermediate step. For the analysis of misalignment, however, it is practical to choose a base year in which there was no misalignment according to prior knowledge. When in such a year of a well-aligned nominal rate the RERI is set equal to 100, one can easily infer the degree of over or under-valuation by measuring the difference between the computed RERI in any year and the base year RERI of 100. This last step of the calculation implies dividing the RER* in the chosen base year by its own value and multiplying it with 100. When this operation is done for the whole time sequence, one can see the degree of over-valuation (RERI > 100) or under-valuation (RERI < 100) in any year. When none of the years, for which data are available, was a well-aligned year, but the degree of over- or under-valuation is known for one year, one proceeds simply by choosing that year as a base year and computing it such that it has a value equal to 100 plus the known degree of over-valuation (or

100 minus the degree of under-valuation). For instance, if we know that in 1980 the exchange rate was overvalued by 20 percent, we simply set the RERI equal to 120 and proceed as before.

The following example may serve to clarify the procedure. In early 1994, the Mexican exchange rate equalled about 3 pesos per U.S.\$. In December 1994 it depreciated to 5 pesos/U.S.\$. The depreciation was one of 40 percent[5] as the value of the peso shrank from U.S.\$0.333 to U.S.\$0.2. Assuming that domestic and foreign prices rose at rates of 15 percent and 3 percent, respectively, and that in 1994 the peso had been overvalued by 20 percent, the 1995 RERI equals then $[(1/5*1.15/1.03)/(1/3)]*120 = 80.4$, indicating that the peso was undervalued by about 20 percent in 1995. The logic of this method of analysis can be seen in the following Table 6.1.

**Table 6.1   Computing the real exchange rate for Mexico**

| Year | E | E* | Pd | Pf | RER* | RERI* | RERI*$_{adj.}$ |
|------|-----------|----------|-----|-----|-------|-------|--------|
|      | (Pesos/\$) | (\$/Peso) |     |     |       |       |        |
| 1994 | 3 | 0.333 | 100 | 100 | 0.333 | 100 | 120 |
| 1995 | 5 | 0.2 | 115 | 103 | 0.223 | 67 | 80.4 |

The theory underlying this approach to analysing misalignment is the purchasing power parity theory (PPP). It assumes that in the long run nominal exchange rates should equal relative prices, that is, E should equal Pd/Pf. In other words, the real exchange rate should have a value close to one[6] and should remain at that level as long as the currency is well aligned. We know, however, that even in the long run exchange rates tend to deviate from the relative price ratio, because they also reflect other factors than relative prices, such as financial flows and real changes in the economies. Since this is the case, one can easily find other criteria for defining a well-aligned exchange rate. The most logical of such criteria is that of external balance, in other words, a situation characterized by the absence of unwanted reserve losses. Although external balance is not unrelated to purchasing power parity, it is clearly not the same. A country may have an exchange rate that reflects well relative prices, but, due to strong capital inflows, its currency appreciates to a point where it is over-valued in terms of PPP, although providing external balance. In that case the purchasing power-based rate is not equal to the one that assures external balance.

---

[5]   For the purpose of computing meaningful rates of devaluation or depreciation, it is practical to use the inverse of the normal exchange rate definition, or the value of the currency in terms of foreign currency.

[6]   It should be equal to one only if the domestic and foreign price indices are based on the same basket of goods and services as the nominal exchange rate.

Given its relative simplicity, the approach based on PPP is frequently used to evaluate currency alignment and misalignment.

The computation of the real exchange rate with the purpose of determining the degree of over- or under-valuation of the currency is important for the policy maker because the real exchange rate is an indicator of how the international competitiveness of economic activities is affected by exchange rate misalignment. Competitiveness can be defined as the ability to sell without making losses, or to produce at unit costs that are lower than those of international competitors. Clearly, international competitiveness is first and foremost a result of high productivity and factor cheapness, which vary from industry to industry. But the exchange rate affects all or most domestic prices relative to foreign prices, and thereby impacts on the competitiveness of all activities. An overvalued exchange rate represents a disincentive to all domestic producers, since it makes imports artificially cheap and lowers the domestic currency price of exports. Inversely, an undervalued exchange rate makes industries internationally competitive, as long as domestic prices do not catch up with world prices and costs. Although the impact of exchange rate misalignment on competitiveness is a temporary phenomenon, it can last for periods of several years. Competitive advantage derived from exchange rate under-valuation is not equal to comparative advantage. While comparative advantage of industries does not disappear with real appreciation of the exchange rate, competitive advantage does. It follows then that policy makers must try to avoid major misalignment of the exchange rate in order to assure stability of economic incentives. In the case of a fixed exchange rate regime overvaluation is eliminated by devaluing the currency and, at the same time, preventing the domestic rate of inflation from exceeding international rates. Let us see now what are the implications of currency devaluation for the economy. Before doing so, however, the reader should be acquainted with one more definition of the real exchange rate, the real effective exchange rate (REER).

The REER follows the same principle as the RER, except that it is trade-weighted and expresses the value of a currency in terms of all other currencies that are important in the country's trade relations. Logically, it is also in index form, just like the RERI, as it cannot be expressed in terms of several foreign currencies at the same time. The computation of REER is complex and requires data on the trade flows and prices of many countries. For that reason, even the IMF is unable to publish it for all of its member countries, which are covered in its International Financial Statistics, a monthly and yearly publication and a major source of international trade and financial data.

**6.5    Currency Devaluation and its Consequences**

The principal remedy to currency over-valuation is devaluation.[7] It is usually a painful remedy because it has strong side effects. Besides raising the prices of tradable goods *vis-à-vis* those of non-tradable goods, as well as stimulating exports and discouraging imports, it also fuels inflation. This follows directly from the rise of import prices, but does not stop there. The extent to which devaluation translates into increased import prices is referred to as pass-through and depends on the willingness of importers to accept losses in market share. To avoid such losses, importers often hold on to import prices or increase them by less than the devaluation. An initial price hike of import prices is eventually transmitted to the whole price system, depending on how strongly prices are linked to import prices, and on what arrangements the government makes to limit inflation. One way of avoiding the inflationary spiral following devaluation is for the government to conclude agreements with producers and unions that limit further price and wage increases in a specified period of time.

In the short run, devaluations can be painful because they reduce real income, leading to a reduction of demand and possibly increased poverty. Aggregate supply may also decline when producers see their costs increase due to price increases of imported inputs. Since the prices of traded goods rise relative to those of non-traded goods, resources will flow from non-traded to traded goods sectors, but the flow takes time and in the meantime, some resources, mainly workers are likely to be idle. In the long run, however, the elimination of misalignment, especially over-valuation, must be expected to have a positive impact on the resource allocation and growth.

A further observation of some interest is the effect of devaluations on the rate and structure of protection. When governments devalue the currency and make arrangements to limit the price and wage increases in the economy by agreements with employers and unions, the usual link between international and domestic prices gets broken. We normally assume that the domestic prices of tradable goods are determined as

(6.4)    Pmd = Pmw e $(1 + tm)$ for importables, and

(6.5)    Pxd = Pxw e $(1 - tx)$ for exportables,

---

[7] The reader is reminded that the terms devaluation and revaluation apply to a discrete change of parity in a fixed-rate regime. In flexible-rate regimes we speak of depreciation, rather than devaluation, and of appreciation, rather than revaluation.

where Pmw and Pxw are the international import and export prices in foreign currency, tm is the ad-valorem import duty and tx is an ad-valorem export tax. Under this assumption, combined with the small-country assumption, that is, importers and exporters are price takers in international markets, the nominal rate of protection (NRP) would remain unchanged by the devaluation. Domestic prices would simply rise at the same rate as the exchange rate. Given the pass-through, however, and especially if it is prolonged by government arrangements to reduce the inflationary impact of the devaluation, the domestic prices remain sticky, while the international prices in domestic currency rise. This leads to the observation of reduced rates of protection, possibly to negative rates of protection, as recorded in Mexico after the devaluations of 1983/84. This is discussed in Case Study 11 of the Mexican devaluation and trade liberalization of the 1980s, following this chapter.

### 6.6     The Dutch Disease Syndrome

The term Dutch Disease refers to a situation in which an export boom based on the discovery and exploitation of a new natural resource causes real currency appreciation, with a subsequent decline of traditional exports. The name is derived from the Dutch experience of the 1970s when, following the discovery of major natural gas reserves in the 1960s, exports rose, but the economy suffered from declining traditional exports, slow growth and unemployment. Not only traditional exports may be affected, but import-competing sectors may also suffer as the appreciation makes it harder for domestic industries to compete with cheaper imports. Some observers have linked the disease to de-industrialization. The phenomenon has been analyzed theoretically by Corden and Neary (1982) and empirically by Roemer (1985) and others. The oil boom of the 1970s may have led to Dutch Disease in several oil-exporting countries such as Nigeria, Indonesia and Mexico. Its causes are not limited to export booms, however, but can also include major capital inflows, or massive aid flows. The Dutch Disease syndrome can be understood as a decline in competitiveness of the traditional sectors in the economy due to currency appreciation caused by the gain in competitiveness of new industries. If the development of new industries is permanent, however, and not just a short-lived phenomenon based on a quickly exhausted resource, then it must be seen as part of the natural structural change, and the name of 'disease' does not appear to be justified. In that sense the term 'Dutch Disease' applies even better to temporary influxes of foreign exchange than the discovery and development of exportable resources. Whether the Dutch Disease significantly affects an economy depends also on the relative importance of the sectors whose competitiveness declines due to the appreciating currency.

## References

Corden, M. and P. Neary (1982), 'Booming Sector and De-industrialization in a Small Open Economy', *Economic Journal*, 92, pp. 825-48.
Dornbusch, R. and L.T. Kuenzler (1993), 'Exchange Rate Policy: Options and Issues', in: Dornbusch (ed.), *Policymaking in the Open Economy*, EDI Series in Economic Development, Oxford University Press.
Edwards, S. (1988), *Exchange Rate Misalignment in Developing Countries,* The World Bank,Occasional Paper No.2.
Roemer, M. (1985), 'Dutch Disease in Developing Countries: Swallowing Bitter Medicine', in: Lundahl (ed.), *The Primary Sector in Economic Development*, London, Croom-Helms.
Swan, T.W. (1963), 'Longer-Run Problems of the Balance of Payments', in: H.W. Arndt and M.W. Corden (eds.), *The Australian Economy: A Volume of Readings*, Melbourne: Chesire Press, pp. 384-95.

# Case Study 12
# Protection, Sector Bias and the Exchange Rate in Mexico's Trade Policy Reform

## Purpose

The present case study deals with the effects of trade policy reform in Mexico in the 1980s. It focuses on three aspects, first, the structure of protection and the resulting sector bias, second, the interaction between protection and the exchange rate, and third, the international competitiveness of Mexican industries during and after the reforms. The purpose of the study is to analyze and interpret the price incentive structure as available to us in the form of data on protection, the exchange rate and price levels. The conclusions of this study are useful mainly by leading to a better understanding of the role the exchange rate plays in trade policy reform, and of the sequencing of such reforms.

**Background**

The Mexican economy grew during the 1960s and 1970s under an inward-oriented trade regime. In the 1980s, it experienced a shift toward outward-oriented trade policies. The trade regime of the 1960s and 1970s included substantial tariffs, quantitative restrictions in form of import licensing, and the use of reference prices for imports. In the early 1980s the trade restrictions were further tightened in response to a balance of payments crisis and the concurrent debt crisis. In 1985, however, the regime was liberalized by reducing the licensing coverage from nearly 100 percent to less than 50 percent by the end of the year, and to less than 25 percent by mid-1988. Import duties were both reduced and made more uniform. The number of tariff levels was reduced from 16 to 5, and the maximum tariff rate was reduced from formerly 100 percent to 20 percent. The production-weighted tariff declined from 28.5 percent in 1984 to about 10 percent in 1988. The trade policy reform was preceded, however, by a substantial currency depreciation, the result of a series of events including both withdrawal of the Central Bank from the market and episodes of complete exchange control. After 1982 the exchange regime continued to be a dual-rate managed float.

**Method of Analysis**

The analysis proposed in this study consists of three stages. At the first stage, the available data on protection are used to calculate sector average NRPs and the sector bias. At the second stage, the degree of currency misalignment is estimated and used for the adjustment of the protection measures. At the third stage, the international competitiveness of Mexican industries is evaluated using the measures of protection as a proxy (inverse) indicator of price competitiveness.

*1)      Protection and sector bias*

Trade policy, like various other policies, tends to confer an incentive bias on the affected sectors. To the extent that price incentives vary among sectors, the variation in incentives creates a differential pull of resources into or out of industries. For a single industry or sector this is measured by the nominal rate of protection (NRP), which compares the domestic price with the international (cif) price of equivalent imports. If the tariff is the only existing distortion and equal to the difference between the domestic and international price of a product, then the nominal tariff can be used instead of the NRP based on price comparisons. In the presence of quantitative restrictions, tax exonerations and smuggling, however, price comparisons are necessary to establish meaningful NRPs. The Mexican data provided in this case study are so-called implicit NRPs based on price comparisons. They were established and published by the Mexican Ministry of Industry (SECOFI), under guidance of Dr. ten Kate. It is clear from the data that the implicit NRPs diverge significantly from the tariff. Their frequently negative values also suggest that they resulted from relative stickiness of domestic prices and strong price increases of international prices due to the devaluation of the peso in 1983. They must be understood as short-run NRPs.

The bias resulting from unequal protection in the two sectors, primary and industrial, can be measured as proposed in Chapter 5, that is, as:

$$B_{prim/ind.} = (NRP_{prim.} + 1)/(NRP_{ind.} + 1) - 1$$

The bias consists of a direct component, that is, the price distortion of the sector itself, in this case agriculture, and an indirect component, the price distortion of the other sector or the rest of the economy, in this case industry. The rationale of this way of measuring biases is that primary sector producers suffer not only from the fact that their output price tends to be below the world price (typically in agriculture, but also the state-controlled and regulated petroleum industry) but also from the fact that they pay industrial product prices that are higher than world prices.

Since the Mexican NRPs are based on price comparisons ('implicit protection') the measurement picks up the effect on prices of various policy measures, such as tariff and non-tariff barriers, currency misalignment, tariff exonerations and smuggling, as well as market pressures. Therefore, the NRPs and the bias measure reflect both, policy distortions and the competitive strength of the sectors and sub-sectors.

*2)    Exchange rate misalignment*

The degree of over- or under-valuation of the peso is to be estimated using the real exchange rate index (RERI), which is based on the purchasing power parity theory. The reader is reminded that this index is defined as the inverse of the real exchange rate, $RER^* = Pd/(E\ Pf)$, which is then transformed into an index number with a value of 100 in the base year. In the present case study it is practical to choose as base year the year 1981, because only for this year we have information on the earlier state of misalignment of the exchange rate. In other words, since the exchange rate was known to be overvalued by 22 percent in 1981, the RERI in that year should be equal to 122.

The degree of misalignment is also used to compute net rates of nominal protection:

$$NRPnet = (1+NRP)/CM - 1$$

where CM is the coefficient of misalignment and equals RERI/100. If, for instance, the data based on an over-valued (by 20 percent) official exchange rate indicate an industry's NRP to be 32 percent, the net rate of protection would be only 10 percent. In other words, when the currency is over-valued, the gross nominal rates of protection (NRP) overstate the true extent of protection, which the net rate is meant to approximate. It is important to realize, however, that the net rate is only an approximation of the 'true rate' of protection, since it represents an adjusted partial equilibrium term. To compute the true degree of protection would require a comparison of distorted prices with true general equilibrium prices and exchange rates, which in turn would need a general equilibrium framework.

*3)      Competitiveness*

Competitiveness of industries *vis-à-vis* imports in domestic markets, or *vis-à-vis* international competitors in export markets, is evaluated best by the concept of cost competitiveness as discussed in Chapter 9. The nominal rate of protection (NRP) can be used, however, as a proxy indicator of price competitiveness. The idea is that strongly protected industries tend to be high-cost and therefore non-competitive, whereas unprotected industries typically owe their existence to a positive degree of competitiveness.

Nevertheless, one may find highly competitive firms in protected industries, which turn their competitive strength into high profits, as long as domestic competition is not very strong. A more problematic issue is the question of whether the gross or the net rate of protection should be used and how the concept of competitiveness compares to that of comparative advantage. The answer to these questions will have to be delayed to further discussion in Chapter 9.

**Assigned Questions**

1)      Compute the (weighted) average NRPs of the primary and industrial (manufacturing) sectors for 1978 to 1987, using the data provided in the following table. For the aggregation of NRPs from 10 primary sector branches to a single average (weighted) NRP use the given output data as weights, which are from 1988, but can be used, for simplicity, for all years. The same procedure applies to the 9 manufacturing divisions. Examine which policy changes may have been responsible for various changes in the rates of protection, paying special attention to the negative rates of protection. Identify the particular branches and divisions of the two sectors, which determine most strongly the average sector NRP.

2)      Compute the bias of the primary *vis-à-vis* the industrial sector. Observe whether there was an anti-primary sector bias before the reform and whether any existing bias may have been reduced or reversed through policy changes.

3)      Compute the real exchange rate index (RERI) using the provided data on the nominal exchange rate and price levels, as well as the procedure recommended in the chapter. Infer the degree of currency misalignment in the years 1981 to 1987 (for 1982 and 1983 data are missing), based on the additional information that in 1981 the currency was overvalued by 22 percent.

4)      Interpret the NRP as a proxy indicator of international price competitiveness and observe which sub-sectors were most and least competitive at the beginning and at the end of the study period. Which policy changes have contributed most to an increase in price competitiveness?

5)      Adjust the sector average NRP for currency misalignment by computing the NRPnet in both sectors and the years 1981 and 1984 to 1987. How does the misalignment affect the sector bias?

**Table CS12a    Nominal rates of protection in Mexico's primary and manufacturing sectors**

| BRANCH/ DIVISION | Output (million pesos) | 1979 | 1980 | 1981 | 1984 | 1985 | 1986 | 1987 |
|---|---|---|---|---|---|---|---|---|
| Primary sector | | | | | | | | |
| BRANCH 1 | 284,107 | -5.0 | 13.0 | 23.0 | -9.5 | -1.3 | -15.8 | -6.3 |
| BRANCH 2 | 225,035 | -2.0 | 14.0 | 31.0 | 1.5 | 12.0 | -17.5 | -19.8 |
| BRANCH 3 | 24,701 | -12.0 | 2.0 | 26.0 | -22.3 | -6.3 | -34.5 | -47.0 |
| BRANCH 4 | 23,870 | -1.0 | -3.0 | -2.0 | -6.5 | -4.8 | -13.0 | 2.8 |
| BRANCH 5 | 10,151 | -55.0 | -53.0 | -51.0 | -1.8 | 0.0 | -19.3 | -22.8 |
| BRANCH 6 | 118,005 | -74.0 | -88.0 | -89.0 | -75.8 | -72.5 | -49.3 | -53.3 |
| BRANCH 7 | 7,551 | -22.0 | -19.0 | 2.0 | -2.0 | 0.0 | -2.5 | 0.0 |
| BRANCH 8 | 83,465 | -4.0 | 0.0 | 1.0 | 1.8 | 1.5 | 3.3 | 4.3 |
| BRANCH 9 | 19,708 | 0.0 | 0.0 | 14.0 | 0.0 | 0.0 | 0.0 | 0.0 |
| BRANCH 10 | 10,687 | -11.0 | -12.0 | -11.0 | -36.8 | -9.5 | -16.8 | -26.3 |
| Industrial (manufacturing) sector | | | | | | | | |
| DIVISION 1 | 804,563 | -5.6 | 4.6 | 17.7 | -26.2 | -20.0 | -37.2 | -36.5 |
| DIVISION 2 | 259,344 | 9.7 | 20.4 | 40.6 | 6.0 | 17.3 | -5.9 | 7.7 |
| DIVISION 3 | 83,582 | 2.8 | 24.4 | 31.5 | -11.5 | 1.8 | -14.2 | -32.2 |
| DIVISION 4 | 133,867 | 12.5 | 18.1 | 22.3 | -15.8 | -16.9 | -37.7 | -22.4 |
| DIVISION 5 | 487,962 | -0.9 | 5.6 | 3.6 | -11.3 | -6.7 | -18.4 | -26.7 |
| DIVISION 6 | 122,439 | 1.1 | 6.7 | 4.4 | -12.9 | -7.3 | -22.2 | -19.7 |
| DIVISION 7 | 187,890 | 3.3 | 6.8 | 12.2 | 5.9 | 2.3 | -13.4 | -14.6 |
| DIVISION 8 | 457,448 | 24.2 | 37.2 | 46.8 | 18.1 | 13.7 | -12.6 | -8.9 |
| DIVISION 9 | 46,517 | 21.0 | 35.0 | 41.0 | -43.8 | -45.0 | -51.5 | -58.5 |

*Source:* SECOFI.

**Table CS12b  Nominal exchange rate and price indices, Mexico and U.S., 1981-1987**

|  | 1981 | 1982 | 1983 | 1984 | 1985 | 1986 | 1987 |
|---|---|---|---|---|---|---|---|
| U.S. prices 1980 = 100 | 109.8 | 114.2 | 116.1 | 118.5 | 119.6 | 117.9 | 120.5 |
| Mexican prices 1980 = 100 | 127.9 | 207.3 | 410.5 | 679.1 | 1071.2 | 1994.7 | 4624.0 |
| Nominal E (pesos/$) | 24.5 | 57.2 | 150.3 | 185.2 | 310.3 | 637.9 | 1405.0 |

Industrial sector divisions:

Division 1:   Food, beverages, tobacco
Division 2:   Textiles, leather, clothing
Division 3:   Wood industries
Division 4:   Paper and printing
Division 5:   Chemicals, petroleum, rubber, plastics
Division 6:   Non-metallic minerals
Division 7:   Basic metals
Division 8:   Metal products, machines, equipment
Division 9:   Other manufacturing

Primary sector branches:

Branch 1     Agriculture
Branch 2     Livestock
Branch 3     Forestry
Branch 4     Hunting and fishing
Branch 5     Coal mining
Branch 6     Oil and gas
Branch 7     Iron ore mining
Branch 8     Non-ferrous mining
Branch 9     Sand and gravel
Branch 10    Other mining

**Case Study 12: Solution**

1)      The weighted average of nominal protection rates (NRP) in the primary and secondary sectors have been computed as follows (in percent):

**Table CS12c     Average nominal rates of protection per sector**

|          | 1979  | 1980  | 1981 | 1984  | 1985 | 1986  | 1987  |
|----------|-------|-------|------|-------|------|-------|-------|
| Primary  | -15.0 | -5.4  | 4.1  | -15.2 | -8.0 | -19.2 | -17.0 |
| Industrial | 4.8 | 14.3  | 22.6 | -8.6  | -5.2 | -23.3 | -22.5 |

For the primary sector, the strongly negative protection in 1979 and 1980 resulted essentially from low and controlled prices in the energy (oil and coal) and mining sector. Agriculture, livestock and forestry also contributed to the negative protection, although at lower rates.

      For the industrial sector, where prices were essentially not controlled and the protective tariff rates were clearly positive, it is more puzzling why the NRPs turned negative from 1985 onwards. As we shall see under the third question, this is explained by the temporary misalignment of the currency.

2)      The sector bias resulting from these NRPs has been calculated as $B_{prim/ind} = (1+NRP_{prim})/(1+NRP_{ind}) -1$ and is shown in the following table.

**Table CS12d     Primary sector bias *vis-à-vis* manufacturing**

| Year     | 1979  | 1980  | 1981  | 1984 | 1985 | 1986 | 1987 |
|----------|-------|-------|-------|------|------|------|------|
| Bias (%) | -18.8 | -17.3 | -15.0 | -7.2 | -3.0 | 5.3  | 7.0  |

The numbers suggest that until 1985 the incentive regime implied a strong but diminishing bias against the primary sector. The bias turned positive in 1986 and 1987, essentially as a consequence of negative protection in the industrial sector, which was stronger than that of the primary sector. It is important to note that this essentially resulted from the peso depreciation.

3)      In order to analyze the misalignment of the currency, the real exchange rate has been computed in its inverse form RER* = Pd/(E Pf), where Pd refers to the Mexican price level, Pf to the U.S. price level, and E to the nominal exchange rate (pesos/U.S.$). In the last two rows of the table the RER* is then shown as an index, first with 1981 as base year and then based on the assumption that in 1981 the peso was overvalued by 22 percent.

**Table CS12e   Measuring Mexico's currency misalignment**

| Index\Year | 1981 | 1982 | 1983 | 1984 | 1985 | 1986 | 1987 |
|---|---|---|---|---|---|---|---|
| Pf | 108.9 | 114.2 | 116.1 | 118.5 | 119.6 | 117.9 | 120.5 |
| Pd | 127.9 | 207.3 | 410.5 | 679.1 | 1071.2 | 1994.7 | 4624.7 |
| E | 24.5 | 57.2 | 150.3 | 185.2 | 310.3 | 637.9 | 1405.8 |
| 1/E | 0.041 | 0.017 | 0.007 | 0.005 | 0.003 | 0.002 | 0.001 |
| RER* | 0.048 | 0.032 | 0.024 | 0.031 | 0.029 | 0.027 | 0.027 |
| RERI | 100 | 66.8 | 49.5 | 65.1 | 60.7 | 55.8 | 57.5 |
| RERIadj. | 122.0 | 81.5 | 60.4 | 79.4 | 74.1 | 68.1 | 70.1 |

The table shows that the peso depreciated in nominal terms over the whole period, especially in 1982 and 1983. However, the prices caught up with the currency depreciation (pass through) and the inflation differential between Mexico and the U.S. diminished the depreciation in real terms. It can be seen that the real depreciation between 1981 and 1987 amounted to 42.5 percent. If one assumes then that the peso had been overvalued by 22 percent in 1981, it follows that it became undervalued since 1982 and remained so until 1987 at rates varying between 19.5 percent (in 1982) and 39.6 percent (in 1983).

The real exchange rate provides us with an explanation of the negative rates of protection observed in the industrial sector that had positive tariff rates. As a consequence of the strong depreciation of the peso the foreign prices were sliding upwards, whereas the domestic prices of industrial goods were voluntarily, but temporarily, kept low. In 1986/87 several industrial divisions appeared to be capable of exporting their produce, although this did not happen yet, because most producers were not yet prepared to confront the export market and domestic prices were catching up with the currency depreciation. The currency depreciation, however, had eliminated most of the protection before the tariffs were lowered, so that the following trade liberalization in 1986/87 became less painful for the producers. One can refer to this phenomenon as exchange rate protection, because the competitive pressure on prices was temporarily shifted from imports to domestic factors.

4)      If one interprets the NRPs as proxy indicators of international competitiveness, then it follows that in 1987, following the real depreciation of the peso and some degree of trade liberalization, the most competitive primary branch was the oil and gas sector and the least competitive branch was that of non-ferrous mining. In the industrial (manufacturing) sector the division 9 (other manufacturing products) was

the most competitive one and the division 2 (textiles and leather clothing) appeared to be the least competitive.

5)        The following table shows the NRPnet, adjusted for currency overvaluation.

**Table CS12f    Net nominal rates of protection, Mexico**

| Sector\Year | 1981 | 1984 | 1985 | 1986 | 1987 |
|---|---|---|---|---|---|
| Primary | -14.6 | 6.7 | 24.2 | 18.6 | 18.3 |
| Industrial | 0.5 | 15.0 | 28.0 | 12.7 | 10.6 |
| Bias (pro-primary) | -15.0 | -7.2 | -3.0 | 5.3 | 7.0 |

The numbers suggest that, without the currency undervaluation, both sectors would have remained positively protected, but that the protection came down in 1986 and 1987 as a consequence of trade liberalization. The bias remains the same as computed earlier, however, since the currency misalignment affects both sectors in the same way. This is a simplifying assumption, however, because in reality industries and sectors may be affected differently by the degree of misalignment of the currency.

# Chapter 7

# Regional Integration and Monetary Union

In Chapter 5 the concept of regional integration was briefly introduced in the context of trade agreements. It is, however, a much wider concept ranging from simple preferential trade agreements and customs unions to common markets and economic unions. It therefore deserves further attention in the present chapter. In the first section the different stages of economic integration are being defined. In the second, the issues of regionalism and multilateralism are discussed with reference to the rules of the GATT and WTO. The welfare effects of preferential trade are examined in the third section, and the issue of intra-industry trade in the fourth section. The fifth section deals with monetary union and the theory of optimum currency areas and the sixth is a short review of the theory of intra-industry trade. The final section presents some evidence of the regional integration attempts by various groups of developing countries in the post-WWII era.

## 7.1    The Stages of Regional Integration

The weakest form of economic integration between two or several countries is a preferential trade agreement. In such an agreement the partner countries agree to trade with each other at more favourable conditions than towards third countries, and they also agree to remain perfectly free in their trade relations with third countries. The trade between the partner countries may be totally free from trade barriers, in which case there is a free trade area (FTA), or it may be less restricted than towards third countries.

The second stage of integration is the customs union (CU), which is a free trade area with a common external tariff towards third countries. The customs union is a logical progression from the FTA, as it eliminates the incentives for transfer trade flows that circumvent the higher external tariff of countries within FTAs with differential external trade barriers. The theory of customs union is the one that has received most attention in the literature and is discussed further in the fourth section.

The third stage of integration is known as common market and adds to the customs union the free flow of factors of production. This implies that not only capital can flow without restrictions between the member countries, but labour can also migrate without restrictions. The traditional barriers to the flow of labour are, however, much more complex than those of capital, and range from open interdictions or licensing regimes to the regulation of professional qualifications and language requirements. Even in otherwise fully integrated areas like nation states inter-regional mobility of labour is often imperfect due to such regulations.

Economic unions, the highest degree of integration, short of the economic and political union, can be defined as a common market, in which the member countries also share the same currency, that is, they are also a monetary union. There are monetary unions, however, in which countries share the same currency, without being an economic union and not even a common market. This fact has led to the theory of optimum currency areas, which examines under which conditions such monetary unions can be beneficial to the participating countries.

In the post-WWII era many countries have attempted to integrate with others, usually regional neighbours, and under different degrees of integration. The best-known and most successful experience is that of the European Union, which has progressed from a simple customs union through various stages of integration to an economic union, and has recently adopted a single currency, the Euro. The success of this union is mainly attributable to a strong political will of the member countries to overcome historical conflicts. Most other attempts of regional integration have been less successful, due to either unequal distribution of integration benefits or due to the lack of political will to surrender national sovereignty.

## 7.2    Regionalism vs. Multilateralism

The international trade relations of the post-WWII era have been dominated by the will to lower trade barriers in a multilateral orderly and negotiated fashion. The negotiations have taken place under the auspices of the General Agreement of Tariffs and Trade (GATT), which was established in 1947 in Geneva and was the driving force of eight rounds of multilateral negotiations for the reduction of barriers to trade during five decades. It gave way to the World Trade Organization (WTO) in 1994.

As under the GATT earlier, a key principle of membership of the WTO is non-discrimination. Preferential treatment *vis-à-vis* one trade partner, is conceded to all members of the WTO, except for members of

FTAs and CUs. The functions of the WTO are described as: administering trade agreements, acting as a forum for trade negotiations, settling trade disputes, reviewing national trade policies, assisting developing countries in trade policy issues through technical assistance and training programs, and cooperating with international organizations. Currently, the WTO consists of 147 member countries, whose trade represents more than 90 percent of world trade. Thirty other countries are still negotiating membership.

Parallel to the multilateral negotiations for trade liberalization there have been many attempts to form regional preferential trade agreements. One can therefore ask whether regionalism is a complement to or a substitute for multilateralism. The pessimistic view is that there will be a movement towards trading blocs that will turn inward and erect barriers with non-members and thus obstruct further liberalization. The more optimistic view is that the initial creation of trading blocs speed up the progress towards global free trade as it is much easier to negotiate with only a few blocs, rather than with numerous countries. The answer to this question is not obvious and depends on the political philosophy of the leading nations' governments. During the first wave of regionalism in the 1960s the European common market was formed and regionalism also spread through Africa and Latin America. The U.S., however, remained a supporter of multilateralism. During the second wave of regionalism in the middle eighties, the U.S. has favoured a regional approach (NAFTA and overtures towards Latin America), while Europe widened and deepened its integration. The reason behind the U.S.' change in opinion was the slow progress at GATT (Krugman, 1993). The large number of members had made the negotiations too difficult and there had also been a change in the character of protection (for instance voluntary export restrictions, anti-dumping mechanisms and other forms of administered protection). The change of U.S. strategy and the further integration of Europe made others, such as East Asia and various developing countries, fear that regional blocs are the only way to access world markets and to be left out. Therefore, we witness at present a new wave of regionalism.

The principle of non-discrimination, which is central to the final conception of the GATT and the WTO, takes the form of the 'most favoured nation' (MFN) status of all member countries. It means that trade preferences granted to a country must be extended to all other members. The only significant exception to the MFN clause is made in article 24, which permits customs unions and free trade areas, as long as they go all the way to elimination of trade barriers. This clause seems to be in contradiction to the principle, but it can also be interpreted to be a practical route toward universal free trade that GATT favoured as its ultimate goal. At this point in history it is not clear whether the existing regional blocs will give way to universal free trade, or whether they will remain organizations for enhanced regional trade (with internal problems) and for powerful trade disputes among the blocs.

## 7.3    The Theory of Customs Unions

Regional integration holds considerable promise for developing countries, because their potential to gain from trade is limited by several factors, such as the traditional structure of their exports (mainly raw materials), and the protection of developed country markets against certain imports from developing countries. In practice, however, economic integration in the South has not had the success it deserves. Some of the problems it encounters are fundamental and of an economic nature, others are purely political.

The major fundamental problem with preferential trade agreements is the fact that *trade creation* among the partners of an agreement usually comes to the detriment of trade with non-member countries (*trade diversion*). While trade creation has the well-known benefits of static efficiency gains, the diversion of trade from lower-cost non-member countries leads to the loss of potential tariff revenue, which is the cost of trade diversion. Preferential trade agreements are therefore beneficial to the members only if the benefits of trade creation exceed the costs of trade diversion.

The argument is based on Jacob Viner's (1950) original approach and demonstrated in the following diagram (Figure 7.1), in which the typical situation of an importable product is shown in the familiar partial-equilibrium setting of a country that faces the prospect of association with a regional neighbour through a free trade area (FTA) or customs union (CU). Its supply curve takes three alternative forms: Before association and with a tariff of tm consumers face a supply curve shown by CC's, while under free trade they would face AA's. Under a FTA or CU with another country that has higher production costs than third countries, the supply curve would be BB's, which represents the cost of production in the member country, when its products enter the home market without any restriction (neglecting transport cost). The domestic price would therefore fall from Pd' to Pd", when regional free is opened up. Imports would rise from formerly (Q3-Q2) to (Q4-Q1), which represents trade creation. It is, at the same time, trade diversion to the extent that the imports from third countries (Q3-Q2) are replaced by imports from member countries and as long as the external tariff remains at its former level. If, however, the external tariff is lowered as well, the effect of trade diversion diminishes. The welfare implications of regional free trade can be computed in the same fashion as done in Chapter 5. The price fall from Pd' to Pd" following introduction of regional free trade implies a gain of consumer surplus shown be area [a+b+c+d], but producers lose producers' surplus of area [a] and the government loses tariff revenue of area [c+h]. On the whole, the introduction of regional free trade results in a welfare gain of [b+d-h]. Whether it is a net gain or loss depends on whether the efficiency gain from trade creation [b+d] exceeds the net loss of tariff revenue [h+c-c], that is, the revenue loss net of [c], which is part of the consumers' gain. It also remains true that regional free trade implies a shortfall of welfare, relative to a situation of total free trade, which sums up to [f+j].

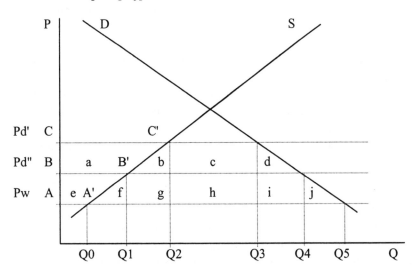

**Figure 7.1   Welfare effects of regional integration**

In practice, and in addition to the ambiguity of a net welfare gain, many trade associations are hampered by the fact that the members tend to have similar industrial structures, so that the more industrialized members tend to reap the benefits of industrialization, whereas the less advanced members tend to become the suppliers of raw materials to their neighbours. Furthermore, there are often important impediments to trade among the members, due to insufficient means of transportation and communication (especially within Africa), as well as insufficient payment and financing agreements. Case Study 13 offers an opportunity to compute the net welfare gain of regional free trade of Uganda in the East African FTA with Kenya and Tanzania.

## 7.4     Regional Integration and Intra-Industry Trade

A further interesting aspect of regional integration is the appearance and importance of intra-industry trade. While most of the traditional trade flows occur between different industries (inter-industry trade) and countries with different resource endowments or factor productivity, intra-industry trade occurs within the same industry and between countries of very similar resource endowment. Since the members of regional associations often are similar in terms of resource endowment and the state of development, this may explain why intra-industry trade is associated with regional integration. An important historical example is the European Union. Its original six member countries, although different in many respects, were nevertheless similar to each other, compared with, for instance, many developing countries. Much of their rapidly growing trade is intra-industry trade. That means that they import and export within the same industry. This phenomenon has been examined extensively by Grubel and Lloyd (1975) and others, but it escapes the conventional explanations of trade, such as the Ricardian and Heckscher-Ohlin models. One of the more popular explanations of intra-industry trade has been provided by Krugman (1980).

The Krugman model assumes that in many modern industries product differentiation prevails in both, consumer preferences and producers' competitive behaviour. Different producers of similar products compete by emphasizing their own brand names and brand characteristics. The consumer, on the other hand, distinguishes between the different brands and develops preferences for them. As a result, the producers of differentiated products enjoy some market power and behave like monopolistic competitors. In addition, the Krugman model also assumes that economies of scale are important, so that average costs decline significantly when the size of plants is increased. Based on these two assumptions, Krugman shows that the enlargement of markets through regional integration leads the producers of differentiated products to concentrate their production in plants of larger size. This allows them to capture the benefits of longer production runs. The larger plants supply then the markets in all member countries of the regional trade association and beyond. Regional integration is instrumental in the process of plant closure in some countries and plant expansion in others.

How important is intra-industry trade for developing countries? The evidence from trade statistics suggests that intra-industry trade occurs mainly between highly industrialized countries and much less between the less developed countries, although they may have similar resource endowments. This follows from the fact that product differentiation is mainly found in industrial products and not in raw materials, which represent a large proportion of the trade of developing countries. Therefore, much of their trade is North-South trade and typically of the inter-industry kind. In trade associations whose members are industry-oriented, such as ASEAN[1] and APEC in Asia and MERCOSUR in South America, intra-industry trade plays an increasingly important role. In the African trade associations, such as ECOWAS or CEAO, intra-industry trade is insignificant at this stage, but it could be used to the advantage of these countries. In some of their typical manufacturing industries producing consumer goods for the domestic market economies of scale exist. They could be used to lower the cost by specializing in and exporting some products while importing other product varieties. If this occurs not only in one country but in several ones and in differentiated products, then intra-industry trade can contribute to overcoming the handicap of small markets. It takes political will to implement trade agreements and to adopt initial incentives, in order to transform regional integration treaties into truly integrated markets.

## 7.5    Monetary Union and Economic Integration

Monetary union can be regarded as an extension of a fixed exchange rate regime and as part of the political process of economic integration. It is often the ultimate step in the process of regional integration, but is sometimes chosen by countries without the previous stages of integration. Such a case is examined in Case Study 14 of the CFA franc zone of African countries. The normal sequence of economic integration includes first preferential trade agreements, then customs union (adding a common external tariff), the common market (eliminating barriers to factor mobility) and finally economic union, where a common currency is regarded as its defining characteristic. Before using a common currency, however, countries tend to tie their currencies together by pegging their exchange rates to an anchor currency, either rigidly or within a narrow margin of flexibility. In the process leading to the European Union the Deutsche Mark (DM) has played this role of anchor currency in the European Monetary System (EMS), due to the historical discipline of German monetary policy and the strength of the German economy.

---

[1]    See section 7.6 for more details about these trade associations.

Whether countries should or should not engage in monetary union, is an interesting question, which was examined in a seminal paper by Mundell (1961). His theory of Optimum Currency Areas, demonstrated in Figure 7.2, suggests that with increased economic integration the benefits of monetary union tend to rise. These benefits are derived from increased efficiency in trade and finance through reduced uncertainty and the ease of using the same currency for trade within the region, thus avoiding transaction costs. Increased integration, however, also implies the loss of the tool of monetary policy and therefore a potential loss of economic stability. When a region within the monetary union experiences external shocks, it cannot counteract them by help of monetary policy, which is a prerogative of the region's central bank. This cost of sharing a common currency declines with the degree of economic integration because integration provides other means of absorbing shocks, such as trade, factor movements and fiscal federalism.

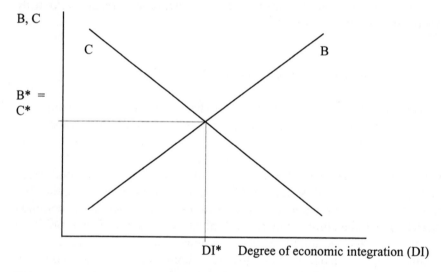

**Figure 7.2      Benefits (B) and costs (C) of using a common currency**

In Figure 7.2, the benefits of monetary union can be seen as a rising function, and the costs of stability loss as a declining function of economic integration. The intersection of these two curves marks the threshold (DI*), at which a group of countries (region) becomes an optimum currency area. Although the European Union has followed the typical sequence of economic integration, it is not clear that it qualifies as an optimum currency area. In the context of developing countries, there are several examples of attempts towards monetary integration. Perhaps the most stable of such arrangements is the African 'zone franc CFA' group of countries whose currency, the franc CFA, is tied to the French franc. A short description of this case is contained in Case Study 14.

## 7.6     Regional Integration Attempts in less Developed Countries

The following description of regional integration schemes in Sub-Saharan Africa, Latin America and Asia is based upon the writings of F. Foroutan, J.J. Nogues, R. Quintanilla and G.R. Saxonhouse (in: de Melo and Panagariya, 1993).

### 7.6.1     Sub-Saharan Africa

In Sub-Saharan Africa, several groups of countries have pursued policies to achieve a degree of regional integration. Some of them came into existence because of geographic proximity. Others were driven by a common colonial history.

In *Western Africa*, three regional blocs have been created: the Economic Community of Western African States (ECOWAS), la Communaute Economique de l'Afrique de l'Ouest (CEAO) and the Mano River Union (MRU). ECOWAS was founded in 1975, driven by Nigeria's aspirations for greater influence in a French dominated region and Nigeria's intentions to reduce its dependence on oil revenues. With its 16 members, ECOWAS became the largest and most diversified economic community in Sub-Saharan Africa. The 1975 and 1979 treaties envisioned the creation of a common market, the reduction of tariffs and non-tariff barriers, a common external tariff, fiscal and monetary harmonization, free movement of persons and a common defense pact. None of these objectives were attained due to economic, cultural, political and ideological differences among member states.

The CEAO came into existence with the 1973 treaty of Abidjan. Its seven members, who were also members of ECOWAS, aimed to maintain the arrangements for monetary and economic cooperation, which were established under French colonial rule. The seven member countries aimed at promoting intra-group trade and factor mobility through preferential tariffs to members. This agreement also had very limited success, as intra-group trade remained unimportant and a common external tariff was never even formulated.

The MRU was formed in 1973 by Liberia and Sierra Leone. Guinea joined the two countries in 1980. Their objectives were the expansion of trade among its members through an elimination of existing barriers, a common protection policy towards the rest of the world and further economic cooperation. This agreement failed as non-tariff barriers remained and there was a lack of complementarity among the three members' production structures. Severe political unrest in Liberia likely contributed to the failure as well.

*Central Africa* has known two regional groupings: The Customs and Economic Union of Central Africa (UDEAC) and the Economic Community of the Countries of the Great Lakes (CEPGL). UDEAC was basically a continuation of cooperation among former French colonies in Central Africa. It was established in 1973 with the treaty of Brazzaville, which stated its objectives as customs union, monetary union, removal of internal barriers for trade and a common external tariff. In 1974 already, the objective of a common external tariff was abolished and the customs union was restricted to a limited amount of goods. CEPGL was formed in 1976 and consisted of the former Belgian colonies Burundi, Rwanda and Congo. Its objectives were the removal of barriers to trade and joint development projects for the region. This agreement failed as well, no progress has been made towards trade liberalization and major political conflicts have arisen in each country.

Three regional associations have been formed in *Eastern and Southern Africa*: the Preferential Trade Area for Eastern and Southern African States (PTA), the Southern African Development Coordination Conference (SADCC) and the Southern African Customs Union (SACU). PTA was formed in 1981 and consisted of 18 countries. Its ultimate goal was the formation of an economic community. This goal was to be achieved by a gradual expansion of the number of goods that were eligible for preferential treatment and a gradual decrease of tariffs. In 1993 the PTA was superseded by the Common Market of Eastern and Southern Africa (COMESA), which has since grown to 22 member countries and in its trade volume, but excludes South Africa and Botswana. The Case Study 13 provides some information on COMESA and Uganda, one of its members.

SADCC was formed in 1980 with the objective of increased cooperation among members in order to lessen their economic dependence on the Republic of South Africa. The main difference with all other Regional Integration Schemes in Sub-Saharan Africa was that SADCC only pursued the modest goal of economic cooperation without even mentioning further integration into customs union or economic union.

SACU was formed already in 1910 and consisted of the Republic of South Africa, Botswana, Lesotho and Swaziland (Namibia joined in 1990). SACU has well integrated goods and factor markets and a common external tariff. The SACU members are also members of the Rand Monetary Area.

The overall evaluation of Africa's integration schemes is fairly dismal. Except for SACU, none of the integration agreements have fully met their objectives. The share of intra-region trade has remained small and stagnant over time. The causes of these failures can be summarized as limited trade potential and a failure to liberalize intra regional trade. If there exist no complementarities between countries and there is little demand for each other's products, even when barriers to trade are broken down, trade will remain low. The regional blocs apparently have failed to liberalize intra-regional trade. Import substitution in the past has been one cause of the failure to liberalize as it contributed to keeping high barriers to each other. The highly inefficient import substituting industries were defended by high protective barriers and overvalued currencies. Tariff revenues often contributed an important share of government revenues. Therefore the governments were reluctant to liberalize. A biased distribution of the possible benefits of liberalization also formed an obstacle to liberalize. As many of the economies are very different in size and structure, when trade is liberalized, some sort of compensation mechanism is needed to evenly divide the benefits and losses among the members of a regional bloc. Such compensation schemes were not existing or not workable.

Besides efforts towards trade integration, the region also knows monetary unions, namely the Rand and the CFA franc zones. Factor market integration has remained limited in Sub-Saharan Africa. Since there are huge differences in standards of living, free and unrestricted movement of labour remains prohibited in order to avoid the disruptive effects of large movements of people. Only the Rand and CFA franc zones allow relatively free movement of capital. The latter of these monetary unions is being discussed in the following Case Study 14.

### 7.6.2 Latin America

In Latin America, several regional arrangements were negotiated after the Second World War. The Latin American Free Trade Area (LAFTA) was created in 1960, the Central American Common Market (CACM) in 1960 as well, the Andean Pact in 1969 and the Caribbean Community and Common Market (CARICOM) came into existence in 1973. Each one of these agreements was inward-oriented and based upon import substitution at the regional level. These import substitution policies did not resolve the region's foreign exchange constraint. There was thus a need for a larger focus on the expansion of exports. None of the agreements' deadlines were met and disagreements over the sharing of the benefits of regional integration among the member countries caused frictions. The external debt crises of the 1980s uncovered the region's vulnerability and stressed the need for further integration. The CACM had become no more than a forum for seeking regional peace rather than the common market it initially envisioned and new efforts to further integrate different regions of Latin America did not go beyond their statements of intent.

Regional integration had clearly failed. Intra-regional trade declined rather than increased during the 1980s. The first country to liberalize unilaterally was Chile, which accelerated its growth considerably after liberalization. Other Latin American countries such as Mexico, Costa Rica, Argentina and Peru also moved significantly close to a liberal trade regime in the 1990s. Unilateral trade liberalization appeared to be the strategy that worked in order to increase the region's economic growth. Multilateral trade liberalization seemed another option for the region, which led Latin American countries to participate in the Uruguay Round and to become GATT members.

Regional integration regained some momentum in the early 1990s with the creation of MERCOSUR and a renewal of the Andean Pact and CACM. MERCOSUR was set up in 1994 by Argentina, Brazil, Paraguay and Uruguay. Motivated by the failure of previous agreements and the need to expand foreign trade in order to alleviate their foreign debt problems, the four countries decided on free trade of goods and services and factor mobility among each other. This integration also coincided with broad economic reforms, deregulation and privatization.

The Andean Pact was renewed in 1991 by Bolivia, Colombia and Venezuela and was joined by Ecuador and Peru in 1992. The renewal consisted of an elimination of all tariffs on trade among each other and the elimination of some non-tariff barriers. Trade among Andean countries remained low though (below 6 percent) because the countries have similar factor endowments and the inward oriented policies of the past had limited the development of exportables. Andean exports consist mainly of minerals that are foremost demanded by Western countries. Another factor that even amplified the direction of trade is that transport costs within the region are higher than shipping costs to the U.S.

The Central American Common Market (CACM) was revived in 1990 with the declaration of Antigua. This revival was motivated by economic reforms after the debt crises of the 1980s and the need to re-establish peace in the region. Its objectives were the renewal of a framework for Central American economic integration, a restoration and expansion of free trade in Central America, a common external tariff and the harmonization of the member countries' trade policies.

## 7.6.3    East Asia

Interest in regional integration for East Asia has been somewhat limited. The so-called Asian Tigers have known considerable success in the global marketplace and the multilateral approach to trade liberalization has paid off well for them. These countries have been very cautious not to undermine the GATT by insisting on their own regional integration schemes. The best known of such schemes is the Association of Southeast Asian Nations (ASEAN), which was originally formed in 1967 to address political and security concerns. In 1977 ASEAN members signed a Preferential Trade Agreement and in 1992 the members decided upon the formation of a Free Trade Area, known as AFTA, over the following fifteen years. Although intra-regional trade has remained relatively small, further breaking down of trade barriers may attract much more investments into the region and affect economic growth in that way.

A second regional scheme is the Asia Pacific Economic Cooperation (APEC). Since 1989 foreign ministers of the Pacific Rim Countries meet and discuss issues of mutual interest. So far, this cooperation has been restricted to regional information exchanges and technical cooperation.

## References

de Melo, J. and A. Panagariya (1993), *New Dimensions in Regional Integration*, Centre for Economic Policy Research, Cambridge University Press.

Grubel, H.G. and P.G. Lloyd (1975), *Intra-Industry Trade: The Theory and Measurement of International Trade in Differentiated Products*, New York, Halstead.

Krugman, Paul (1980), 'Scale economies, product differentiation, and the pattern of trade', *American Economic Review*.

Krugman, Paul (1993), 'Regionalism versus multilateralism: analytical notes', in: de Melo, Panagariya, op. cit.

Mundel, Robert (1961), 'The Theory of Optimum Currency Areas', *American Economic Review,* 51, September.

Viner, Jacob (1950), *The Customs Union Issue*, New York, Carnegie Endowment for International Peace.

# Case Study 13
# Regional Integration in East Africa:
# The Case of Uganda

The Preferential Trade Area for Eastern and Southern African States (PTA) was established in 1982 and had twenty member countries. Although the agreement had brought about disappointing results in economic integration, the member country governments decided to transform the free trade area into a common market. The COMESA (Common Market of Eastern and Southern Africa) treaty was signed in 1993 and its aims were very ambitious. The member countries were to evolve from a preferential trade area into a customs union, a common market and eventually into an economic and monetary union. The political will to implement these changes was not strong enough in all countries to guarantee progress. Because of their common history, Kenya, Uganda and Tanzania agreed to integrate faster than other COMESA-members and decided in 1993 to promote cooperation in political, economic, social, cultural and security issues (Ifo Institute, 1997). In 1996, however, Uganda still applied COMESA import duties for products originating from Kenya and Tanzania.

In this case study we estimate the welfare gains and losses that would occur to Uganda, if the three East African countries engaged in regional free trade in 1997 and abolished the existing import barriers such as tariffs and quota.

## Assigned Questions

1)      The British-American Tobacco Company (BAT Uganda) is the only producer of cigarettes in Uganda and supplies only the Ugandan market. Imports of cigarettes are licensed to Philip Morris and Mastermind of Kenya, both Kenyan companies. BAT also operates a much larger production plant in Kenya. Due to economies of scale and a longer history of industrial production in Kenya, the unit cost of cigarettes produced by BAT's Kenyan plant is lower than that of the Ugandan plant. The Ugandan government faces the decision to either eliminate the tariff on cigarettes from Kenya (open borders) or to continue to provide protection to the Ugandan plant.

        The Ifo Institute for economic research has projected supply, demand and prices under two possible situations: open borders and continued protection. The following table[2] shows the projections for 1997.

**Table CS13a    Cigarette production and trade in Uganda**

|  | Open borders | Continued protection |
|---|---|---|
| Demand[3] | 2.34 | 2.22 |
| Supply: | 2.34 | 2.22 |
| from Uganda | 1.38 | 1.74 |
| Imports | 0.96 | 0.50 |
| Ugandan Price[4] | 45.00 | 50.80 |

a.     Calculate the welfare loss or gain from eliminating cigarette protection and opening borders to Kenya. Explain your findings by help of a diagram. Assume that (i) imports from third countries would be more expensive, (ii) that the difference between the open borders price and the price under protection is entirely due to import tariffs and (iii) that we have linear demand and supply functions.

b.     In 1996, Uganda counted 30,000 tobacco farmers who sold their crop to BAT's Ugandan production plant. The Ifo study predicts that, under open borders, BAT will have shifted its entire production of cigarettes for the Ugandan market to its Kenyan production facility by 1999 and Ugandan tobacco inputs for BAT's cigarettes would no longer be needed. If the Ugandan tobacco farmers would find no other buyer for their crops, tobacco production will fall sharply. Does your welfare analysis take this into account? Is it a valid argument for continued protection?

2)     Iron sheets, used for the roofing of houses, are the third most important item of household expenditure, after cooking utensils and clothes in Uganda. Iron sheets are being produced by Ugandan producers and imported from Kenya, Tanzania, Netherlands, China and Japan. Import duties from COMESA countries are three percent, and five percent from the rest of the world. In 1996,

---

[2]   Source: 'Impact of East African regional integration on the Ugandan economy', vol.2, sectoral studies, Ifo Institute for Economic Research, Munich, and International Development Consultants, Kampala, May 1997.

[3]   Billions of sticks.

[4]   Ugandan shillings per stick.

around 70 percent of iron articles imports came from outside COMESA. For purposes of our welfare analysis, we assume that iron sheets from within and outside COMESA are equal in quality. We also assume that after opening up borders within COMESA (zero percent import duty) all imports of iron sheets will come from COMESA countries. The following table contains the Ifo Institute's projections for 1997 (units are in thousands of tons).

**Table CS13b    Iron sheet production and trade in Uganda**

|  | Open borders | Continued protection |
|---|---|---|
| Demand | 120.2 | 111.6 |
| Supply: | 120.2 | 111.6 |
| from Uganda | 28.2 | 56.2 |
| Imports | 92.0 | 55.4 |

Based on other sources of information, the price of iron sheets is 1200/tonne in Kenya and Tanzania and 1177/ton outside COMESA countries, such that in Uganda iron sheets from COMESA and the rest of the world both cost 1236/ton.

a.    Compute the welfare gain or loss from eliminating protection of iron sheet production and opening borders. Explain your findings by help of a diagram.

b.    How does the situation differ from the former case of cigarettes and how can you explain the result of your calculation?

3)    Uganda's extensive limestone deposits could provide the country with enough cement to be self-sufficient and to export. However, because of high unit production costs, Uganda imports cement from Kenya and Tanzania. The following table displays the Ifo Institute's projections for 1997 (quantities in thousands of tons).

**Table CS13c    Cement production and trade in Uganda**

|  | Open borders | Continued protection |
|---|---|---|
| Demand | 445 | 442 |
| Supply by: | 445 | 442 |
| Uganda | 140 | 175 |
| Imports | 305 | 267 |

The Ugandan price of cement is 170,000 Ugandan Shilling/ton, while the foreign price of cement is 160,000 Ugandan Shilling/ton CIF border. The COMESA import tariff is 3 percent.

a.    Calculate the welfare loss or gain from regional free trade in cement. Explain your findings by help of a diagram.

4)    Use your findings and knowledge of economic integration to argue whether Uganda should or should not engage in free trade with Kenya and Tanzania in the short run, and with all COMESA-members in the long run. You may assume that the three industries are representative of the whole manufacturing sector.

## Case Study 13: Solution

*1    Cigarettes*

a)    The effects of moving from protection to open borders is explained by help of the following diagram:

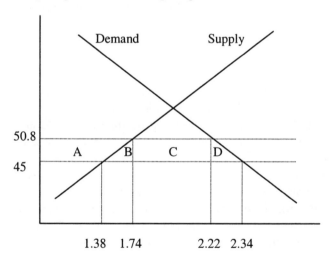

**Figure CS13a    The cigarette market in Uganda**

Gain of consumer surplus: A + B + C + D
Loss of producer surplus: - A
Loss of government revenue: - C
⟶    Total welfare gain: B + D

Area B = efficiency gain because of a reduction of the consumption distortion. Because of the lower price, consumers demand more cigarettes. B = (1.74 − 1.38) * (50.8 − 45) / 2 = 0.36 * 5.8 / 2 = 1.044 billion Ugandan Shillings.

Area D = efficiency gain because of a reduction of the production distortion. Because of the lower price, BAT produces less cigarette output. D = (2.34 − 2.22) * (50.8 − 45) / 2 = 0.12 * 5.8 / 2 = 0.348 billion Ugandan Shillings.

The total welfare gain of regional free trade of cigarettes within COMESA sums up to 1.392 billion Ugandan Shillings.

b)       Ugandan tobacco growers could still sell their crops to BAT Kenya or to other foreign cigarette producers such as Philip Morris and Mastermind of Kenya. However, they will probably have to cut their prices to be able to compete with Kenyan tobacco growers, which leads to reduced income for Ugandan tobacco growers. If they cannot export tobacco to Kenya or other foreign countries, they will be forced to either cultivate other crops or find other jobs. The welfare analysis of question (a) does not address this particular question as it treats the tobacco input as a cost, irrespective of where the tobacco comes from.

Is the potential loss of income for Ugandan tobacco growers a valid argument for continued protection of the tobacco industry? As Kenya is better at producing cigarettes, Uganda does not seem to have a comparative advantage in this industry and protecting that production comes at a cost, which is largely born by Ugandan consumers. Also, continued protection of the cigarette industry does not guarantee the jobs in tobacco agriculture, since private firms cannot be obliged to buy their inputs locally. If the government of Uganda is concerned with the welfare of the tobacco growers, which it should be, given the large number of them and the potential impact on the rural areas, it should design methods that help them to either become competitive exporters or grow other crops.

2       *Iron sheets*

a)       The situation in Uganda's market for iron sheets is shown in the following diagram:

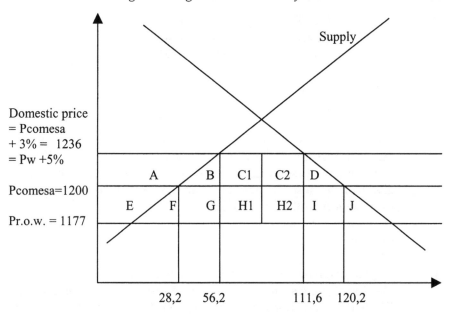

**Figure CS13b    The iron sheet market in Uganda**

Under continued protection, Ugandan consumers demand 111,600 tons of iron sheets. Ugandan producers supply 56,200 tons and 55,400 tons are imported (70 percent from outside COMESA, 30 percent from COMESA).

Under open borders, Ugandan consumers would demand 120,200 tons of iron sheets, of which 28,200 tons would be produced by Uganda and 92,000 tons would be imported from COMESA countries. The price would decline from 1236 to 1200 U.Sh., due to the elimination of the COMESA tariff. Since imports from Kenya (or other COMESA countries) would then be less expensive than imports from third countries after the tariff, some imports (i.e. the 70 percent of present imports) would be diverted from third countries towards Kenya.

While the net benefits of trade creation due to free trade between Kenya and Uganda are shown here by the triangles B and D, the country also faces trade diversion because the presently 70 percent of imports which come from third countries would be replaced by imports from Kenya or other COMESA countries. This replacement leads to a loss of tariff revenue, which is shown in the diagram as the area H2. Therefore, the net benefits from trade creation and trade diversion are to be calculated as B + D − H2.

$B = (1236-1200)*(56.2-28.2)/2 = 504$
$D = (1236-1200)*(120.2-111.6)/2 = 154.8$
$H2 = (111.6-56.2)*.7*(1200-1177) = 891.9$

Total net gain or loss from moving to regional free trade:
$B+D-H2 = 504 + 154.8 - 891.9 = -233.1$, which is a net loss.

b)      While in the case of cigarettes there was no trade diversion due to the fact that all imports are already coming from COMESA countries, the case of iron sheets involves some amount of trade diversion because 70 percent of the present imports are coming from countries other than COMESA.

3       *Cement*

a)      For the diagram we refer to the one of the first case, because just like for cigarettes, there is no trade diversion in the present case. While the international price is 160,000 shillings/ton, the Ugandan price is taken to be the price that would prevail without imports. The price of cement imports with COMESA tariff is 160,000 $(1+0.03) = 164,800$ shillings/ton.

Gain of consumer surplus: $A + B + C + D$
Loss of producer surplus: $- A$
Loss of government revenue: $- C$
⟶      Total welfare gain: $B + D$

Area $B =$ efficiency gain because of a reduction of the consumption distortion. Because of the lower price, people shift their consumption away from other goods and consume more cement. B $= (175,000 - 140,000) * (164,800 - 160,000) / 2 = 84$ million Ugandan Shillings.

Area $D =$ efficiency gain because of a reduction of the production distortion. Because of the lower price, Uganda produces less cement.

$D = (445,000 - 442,000) * (164,800 - 160,000) / 2 = 7.2$ million Ugandan Shillings.

The total welfare gain of free trade in cement within COMESA sums up to 91.2 million Ugandan Shillings.

If the three industries seen above were representative of the whole manufacturing sector, there would be a net gain of $1,392 - 233 + 91 = 1,250$ million U.Sh. from opening up the border. In other words, it would be beneficial for Uganda to establish regional free trade with its neighbours.

Uganda should engage in free trade with Kenya and Tanzania in the short run and with the entire COMESA community in the long run because the welfare analysis shows net welfare gains. Ugandan industry will produce where comparative advantage lies (agriculture) and will import other goods. If Ugandan producers face competition of foreign products, production will become more efficient in the long run, and that may lead to comparative advantage in industries that do not have such advantage at present. One may also invoke the possibility of further trade creation within the region due to intra-industry trade developing between Uganda, Kenya and Tanzania. Economic integration could be an engine for peace in the region.

# Case Study 14
# Monetary Union:
# The Case of the CFA Franc Zone

The purpose of this case study is to analyze the benefits and costs for the member countries of membership in the Franc CFA monetary union. In the context of this case study we examine the alignment or misalignment of the exchange rate, as well as the terms of trade, of various member countries and draw conclusions about their economic policies.

## Background

The Communaute Financiere Africaine, or CFA Zone, is a monetary union made up of fourteen African countries. The Zone is divided into two separate groups of Sub-Saharan African countries as well as the island republic of the Comoros.

The West African Monetary Union, or UMOA, is the first group of countries, and consists of Benin, Burkina Fasso, Cote d'Ivoire, Mali, Niger, Senegal, and Togo. Its central bank is the BCEAO, the Central Bank of West African States. The second grouping of countries is the Customs and Economic Union of Central Africa (UDEAC) and its central bank is the BEAC, the Bank of Central African States. The UDEAC consists of

Cameroon, Central African Republic, Chad, Congo, Equatorial Guinea and Gabon.

The central banks each operate like any other 'normal' central bank, issuing currency (both banks however issue the same currency, the CFA Franc), enacting financial legislation, governing and aiding the establishment of banks and financial institutions, as well as collecting and disseminating economic data. The final authority on monetary issues rests with the Bank Councils of Administration, which are composed of ministers of finance from each member nation as well as France.

The initial goal of the monetary union was to create a stable economic climate so as to foster growth and investment throughout the region. Through the creation of a 'compte d'opérations' to be maintained at the French Treasury, the Zone members were given guaranteed convertibility of their currency and a theoretically unlimited line of credit from France. Established in 1948, the CFA Franc has a fixed exchange rate and, until 1994, was pegged to the French Franc at a value of fifty CFA Francs per French Franc (50 CFAF = 1 FF). In return, CFA Zone members would hold a minimum of 65 percent of their monetary reserves in French Francs and effect their exchange transactions on the Paris market.

The relationship between France and its former colonies is an interesting one. The guarantee of convertibility extended to the CFA Franc means that if the funds in the compte d'opérations fall too far, and if 'all other means of payment have been exhausted', France will extend an overdraft to the Zone members to cover their balance of payments deficits. This is not meant to be a development or aid fund, but rather a mechanism to smooth over temporary and unforeseen balance of payment problems, much like an IMF resource.

Why France would extend such a seemingly open-ended line of credit to all the countries of the Zone is largely a political question rather than an economic one, as there is in France a perception of grave responsibility towards its former colonies. However, the compte d'opérations has yet to be a financial drain on the French Treasury, since whatever deficit certain CFA countries have incurred in the account has always been financed by the surplus of other CFA countries. Furthermore, the magnitude of the account is so small that it does not truly affect France's economy.

Mundell has argued (1972) that the CFA Zone developed because the former French colonies, upon gaining independence, were not financially developed enough to run their own banking and financial systems. This was due to the French policy of administrative centralization, and, in direct contrast to former British African colonies, left the countries of the Francophonie heavily dependent on France. Today, the monetary union is only one of a wide range of ties the CFA Zone has with France. Besides financial aid, technical and administrative expertise received by the member countries, trade both to and from the Zone is largely with France. The influences of the French language and culture are also seen in the former colonies, especially evident among the area's elite.

Until recently, the CFA Zone has been a politically stable area, due partly to the French military presence there. The population of approximately 80 million is generally sparse and poor, with half the countries belonging to the lowest income per capita grouping in the world. The Human Development Index, as measured by the United Nations Development Programme (UNDP), also classifies many of the Zone members among the world's least developed. The political stability of the region has been a major economic asset, especially combined with the liberal economic policies proposed by governments eager to attract private and official capital. Overall, though, the area is highly dependent on a narrow range of agricultural and mineral commodities, especially cocoa, coffee, petroleum, bauxite and uranium. These generate the bulk of national income, government revenue and foreign exchange earnings. The absence of a well developed and diversified industrial base has led the Zone to depend on imported machinery, transport equipment, and other manufactures.

Although the pros and cons of the CFA Zone have often been debated, there can be no disputing that throughout the 1960s and 1970s, Zone members showed consistently higher growth rates as well as much lower rates of inflation than their non-member neighbours. From 1970 to 1985, income per capita of Zone members rose an average of two percent, despite variations caused by two oil shocks, a primary commodity boom and the start of a debt crisis. Since 1986, however, income per capita has decreased by an average of seven percent per year, and has dropped by 40 percent overall.

Devarajan and Hinkle (1994) have argued that the poor performance of Zone members was mainly due to their currency being overvalued. The overvalued currency, in turn, is attributed to three factors: many years of inappropriate economic policies, a substantial decline in the Zone's terms of trade, and an increase in the real exchange rate. Throughout the late 1970s and 1980s, the response of various Zone governments to commodity booms was expansionary macroeconomic policies, and this left many Zone countries with inflated and unsustainable cost structures in both the public and private sectors. The terms of trade decline, a reversal of a fifteen-year trend, was brought on by a 40 percent decline in the world prices of major exports: coffee, cocoa, and oil for Gabon. The exchange rate, pegged to the French Franc, instead of depreciating with the terms of trade decline, appreciated as the FF appreciated by 70 percent relative to the U.S. dollar after 1985. When competing Asian, Latin American and African developing countries devalued their currencies, further depreciating their real exchange rates, the CFA Franc countries lost more and more of their traditional market share. Devarajan says that even in export sectors where Zone countries had a strong comparative advantage, they lost competitiveness as a result of the increasingly overvalued real exchange rate.

Finally, by 1993, the situation was judged to be untenable. On January 11, 1994, the CFA Franc was devalued to a new parity of 100 CFAF per French Franc (100 CFAF = 1 FF). With this devaluation, it was hoped that the Zone will be able to revitalize itself and repeat its earlier impressive growth performances. The stable economic environment provided by the structure of the Zone still has the potential to be a positive mechanism. As well, it is hoped that the fiscal and monetary discipline enforced by Zone regulations should keep Zone governments from pursuing policies that result in rampant inflation.

## Method of Analysis

In order to analyze the benefits and costs of monetary union membership in the context of the Zone Franc, we proceed in three stages. First, we examine the exchange rate alignment or misalignment. Second, we compute the changes in the terms of trade and consider the consequences thereof. Third, we review the expected benefits and costs of monetary unions on the basis of the theory of optimum currency areas. The information regarding the benefits and costs of the FCFA monetary union is contained in Devarajan and de Melo (1991) and in Devarajan and Hinkle (1994). Data on the exchange rate and terms of trade for five member countries are provided in spreadsheet format in the following tables. The data are taken from the International Financial Statistics Yearbook of 1999.

## Assigned Questions

1)   Compute the real exchange rate index, RERI*, for the five countries, using the data in columns NERI*, PDI, and PFI of Table CS14a.

2)     Explain the difference between RERI* and REERI, which is published by the IMF for only some countries (only Cameroon, Côte d'Ivoire and Gabon in our sample), focusing on the definition of these two indices. Considering that these countries' main trade partner is France, explain why REERI behaved differently from the RERI* between 1985 and 1992. (Hint: remember that NERI* is the exchange rate *vis-à-vis* the U.S.$ and that the dollar depreciated strongly *vis-à-vis* most other currencies from 1985 onwards.)

3)     Assuming that the FCFA exchange rate was well-aligned in 1994, after the devaluation in early 1994, was the FCFA over- or undervalued in 1999, and by how much? Your answer will differ for the five countries. Why?

4)     As an alternative method of estimating the degree of misalignment, assume now that in 1985 the U.S.$ was 20 percent over-valued *vis-à-vis* the FCFA, by how much was the currency over- or undervalued in 1999 in the five countries of our sample.

5)     Use the export price index, PXI, and import price index, PMI, in the countries for which they are shown (Burkina Fasso and Sénégal), to compute the terms of trade index (ToTI), and determine whether these countries have experienced ToT gains or losses.What are the implications of the latter finding for having an implicitly fixed exchange rate by using the FCFA, which had a fixed parity to the FF (now to the EURO)?

6)     What are the benefits and costs of the membership for member countries of the monetary union? Base your answers on your own calculations as well as on the readings.

## Definition of the Variables and Data Sources

The variables in the following tables are to be interpreted and their data sources are as follows:

| Variable | Meaning | Source |
|---|---|---|
| NERI* | Nominal Exchange Rate Index (U.S.$ per FCFA) | line rf, IFS 2002 |
| PDI | Domestic Price Index (Consumer Price Index) | line 64, IFS 2002 |
| PFI | Foreign Price Index (Industrial Country CPI) | line 110, IFS 2002 |
| RERI* | Real Exchange Rate Index (to be computed) | |
| RERI*adj | Adjusted Real Exchange Rate Index (to be computed) | |
| PXI | Export Price Index (Unit value of exports) | line 74, IFS 2002 |
| PMI | Import Price Index (Unit value of imports) | line 75, IFS 2002 |
| ToTI | Terms of Trade Index (to be computed) | |
| REERI | Real Effective Exchange Rate Index | line rec, IFS 2002 |

## References

Devarajan, Shantayanan and de Melo, Jaime (1991), 'Membership in the CFA Zone: Odyssean Journey or Trojan Horse?', in: A. Chibber and S. Fischer, (eds.), *Economic Reform in Sub-Saharan Africa*, The World Bank.

Devarajan, S. and L.E. Hinkle (1994), 'The CFA Franc Parity Change: an Opportunity to Restore Growth and Reduce Poverty', The World Bank.

International Monetary Fund, *International Financial Statistics, Yearbook*, 2002.

**Table CS14a**    **Exchange rate, foreign (OECD) and domestic prices in five countries of the FCFA zone**

| Year | NERI* | PFI | Burkina Fasso PDI | Came-roon PDI | Côte d'Ivoire PDI | Gabon PDI | Sénégal PDI |
|------|-------|-----|-------|-------|-------|-------|-------|
| 1970 | 98.2 | 29.53 | n.a. | 11.3 | 12.4 | 15.7 | 15.6 |
| 1971 | 98.6 | 30.57 | n.a. | 11.7 | 12.3 | 16.3 | 16.2 |
| 1972 | 107.7 | 31.76 | n.a. | 12.7 | 12.4 | 16.9 | 17.2 |
| 1973 | 122.2 | 35.48 | n.a. | 14.0 | 13.7 | 17.9 | 19.1 |
| 1974 | 112.8 | 41.93 | n.a. | 16.4 | 16.1 | 20.1 | 22.3 |
| 1975 | 233.0 | 45.66 | n.a. | 18.6 | 18.0 | 25.8 | 29.3 |
| 1976 | 209.0 | 48.59 | n.a. | 20.4 | 20.2 | 31.0 | 29.6 |
| 1977 | 203.0 | 51.99 | n.a. | 23.5 | 25.7 | 35.3 | 33.0 |
| 1978 | 221.4 | 54.95 | n.a. | 26.4 | 29.1 | 39.0 | 34.1 |
| 1979 | 234.6 | 60.78 | n.a. | 28.1 | 33.8 | 42.2 | 37.4 |
| 1980 | 236.4 | 69.22 | n.a. | 30.8 | 38.8 | 47.4 | 40.7 |
| 1981 | 184.6 | 75.25 | n.a. | 34.1 | 42.2 | 51.5 | 43.1 |
| 1982 | 152.6 | 78.93 | n.a. | 38.6 | 45.4 | 60.1 | 50.6 |
| 1983 | 131.5 | 81.14 | 67.4 | 45.0 | 48.0 | 66.5 | 56.5 |
| 1984 | 114.5 | 84.55 | 70.6 | 50.2 | 50.0 | 70.4 | 63.1 |
| 1985 | 111.9 | 86.24 | 75.5 | 54.4 | 51.0 | 75.5 | 71.3 |
| 1986 | 144.3 | 83.74 | 73.5 | 58.7 | 55.9 | 80.3 | 75.7 |
| 1987 | 166.1 | 84.58 | 71.6 | 66.4 | 59.8 | 79.5 | 72.6 |
| 1988 | 167.8 | 87.11 | 74.5 | 67.5 | 63.9 | 72.6 | 71.3 |
| 1989 | 156.5 | 91.04 | 74.3 | 66.4 | 64.4 | 77.4 | 71.6 |
| 1990 | 183.7 | 93.58 | 73.6 | 67.1 | 64.1 | 83.4 | 71.8 |
| 1991 | 177.4 | 94.52 | 75.5 | 67.1 | 65.2 | 73.7 | 70.6 |
| 1992 | 188.9 | 94.99 | 74.0 | 67.1 | 67.9 | 66.6 | 70.5 |
| 1993 | 176.3 | 95.66 | 74.4 | 65.0 | 69.4 | 67.0 | 70.1 |
| 1994 | 90.0 | 96.81 | 93.1 | 87.8 | 87.5 | 91.2 | 92.7 |
| 1995 | 100.0 | 100.0 | 100.0 | 100.0 | 100.0 | 100.0 | 100.0 |
| 1996 | 97.6 | 102.2 | 106.2 | 103.9 | 102.5 | 100.7 | 102.8 |
| 1997 | 85.5 | 104.2 | 108.6 | 108.9 | 106.6 | 104.7 | 104.4 |
| 1998 | 84.6 | 105.7 | 114.1 | 112.4 | 111.6 | 106.2 | 105.6 |
| 1999 | 81.1 | 107.2 | 112.9 | 114.1 | 112.5 | 104.2 | 106.5 |

**Table CS14b    Real effective exchange rate of Cameroon, Cote d'Ivoire and Gabon**

| Year | Cameroon REERI | Côte d'Ivoire REERI | Gabon REERI |
|------|------|------|------|
| 1980 | 131.6 | 149.2 | 204.6 |
| 1981 | 120.9 | 128.2 | 182.1 |
| 1982 | 118.2 | 116.7 | 183.7 |
| 1983 | 122.9 | 112.6 | 180.8 |
| 1984 | 125.0 | 108.4 | 173.5 |
| 1985 | 130.7 | 108.3 | 178.9 |
| 1986 | 144.7 | 130.2 | 194.7 |
| 1987 | 161.8 | 144.5 | 191.3 |
| 1988 | 157.8 | 147.9 | 165.4 |
| 1989 | 145.5 | 139.5 | 167.2 |
| 1990 | 149.5 | 141.3 | 181.4 |
| 1991 | 143.1 | 136.3 | 153.4 |
| 1992 | 144.2 | 142.3 | 138.5 |
| 1993 | 134.5 | 140.3 | 134.3 |
| 1994 | 86.6 | 86.5 | 90.6 |
| 1995 | 100.0 | 100.0 | 100.0 |
| 1996 | 101.5 | 100.5 | 98.9 |
| 1997 | 96.9 | 98.9 | 97.4 |
| 1998 | 102.1 | 105.5 | 100.7 |
| 1999 | 106.7 | 103.5 | 96.3 |
| 2000 | 95.6 | 96.5 | 89.7 |
| 2001 | 98.7 | 99.9 | 91.0 |

**Table CS14c    Export and import unit prices of Burkina Fasso and Senegal**

| Year | Burkina Fasso | | Senegal | |
|------|------|------|------|------|
|      | PXI  | PMI  | PXI  | PMI  |
| 1972 | 56.4  | 32.5  | 21.1  | 42.1  |
| 1973 | 70.2  | 39.3  | 25.0  | 54.3  |
| 1974 | 95.6  | 45.7  | 47.5  | 71.9  |
| 1975 | 108.3 | 59.4  | 40.2  | 85.5  |
| 1976 | 125.0 | 60.5  | 39.2  | 80.7  |
| 1977 | 136.4 | 64.7  | 47.1  | 85.4  |
| 1978 | 141.4 | 68.9  | 50.8  | 91.8  |
| 1979 | 153.6 | 78.8  | 54.4  | 109.4 |
| 1980 | 168.6 | 83.8  | 53.2  | 143.3 |
| 1981 | 144.6 | 78.3  | 73.0  | 124.9 |
| 1982 | 137.7 | 78.7  | 70.7  | 116.7 |
| 1983 | 135.2 | 74.4  | 78.7  | 110.1 |
| 1984 | 121.3 | 67.4  | 100.3 | 105.3 |
| 1985 | 138.6 | 70.5  | 100.0 | 100.0 |
| 1986 | 126.6 | 87.7  | 70.0  | 93.9  |
| 1987 | 151.1 | 90.1  | 66.6  | 102.9 |
| 1988 | 147.8 | 90.9  | n.a.  | n.a.  |
| 1989 | 128.3 | 92.0  | n.a.  | n.a.  |
| 1990 | 165.5 | 115.1 | n.a.  | n.a.  |
| 1991 | 156.1 | 103.0 | n.a.  | n.a.  |
| 1992 | 127.0 | 105.5 | n.a.  | n.a.  |
| 1993 | 114.1 | 100.2 | n.a.  | n.a.  |
| 1994 | 76.3  | 84.1  | n.a.  | n.a.  |
| 1995 | 100.0 | 100.0 | n.a.  | n.a.  |
| 1996 | 95.4  | 101.1 | n.a.  | n.a.  |

Chapter 8

# Stabilization, Structural Adjustment and the Role of the IMF

Having examined fiscal, financial and trade policies separately, we shall now discuss policy reforms that bring all these policies together. Structural adjustment programs (SAPs) are such sets of policies that focus on several economic goals, in particular economic stability, efficient use of resources, internal and external balance. The components of structural adjustment programmes are best described by their objectives. Economic stabilization focuses mainly on internal balance, meaning price stability and high employment. External balance means the continuous provision of foreign exchange for imports, as well as the avoidance of financial crises. Both objectives require macroeconomic policies, whereas the goal of efficient resource use is essentially microeconomic in nature. Structural adjustment in a narrower, and microeconomic, sense involves structural change by way of changing relative prices and other incentives. An important link between the micro and macro policies is the exchange rate, which plays the double role of influencing both macro variables and relative prices. A further component of SAPs is privatization, which has the ultimate goal of increasing the efficiency of resource allocation, while also affecting the fiscal balance and thereby internal and external equilibrium. We discuss first the macro issues of stabilization, external and internal balance, and then deal with structural adjustment in the narrower microeconomic sense. The chapter is completed by discussing the role of the International Monetary Fund (IMF) in structural adjustment programmes and by an attempt to evaluate the progress in structural adjustment in the context of Sub-Saharan Africa.

## 8.1    External Balance and Stabilization Policies

Macroeconomic theory provides us with various models to analyze the effectiveness of policies from a theoretical point of view. The best known of these models is the Keynesian IS-LM model, which in its open-economy version is known as the Mundell-Fleming model. A slightly different approach has been proposed by Krugman and Obstfeld in their popular textbook (2003 and earlier editions). Their model, which carries the name of AA-DD model, puts more emphasis on the market of financial assets. The two approaches come to similar conclusions, although they differ not only in the exposition but also in some of the underlying assumptions. It would go beyond the scope of this chapter to discuss the two approaches and to reconcile their differences. The essential message of the Mundell-Fleming model is that fiscal policy is most potent under a fixed exchange rate and strong capital mobility and monetary policy is most effective under a flexible exchange rate and strong capital mobility, but that in the latter case capital mobility matters less.

The Swan diagram, which is based on the Australian model of small open economies proposed by Trevor Swan (1956), W.E.G. Salter (1959) and Max Corden (1977) and has been introduced in Chapter 6, is another instrument that helps us understand the policy tools to achieve the goals of internal and external balance. The model permits us to identify various combinations, in terms of their intensity, of the two policy tools, fiscal expansion or contraction, and exchange rate devaluation or revaluation, in order to reach general equilibrium.

It is also interesting to examine the assignment and optimal sequencing of policy interventions. Should the finance minister pursue fiscal expansion or restraint to achieve the internal or the external balance objective, and should the central bank pursue only the internal or external balance objective or both? And which intervention should come first? If one assumes that the policy tools should be applied sequentially, in other words, that one authority acts first and the second acts only when the first authority has attained its objective, then it follows that the policy interventions will lead to an oscillation between various disequilibria. Depending on the slopes of the IB and XB-lines, certain policy sequences may even lead away from the desired general equilibrium. In order to avoid such fluctuations in policies and their impacts, it appears to be most advantageous for the authorities to coordinate their policies and to apply them simultaneously. If such coordination is realized, the state of general equilibrium may be reached in a more direct fashion and without major inversions of policies. For instance, some degree of devaluation combined with some fiscal restraint is required in order to reduce an external deficit and unemployment.

Under a flexible exchange rate regime, the exchange rate is not a policy instrument, but it can be replaced by monetary policy. Whether fiscal policy can be effective in that context depends on the degree of capital mobility and on how expectations change as a reaction to policy interventions. Krugman and Obstfeld argue that permanent policy changes lead to changes in expectations, which under a flexible exchange rate would make fiscal expansion ineffective for raising the income level. A similar conclusion is reached in the Mundell-Fleming model, but for a different reason. In this model, the effect of fiscal expansion on income vanishes under perfect capital mobility, because it leads to a current account surplus and currency appreciation, which diminishes aggregate demand. To the extent, however, that fiscal policy retains some of its effects on income under a flexible exchange rate (assuming less than perfect capital mobility or a weak response to expectations), the Swan diagram can then be used in a modified form, replacing the variation of the exchange rate on the vertical axis by changes in the money supply. A situation of external deficit and some unemployment would then require monetary expansion combined with some fiscal restraint.

A further conclusion one can draw from the discussion of the Swan diagram is that the application of any one of the policy tools always affects both, internal and external balance. A currency devaluation, for instance, will improve the current account, but will also increase aggregate demand, thereby creating inflationary pressure, unless there is underemployment. This idea is sometimes overlooked when it is argued that inflation is a monetary phenomenon and should be addressed by monetary policy only. Equally, it is important to remember that external imbalance is closely related to monetary policies, through the role of external reserves as part of the monetary base. In the same sense, external imbalance is also related to the fiscal deficit. To see this more clearly let us remember the fundamentals.

Starting from the fundamental macroeconomic ex-post equality, we see that a current account deficit corresponds to an excess of investment over saving, and a current account surplus corresponds to an excess of saving over investment. For simplicity, we equate again the current account with the trade balance:

$$(8.1) \quad M - X = I - S$$

Since consumption and investment taken together is known as domestic absorption (A), we also see that a current account deficit implies that domestic absorption exceeds GDP, or aggregate demand exceeds aggregate supply:

$$(8.2) \quad M > X \leftrightarrow I > S \leftrightarrow GDP < A$$
$$\text{and} \quad M < X \leftrightarrow I < S \leftrightarrow GDP > A,$$

where the two-sided arrows mean implication. In order to reduce a current account deficit, GDP needs to grow faster than absorption, or absorption needs to be reduced relative to GDP. Enhancing GDP growth is of course the most desirable course of action, but it is also difficult and takes more time to materialize. It requires increased availability of the factors of production, technical progress or more efficient use of the factors, as we saw earlier.

To reduce absorption implies reducing either investment or consumption, where the latter is certainly preferable, though also less popular. It can be achieved by increased taxation or by government spending cuts, both reducing the government deficit. Such expenditure-reducing policies always tend to reduce employment, and they carry therefore a high social cost. A combination of growth-enhancing and absorption-reducing policies may be most desirable.

In addition to reducing expenditure, policy can also switch expenditure from foreign to domestic goods and services, or inversely. This can be done either by devaluation, which makes foreign goods more expensive, or by restrictive trade policy. The latter option introduces price distortions and implies a cost in terms of lowered efficiency. Devaluation, on the other hand, by raising the prices of tradable goods, encourages inflation. Each of these measures needs to be applied in a very controlled fashion, and a mix of growth-enhancing, expenditure-changing and expenditure-switching policies seems to be best suited for the goal of external balance.

The achievement of external balance may interfere with the goal of internal balance, taken to mean full employment and price stability. Full employment is hampered by expenditure reduction and price stability by devaluation. The latter effect follows from the relationship between foreign reserves and the money supply. To demonstrate this, consider the components of money supply. The commercial banks take deposits (DD) from the public and make loans to investors (bank credit or BC), keeping a fraction of the deposits as bank reserves (BR):

(8.3)   $DD = BC + BR$

The central bank issues money to the public, gives credit to the government, and exchanges foreign against domestic currency, keeping therefore a reserve of foreign currency (FR). Its liabilities include the bank reserves (BR) and the currency in circulation (CU), and its assets include central bank credit (CC) and foreign reserves (FR):

$$(8.4) \quad CU + BR = CC + FR$$

The consolidated account of the central and commercial banks reduces therefore to:

$$(8.5) \quad DD + CU = BC + CC + FR = DC + FR$$

where $(DD + CU)$ is the money supply (MS), and $(BC + CC)$ represents total domestic credit (DC). It follows then that any increase in either domestic credit or in foreign reserves results in an increase in the money supply:

$$(8.6) \quad \Delta DC + \Delta FR = \Delta MS.$$

We also remember from the preceding chapter that a change in foreign reserves $(\Delta FR)$ equals the difference between the current account balance and capital inflows (F). In case of a current account deficit exceeding capital inflows (F) foreign reserves decline:

$$(8.7) \quad (M - X) - F = -\Delta FR.$$

Substituting (8.6) into (8.7), we obtain:

$$(8.8) \quad (M - X) = \Delta DC - \Delta MS + F.$$

This means that for a given money supply (i.e. $\Delta MS = 0$) and capital inflow (F), the expansion of domestic credit leads to an increased current account deficit. Monetary policy is not independent of the external account, because in a fixed exchange rate context the fluctuations in foreign reserve holding affect the money supply. In order to reach a current account balance target the government must control the expansion of domestic credit. This important message is known in the literature as the monetary approach to the balance of payments and has led to the development of the so-called Polak model of financial programming by the International Monetary Fund, when it advises countries on how to overcome external imbalances.

The Polak model, in its simplest form, consists of the identities (8.6) and (8.7) and two behavioural equations:

$$(8.9) \quad \Delta MS = k \, \Delta Y$$

(8.10)   $M = m\,Y$

where (8.9) is based on the quantity theory of money reflecting money market equilibrium, with k being the inverse of the velocity of circulation of money, and (8.10) is a simple import function with m being the marginal propensity to import. Following Agenor and Montiel (1996), one can illustrate the interaction between money-market equilibrium (8.9) and the balance of payments identity (8.7) in determining nominal income and the balance of payments as shown in Figure 8.1.

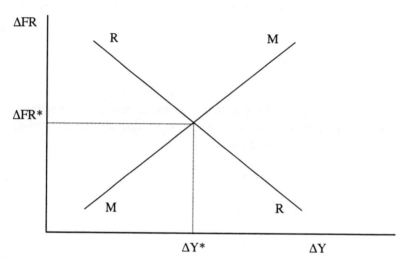

**Figure 8.1    The Polak model**

In this diagram, the two endogenous variables, $\Delta Y$ and $\Delta FR$, are measured on the axes, while exports (X) and capital flows (F) are exogenous, $Y_{t-1}$ is pre-determined (semi-exogenous) and $\Delta DC$ is a policy variable (exogenous). The money market equilibrium is presented as the positively sloping line MM,

(8.11)   $\Delta FR = \Delta MS - \Delta DC = k\,\Delta Y - \Delta DC$

and the balance of payments is presented as the negatively sloping line RR,

(8.12)   $\Delta FR = X - m\,Y + F = X - m\,(Y_{t-1} + \Delta Y) + F$

where both equations are derived from (8.6) to (8.10). Simultaneous external and money market equilibrium is shown by the combination of

$\Delta Y^*$ and $\Delta FR^*$. It is easily seen that an increase in the rate of credit expansion (i.e. a downward shift of MM) will cause the balance of payments to deteriorate and income to rise, whereas an increase in exports or capital inflows (i.e. an upward shift of RR) will cause the balance of payments to improve and income to rise. The model permits us to draw several conclusions, some of which are, in Polak's own recent words counterintuitive and 'therefore constitute a useful bag of knowledge for international officials in their relations with national policy makers, who may be more inclined to project first-round results into the indefinite future' (Polak, 1998):

a.  Rapid domestic credit expansion is likely to result in large deficits in the balance of payments.

b.  A permanent increase in output and exports, such as through the discovery of petroleum, will raise income, but will provide only a temporary relief to the balance of payments.

c.  The stock of money is endogenous; therefore, 'while control over the expansion of credit can achieve a desired balance of payments result, control over the money supply cannot (Polak, 1998).

Polak admits that the model reflects a very simplified view of an economy and that the basic relationships need to be checked in every application of the model. This also allows the financial programmer to introduce further details and specific aspects of economies, for instance how much of any increase in income will be real as opposed to price increases. Much criticism of the IMF's financial programming model and its application has been voiced by structuralists and social activists. It has been argued that while the model may fit some economies, it is unlikely to fit many less developed economies, due to the presence of structural rigidities. For instance, export bottlenecks represent a plausible case against a simplistic application of the model for the purpose of advising governments. The Polak model has also been modified over time to accommodate an additional policy variable, the exchange rate, as well as two policy objectives, medium-term growth and the control over inflation.

In summary, we find that the achievement of external balance requires a mix of growth-enhancing, expenditure-reducing and expenditure-switching policies, combined with the control of domestic credit. Besides encouraging economic growth, governments must reduce their budget deficits, devalue the currency if misaligned and control domestic credit, in order to reach external and internal balance with price stability. Alternatively, the stabilization of domestic prices in a fixed exchange rate regime cannot succeed without budget balancing, which in turn requires an efficient tax system and reduced, as well as productive, government spending.

Monetary policy alone cannot be expected to succeed in bringing high rates of inflation down, and this for two reasons. First, due to the weakness of financial markets in developing countries, the full range of monetary intervention is not available to developing country governments. In particular, open-market operations, which require a well-developed financial market, may have to be replaced, in the short run, by unorthodox policies such as credit ceilings and interest rate regulation. As we have seen, these interventions give rise to financial repression and are therefore not recommended in general. They may be necessary, however, in order to bring inflation rapidly under control.

Another equally unorthodox tool of anti-inflation policy is the use of incomes policies (e.g. freezing wages), combined with pegging the exchange rate to a major stable foreign currency as an 'anchor'. As Dornbusch (1993) has argued, the design of a stabilization programme comprises the following elements: setting of a post-stabilization inflation target, defining the extent and manner of fiscal stabilization, applying appropriate monetary policy, setting the exchange rate at an appropriate level and using incomes policies.

## 8.2     The Microeconomics of Structural Adjustment

The main microeconomic goal of structural adjustment is, as we saw earlier, a more efficient allocation of resources. This objective requires two sets of policies, first the removal or reduction of distortions in the incentive structure, and second, the privatization of publicly owned enterprises. Distortions in the structure of prices and incentives are reduced by trade liberalization, elimination of price controls and by deregulation of over-regulated activities. Privatization involves the selling of state-owned enterprises, as well as outsourcing of some public services. Both sets of policies amount to a reduction in the involvement of government in the economy in favour of the market. It is therefore appropriate to review briefly the rationale of government action as opposed to the role of markets.

The basic argument for government intervention in the economy is the provision of public services and the regulation of markets, where the market cannot or does not fulfil its role of allocating resources efficiently. Markets cannot play this role in the presence of externalities and, in addition, they often do not play it well when markets are imperfect. Cases of market failure are externalities such as pollution on the cost side, or external economies like learning effects on the benefit side. In both cases, the price signals of the market do not fully capture the costs and benefits, so that resources are not allocated optimally. Market imperfections like monopoly or monopsony have a similar effect and are particularly frequent in developing countries, due to the smallness of markets and lack of transparency and information. While market failure can be addressed by governments providing public goods, market imperfections are usually dealt with by regulation. Public transport and communication, as well as energy distribution, are typical areas in which governments regulate in order to achieve a better allocation than by relying on the market. Education and public services are domains in which governments not only regulate but also take ownership and control. In less developed countries it is frequent that governments also own and control businesses that could be owned by private entrepreneurs. The reason for such involvement is sometimes ideological, like in socialist countries, but also lies in the scarcity of trained entrepreneurs. Often public ownership of business stifles the emergence of private entrepreneurship.

When governments excessively regulate the economy, deregulation is the appropriate answer, and it is often part of structural adjustment programs. The goal of deregulation is to bring the prices as much as possible in line with the scarcities of resources and the social objectives pursued by governments. We have seen earlier that there is a welfare cost of taxes and subsidies, including trade taxes and other trade restrictions. Due to the wide-ranging influence of trade restrictions, trade liberalization is the centrepiece of structural adjustment. It involves in particular the elimination or reduction of the existing biases against certain economic activities or whole sectors, as seen in Chapter 5.

A further area in which deregulation is of great importance is the financial sector. Financial liberalization, or the elimination of financial repression, is more than a mere sector-specific policy; it has economy-wide repercussions in that it affects the cost of production and the international competitiveness of industries through the interest rate, as well as the level of investment and total income.

When governments not only regulate, but extensively own and control business, while that function can be exercised by the private sector, privatization is the appropriate answer. The chief rationale of privatization is the empirically documented fact that public ownership tends to be inefficient because it is able to use public funds to pay for deficits. By relying on public funds, public ownership eliminates the incentives for continuous cost cutting and productivity improvement.


## 8.3    The Effects of Structural Adjustment: Empirical Evidence

Structural adjustment programs (SAPs) have been accused of aggravating poverty and of hampering, rather than enhancing, economic development. It is true that few of the countries that adopted such programs have instantly gained in terms of increased growth and accelerated development. The expected short-run effects are improvements in terms of external balance and lowered inflation, growth of exports and imports, the latter to the detriment of import-substituting industries. In the long run, the increased competitiveness of industries is expected to result in aggregate real growth.

To show the expected effects empirically needs overcoming two important problems. First, the outcome of a reform depends on the completeness of implementation. Not all countries that have adopted SAPs have implemented them according to their design. Second, even if that is the case, the success of a reform program depends also on unpredictable factors both inside and outside the economy. We never know how a reforming country would have done without the SAP. Actual post-reform performance should be compared with the counterfactual, which, however, is not observable. Four approaches exist to overcome the latter problem: (a) before-after comparison, (b) comparison between countries with and without reforms, (c) comparison of actual performance with the set targets, and (d) comparison between various simulated outcomes, that is, model-based analysis. In an early IMF survey of 14 studies of 69 countries, using different approaches, Khan (1990) concluded that the empirical evidence of programme success is fairly inconclusive. Improvement of the current account is the most likely positive outcome, whereas inflation reduction and economic growth are less likely to be achieved. The reasons for this weakness of empirical support lie in both the analytical problem and the diversity of implementation records.

In a more critical survey of structural adjustment programs in Africa, Helleiner (1990) argued that they rely too much on reforms in incentive structures and not enough on institutions; and that they neglect important bottlenecks and the provision of crucial public goods. He recommends more emphasis on human capital development, poverty reduction and structural change, especially from traditional to non-traditional exports.

Concerning financial liberalization, the short-term empirical record is not very convincing. Liberalizing countries may not typically experience immediate acceleration of growth. This is not surprising because increased real interest rates can hardly be expected to raise saving and investment. In the longer run, however, the deepening of financial intermediation should improve the resource allocation and strengthen long-run growth.

As to trade liberalization, we remember that the elimination of biases against agriculture and exports and, more generally, neutralization of existing incentive biases, are prime objectives. Incomplete implementation of trade liberalization may result in little change in the structure of incentives and, possibly, even in increased distortions, as the case study of Senegal's New Industrial Policy shows. The World Bank (cf. World Development Report 1987) has compared the macroeconomic performance in forty countries and points to the stronger performance of countries with outward-oriented trade regimes, as opposed to inward-oriented ones. According to this evidence, real per capita income growth was clearly highest in countries with most openness, and lowest in the strongly inward-oriented countries (ibid. p. 84). Conversely, the latter group of countries experienced the highest ICORs, which is consistent with low growth. They also registered slightly higher inflation, with the exception of the moderately outward-oriented group including Brazil, which experienced high inflation in the 1970s and early 1980s. Growth of manufactured exports was also highest in the outward-oriented countries. The anti-agriculture bias of inward-oriented regimes is well documented (cf. World Development Report 1986), and trade liberalization is clearly expected to benefit farmers and peasants through improved price incentives. Whether their supply response is positive and significant depends on price elasticities and has been the subject of extensive research. The prevailing viewpoint based on numerous empirical studies is that the single crop response is fairly elastic, but that total supply response to price change is inelastic as long as complementary inputs are not increased, such as marketing information, transport, irrigation and others.

In a more recent review of structural adjustment programs in the top 20 recipient countries of adjustment loans between 1980 and 1999, Easterly (2002) found that the evidence of positive effects is very weak. In comparison with all developing countries these twenty top recipients experienced very similar effects in terms of per capita growth (0.1 percent vs. 0.3 percent of all countries), current account deficits (6.1 percent vs. 6.0 percent), budget deficit (4.6 percent in both samples), inflation (24 percent vs. 32 percent) and exchange rate misalignment (-3 percent vs. +1 percent). Their average number of adjustment loans was 19, in comparison with seven in all countries. As the author admits, the large number of repeated loans (the maximum being 30 in the case of Argentina) can be seen as a negative bias of the sample. Countries with fewer adjustment loans, or none at all, are likely to have performed better. On the other hand, it is also likely that the top recipients would have performed much worse without the loans and SAPs. The evidence from this study suggests that the crisis countries were able to achieve no more than average performance in most aspects, rather than turning their adjustments into success stories.

## 8.4     The Timing and Sequencing of Reforms

The success of a reform program depends not only on the right combination of policy changes, but also on their timing and sequencing. Rapid implementation of reforms is often seen as a sign of credibility and commitment on behalf of governments. On the other hand, structural changes require the building of institutions and human capacities, which take time, so that excessive speed may jeopardize the expected outcome. While capital potentially moves fast into profitable activities, labour needs retraining and orientation. The evidence from developing and transition economies suggests that the gradual approach is more promising than the shock approach, which has led several countries like Russia into mafia capitalism and much suffering of the poor.

Of equal importance is the right sequence of reform components. If the capital account is opened at an early stage of reforms, that is, before some stability has been achieved and before major distortions have been eliminated, capital flight is likely to occur, which in turn impedes the structural adjustment. In trade liberalization, it is important to start with the elimination of quantitative restrictions before lowering and harmonizing the tariff. By this course of action the incentive structure becomes first more transparent and then more uniform, before the general level of protection is lowered. Equally, labour market reforms should precede the trade reform so that labour can move more easily out of declining and into rising industries (cf. Agénor, 2000). Our understanding of the optimal reform sequence is still incomplete, but it is generally accepted that macroeconomic stabilization has to precede trade and financial liberalization, as well as privatization.

## 8.5 Social Impact and Transition Cost

One of the problems in the implementation of SAPs is the fact that in the adjustment process there are winners and losers, and there are no automatic compensation mechanisms. From the social point of view, governments should be most concerned with the impact on the poor in order to avoid an increase in poverty. In practice, governments are more often influenced by the concern of the more vocal and more organized middle class. There are two ways of dealing with the social impact of reforms; the first is to accelerate and facilitate the transition; the second is to compensate those losers who are most seriously hurt. The first of these objectives is served by policies enhancing the mobility of capital and labour, such as financial deregulation, labour retraining programs and diffusion of information about labour market opportunities. The objectives of compensating the most affected losers and to diminish the extent of poverty require special programs, which are not easily effective and equitable. An example of such a program is the 'Program of Actions to Mitigate the Social Costs of Adjustment' (PAMSCAD) in Ghana (see Case Study 15).

## 8.6 The Role of the IMF in Structural Adjustment Programmes

The International Monetary Fund (IMF) is an international institution that was founded at the Bretton Woods conference in 1944. Its main function has always been to oversee and guarantee the stability of the international monetary and financial system. Under the Bretton Woods regime of fixed exchange rates, its responsibility was particularly heavy because the member countries were obliged to seek the Fund's assistance whenever their external account was in serious difficulties. In these cases, the countries' economic and financial situation was scrutinized, a structural adjustment programme was agreed upon between the respective governments and the Fund, financial aid was provided in the form of stand-by credit or structural adjustment loans, and the programme of reforms was supervised by the Fund before the release of consecutive loan 'tranches'. The reform programmes and agreements with the respective governments are known as conditionality, which is a way of influencing the borrowing countries' policies.

Critiques of such reform programmes have often denounced the IMF for imposing too harsh conditions on the economies concerned and for showing too little flexibility in adjusting the IMF's prescriptions to the specific country conditions. One of the most outspoken and authoritative critics has been Stiglitz, the former U.S. presidential advisor and chief economist of the World Bank. In his wide-ranging evaluation of globalization Stiglitz (2002) attributes the failures of many stabilization programmes, especially the Asian crisis of the late 1990s, to the dogmatism of IMF prescriptions and the adherence to commercial and financial interests by the IMF. As a solution he advocates fundamental changes in the governance of the Fund, as well as changes in procedures and reform of the global financial system. Besides greater transparency in IMF governance he recommends caution with regard to capital market liberalization, bankruptcy procedures rather than reliance on bailouts, improved banking regulation and risk management, strengthened social safety nets and an improved response to crises.

Another form of conditionality exists under the so-called HIPC Debt Initiative. This initiative was adopted by the IMF and World Bank in 1996 in order to alleviate the debt burden of the highly indebted poor countries (HIPCs). Since multilateral debts play an important role for many debtor countries, the two institutions monitor the policy performance of eligible countries and help them to reduce their debt burden in a two-stage process of implementation over a period of six years.

## 8.7     Structural Adjustment in Sub-Saharan Africa in the 1980s

Due to the complexity and wide-ranging nature of structural adjustment programs it is difficult to assess the progress of such reforms in any part of the world. The following short account surveys the reform efforts made in Sub-Saharan Africa (SSA) in the 1980s. The number of stabilization and structural adjustment programmes implemented in the roughly 40 countries of the SSA region is in the order of 250, most of them in cooperation with the IMF and the World Bank. Only a handful of countries had not initiated any adjustment programme by 1989 or introduced a 'home-grown' program (Jesperson, 1992). On average, the countries adopted seven programs during the 1980s, which often included similar components. While IMF-supported programmes focused mainly on stabilization, the World Bank-supported programs dealt mostly with the efficiency aspects of structural adjustment. Most of the countries experienced major internal and external imbalances in the early 1980s, as evident through overvalued exchange rates, large fiscal deficits and substantial rates of inflation, as well as structural distortions as evident from high levels and variation of the rates of protection and the presence of price controls.

**Table 8.1    Stabilization and structural adjustment policies in Sub-Saharan Africa in the 1980s**

| Countries | (1) | (2) | (3) | (4) | (5) | (6) | (7) |
|---|---|---|---|---|---|---|---|
| Benin | ** | *** | ** | *** | **** | * | ** |
| Burkina Fasso | *** | **** | ** | * | ** | * | * |
| Burundi | *** | **** | @@@ | **** | **** | ** | * |
| Cameroon | * | *** | * | ** | * | * | ** |
| Cent. Afr. Rep. | ** | **** | ** | *** | n.a. | ** | * |
| Congo | * | *** | * | *** | ** | ** | * |
| Cote D'Ivoire | * | **** | * | ** | ** | *** | ** |
| Gabon | *** | **** | ** | *** | *** | n.a. | ** |
| Gambia | **** | *** | @@@ | **** | n.a. | n.a. | *** |
| Ghana | **** | *** | @@@@ | **** | **** | ** | ** |
| Kenya | ** | *** | @@@@ | ** | **** | * | ** |
| Madagascar | ** | *** | @@@@ | **** | ** | * | * |
| Malawi | *** | *** | @@@ | *** | *** | **** | ** |
| Mali | ** | **** | ** | **** | **** | n.a. | ** |
| Mauritania | **** | *** | @ | **** | **** | n.a. | ** |
| Mozambique | * | ** | @ | * | **** | *** | ** |
| Niger | * | *** | *** | *** | *** | n.a. | ** |
| Nigeria | ** | *** | @@@ | *** | ** | ** | *** |
| Rwanda | ** | *** | @@ | *** | **** | n.a. | ** |
| Senegal | **** | *** | * | *** | ** | ** | ** |
| Sierra Leone | * | * | @ | **** | n.a. | *** | *** |
| Tanzania | **** | ** | @ | *** | * | *** | ** |
| Togo | *** | *** | ** | *** | **** | n.a. | ** |
| Uganda | ** | *** | @@@ | **** | *** | **** | *** |
| Zambia | * | * | @ | **** | **** | *** | ** |
| Zimbabwe | * | *** | @@@ | *** | *** | ** | ** |

| *Scores*: | **** | *** | ** | * |
|---|---|---|---|---|
| (1) Budget Deficit (% of GDP) | < 1.5 | < 3.5 | < 7.0 | > 7.0 |
| (2) Monet. Policy | Good/Adeq. | Fair | Poor | Very Poor |
| (3) E-Rate Policy | | | | |
|     Flexible: PMP (in %): (@) | 0-10 | 11-30 | 31-50 | >51 |
|     Fixed: REER Deprec. (*, 1980-91) | >40% | 21-40 | 6-20 | 0-5 |
| (4) Price Controls | None | Few | Limited | Extensive |
| (5) Non-Tarrif Barriers | None | Few | Moderate | Extensive |
| (6) Total Import Charges | 0-20 | 21-30 | 31-40 | >41 |
| (7) Sect. Gov. Intervention | Little | Medium | Heavy | |

*Source*: World Bank, Adjustment in Africa, 1994.

Perhaps the most extensive evaluation of the reform implementation and success was undertaken by the World Bank in 1994

(The World Bank, 1994); the preceding table summarizes the conclusions of this document. In the area of macroeconomic policy slightly more than half (15/26) of the countries reviewed improved their performance, but in only six of them the improvement was substantial. In eleven countries the policy stance deteriorated. This evaluation includes the fiscal deficit, monetary/financial policy and the exchange rate. The macroeconomic performance is shown in the first three columns of Table 8.1.

Budget deficits (col.1) were reduced from a median 6.4 percent of GDP in 1980/86 to 5.2 percent in 1990/91. But the performance varied widely, and in only ten countries the fiscal policy stance of 1990/91 was rated as good, adequate or fair. The best performing countries were The Gambia, Ghana, Mauritania, Senegal and Tanzania, whereas Cameroon and Ivory Coast experienced the largest increases in deficits. Most of the deficit reduction resulted from expenditure cutting, while revenues remained more or less constant. Since interest payments increased in all countries, the brunt of expenditure cutting fell on capital expenditure and, to a lesser extent, on non-interest current expenditure. Median capital expenditure declined form 8.7 percent of GDP in 1981/86 to 6.1 percent in 1990/91, whereas current non-interest expenditure declined from 16 to 14 percent. On the other hand, grants, on which most African countries rely heavily, increased by a median 1.3 percent. Without grants, the fiscal deficit would have remained high at a median 8 percent.

In monetary and financial policy, the SS-African performance appears to be more satisfactory than in the fiscal domain. As column 2 shows, in most countries (22/26) the policy stance in 1990/91 was found to be fair or better by the World Bank. The criteria for fair or better performance include low seigniorage (less than 1.5 percent of GDP), low inflation (less than 25 percent) and reasonable interest rates (approximately between -10 and +8 percent in real terms). The issues of seigniorage and interest rates deserve further comments. When seigniorage is an important source of government finance, measured as a proportion of GDP, it is deemed to reflect inflationary monetary policy, at least if it is sustained for longer periods of time. Reasonable interest rates, on the other hand, are defined as neither too high, thereby not inhibiting investment, nor too low, which would tax depositors. The middle range of interest rates is deemed to reflect a modestly encouraging, but not overly expansionary, monetary policy. As the World Bank has argued, in most SS-African countries the interest rate is set by governments and does not reflect the true scarcity of capital, but interest rate distortions have been reduced, so that there are much fewer cases of negative real rates by 1990/91 than a decade earlier.

As to exchange rates, the progress achieved differs markedly between the two groups of countries, those with flexible and those with fixed exchange rates. Paradoxically, the flexible regime countries entered the 1980s with higher degrees of overvaluation than the fixed-rate countries. This occurred because the so-called flexible regimes were not fully flexible, but included regimes of managed float and adjustable peg. They had run up high parallel market premia (PMP), in some cases of 1000 percent and more. They also made drastic adjustments, in particular Ghana, Mozambique, Guinea, Nigeria, Tanzania and Uganda. Their average premium fell from 300 percent in 1981-86 to 46 percent in 1990-91, so that in the latter period, in 11/17 countries the premium was no higher than 30 percent, which the World Bank considers fair to good performance.

In the fixed-rate countries examined, on the other hand, which are all members of the FCFA zone, the degree of overvaluation was modest in the 1980s, but grew rapidly in the early 1990s. Due to the convertibility of the FCFA guaranteed by France, there was no parallel market and the implicit premia or degrees of overvaluation are more difficult to assess. The World Bank has estimated, by comparison with other countries with similar terms of trade losses, that their real effective exchange rates indicated substantial overvaluation of about 50 percent in the early 1990s. Although the analytical basis of this conclusion is uncertain, this estimate comes close to what other studies have found about the FCFA. It is therefore probably true that the fixed-rate countries registered greater losses of competitiveness than their flexible-regime neighbours during the decade of the 1980s. The FCFA was devalued by 50 percent in early 1994, but this adjustment is not yet reported in the World Bank study, so that the progress in adjustment shown in col.3 is less satisfactory for the fixed-rate countries than what would have been concluded by the end of 1994.

As to the structural reforms, most countries (27/29) have eliminated or reduced price controls in goods markets. In agriculture, pricing and marketing systems were reformed with the effect of bringing the producer prices closer to world market prices, although for more than half of the countries the real producer prices of export crops declined. This contributed, nevertheless, to a reduction of the anti-export and anti-agriculture incentive bias. The majority of adjusting countries (17/28) reduced the overall taxation of agriculture. In trade policy reform, most countries (19/29, with no information on 7) have reduced their reliance on non-tariff barriers, softening their import licensing systems or replacing them by tariffs. Tariff regimes have also been rationalized, tariff dispersion reduced and the average tariff level has been reduced in some countries. The intervention of governments in specific sectors by industrial policies has been diminished in most (25/29) countries as column 7 shows. On the whole, we conclude, therefore, that the structural reforms have led to less government interference, reduced price distortions and more openness towards world markets in the majority of countries in Sub-Saharan Africa.

## References

Agénor, P.R. (2000), *The Economics of Adjustment and Growth*, Academic Press, San Diego.
Agénor, P.R. and P.J. Montiel (1996), *Development Macroeconomics*, Princeton University Press, New Jersey.
Corden, W.M. (1977), *Inflation, Exchange Rates and the World Economy*, University of Chicago Press, Chicago.
Dornbusch, R. (1993), *Stabilization, Debt, and Reform,* Prentice Hall, Englewood Cliffs, New Jersey.
Easterly, W. (2002), 'What did structural adjustment adjust?', Institute for International Economics, Center for Global Development.
Helleiner, G.K. (1993), 'Structural adjustment and long-term development in Sub-saharan Africa', paper presented at the international seminar *Structural Adjustment and Beyond*, The Hague, Netherlands.
Jespersen, E. (1992), 'External Shocks, Adjustment Policies and Economic and Social Performance', in: Cornia et al., *Africa's Recovery in the 1990s: From Stagnation and Adjustment to Human Development*, St. Martin's Press.
Khan, M. (1990), 'The Macroeconomic Effects of Fund-Supported Adjustment Programs', *IMF Staff Papers*, vol.37, No.2, June.
Krugman, P.R. and M. Obstfeld (2000), *International Economics, Theory and Policy*, 5th edition, Addison-Wesley.
Polak, J.J. (1998), 'The IMF Monetary Model at 40', *Economic Modelling*, 15, 395-410.
Salter, W.E.G. (1959), 'International Balance and External Balance: The Role of Price and Expenditure Effects', *Economic Record,* August, 226-38.
Stiglitz, J.E. (2002), *Globalization and its Discontents,* Norton, New York.
Swan, T.W. (1956), 'Economic Control in a Dependent Economy', *Economic Record*, November, 339-56.
World Bank (1986), *World Development Report*, Oxford University Press.
World Bank (1994), *Adjustment in Africa: Reforms, Results, and the Road ahead*, Oxford University Press.

# Case Study 15:
# Structural Adjustment in Ghana

## Purpose

In contrast to the more specific reforms dealt with in case studies 6, 7, and 8, the present case study focuses on a variety of policy changes and the interactions between them. This is typical for Structural Adjustment Programmes which usually include macroeconomic stabilization as well as structural adjustment in a narrower sense, that is, measures taken to change the sectoral structure and the structure of relative prices in the economy.

## Background

A Structural Adjustment Programme (SAP) is the general term used for a package of economic policy reforms that targets several economic goals. The main microeconomic goal of a SAP is an efficient resource allocation – most often accomplished through structural reforms and changes in the price and incentive structure. The main macroeconomic goals are external balance as well as internal balance – notably a balanced budget and a reasonable rate of inflation.

SAPs are not, however, without their critics: they have been accused of aggravating poverty and hampering, rather than enhancing, economic development. The policy reforms implemented under SAPs endorsed by the World Bank have also been criticized as overly draconian and not attentive enough to distributional issues. This is not surprising: in the short run, an improvement in a country's external balance and the lower rates of inflation that we expect from a SAP would tend to lower the rate of real growth – however, in the long-run, this 'strong medicine' is expected to lead to increased real rates of growth. The data is, unfortunately, unclear on either issue.

What led Ghana to structural adjustment? Since 1970, national income had declined by approximately 0.5 percent per year, and in the same time period, per capita income fell by over 30 percent. Agricultural output fell also as currency overvaluation and the harsh macroeconomic policy it ensued benefited manufacturers at the expense of farmers. Drought, fire, and bad crop yields also served to decrease output and exports of cocoa, the country's main tradable. Continually high and rising inflation and an almost non-existent level of private investment further served to distort the price and incentive structure.

The 1983 SAP implemented in Ghana, according to the World Bank, was one of the most successful in Sub-Saharan Africa. During the decade of 1983-93 stabilization measures have led to budget balance, export growth, and external balance. Structural reforms including privatization and the closure of loss-making publicly owned companies have led to increased efficiency and resource allocation, as well as increased the level of private investment. Nevertheless, Ghana is still among the world's poorest countries, with per capita income of $390. Real growth has remained at 5 percent per year and 2 percent per capita. At this growth rate, 'the average poor Ghanaian will not cross the poverty line for another fifty years'.

**Method of Analysis**

Since this case study does not require a specific model or quantitative method of analysis, students are expected to read the following texts, to examine the economy and policies by focusing on a few key areas and to answer the assigned questions accordingly. The references are:

**References**

C. Leechor (1993), 'Ghana: frontrunner in adjustment', in: I. Husain and R. Faruqee (eds.), *Adjustment in Africa, Lessons from Country Case Studies,* The World Bank, Washington, D.C.
Commander, Simon et al. (1989), 'Ghana', *Structural Adjustment and Agriculture*, Overseas Development Institute, London.

**Assigned Questions**

1)   Explain three underlying micro/macroeconomic problems that you believe led Ghana to structural adjustment. How was the policy reform intended to remedy these problems?
2)   Why was the official exchange rate overvalued prior to the reform? What was the effect of the subsequent devaluation on the economy, in particular the trade balance? How did the exchange rate devaluation serve as a form of protection to domestic producers?

3)      Explain the private sector investment problem. What policies were applied by the government and how successful were they?

4)      Discuss the bias present in the Ghanaian economy prior to the reform. What policy reforms were implemented to deal with it? What was the expected result of these reforms? How did producers actually respond to them?

5)      Does the SAP appear to have been successful? Why or why not? How close were the planned reforms to those actually implemented? In the long run, what do you think will happen in Ghana?

6)      Consult a recent issue of the Country Report by the Economist Intelligence Unit to find out whether the reforms have had a lasting effect on Ghana's economy. Has the reform led to sustained economic growth or can you identify certain factors that have prevented such growth?

# Chapter 9

# Cost-Benefit Analysis and Competitiveness

Project analysis is one of the most fundamental tools of economic analysis. Its goal is to examine whether the benefits of a project, over its lifetime, exceed its costs or, alternatively, whether the return to an investment is larger than the opportunity cost of the capital invested in it. It is a calculation that is performed, in one way or another, by every investor. There is a difference, however, between project analysis for private investors and the analysis of public sector projects, which is known as social or economic cost-benefit analysis (SCBA). The latter differs from the former in that it considers the benefits and costs of investments not from the individual entrepreneur's point of view but from the whole community's vantage point. While private cost-benefit analysis takes into account only the benefits and costs incurred by the investors themselves, SCBA includes also external benefits and costs, and it attributes different values to certain benefits and costs. Our discussion starts with a short presentation of the basic cost-benefit calculation featuring the discounting of future cash flow, and it focuses then on the rationale and estimation of shadow prices. In section 5 the concepts of competitiveness and comparative advantage are discussed. They are linked to SCBA through the same important distinction between private and social net benefits. In this discussion it is also shown that the principle of comparative advantage, which is fundamental to the gains from trade, is closely linked to the idea of social net benefits.

## 9.1 Approaches to Project and Industry Evaluation

One approach to SCBA is to measure all external effects and to add them to the private net benefits. This is a difficult task because external effects easily escape measurement. One of the methods of project analysis known in the literature as the effects method follows this principle and is frequently used by French development planners. The most common approach, however, is to use shadow prices in the evaluation of all costs and benefits. The underlying idea is that in the presence of external benefits and costs, resources are used at distorted prices. The elimination of the price distortions is equivalent to capturing external benefits and costs. For instance, activities that contribute to environmental deterioration or to reduced public health tend to under-value their costs to society. The use of shadow prices is meant to adjust the net benefits of such projects by attributing higher values to the costs incurred.

The measurement of comparative advantage and competitiveness has a similar purpose as cost-benefit analysis, but it proceeds differently. It also attempts to answer the question whether an activity is commercially and economically profitable. It differs from cost-benefit analysis, however, in that it limits itself to the analysis of benefits and costs in a single time period considered representative, but it extends the analysis beyond that of projects to entire industries and sectors. We shall see that the analysis of comparative advantage requires the application of shadow prices. In that respect it is similar to social cost-benefit analysis. The chapter proposes a method of analysis that integrates the concepts competitiveness and comparative advantage and results in a quantitative analysis of competitiveness according to its sources. This method is a potentially important tool for policy makers when they design industrial policies but wish to minimize price distortions.

## 9.2     The Net Present Value (NPV) Method

Every investment project can be viewed as a stream of costs and benefits over time. To sum up the net benefits requires discounting, because future amounts are worth less than present ones. The rationale of discounting is based on the fact that any financial fund is a potential factor of production able to generate income. A fund that becomes available in a year from now is therefore less worth than the same sum available now because it fails to generate income in that year. For instance, if we are owed $100 now, but the debtor pays us only next year, we are losing the potential return, which the $100 could have earned.

The discount factor is related to the rate of return to capital, as well as to the time preference revealed by all economic agents. These are reflected by the market interest rate, assuming that there are no major distorting interventions in the capital market. The discount factor (DF) is then equal to the inverse of one plus the interest rate (i, expressed as a decimal number) to the power of the number of years (t):

(9.1)    $DF = 1/(1 + i)^t$.

A future value is transformed into its present equivalent by multiplying it with the discount factor. The net present value (NPV) of an investment project is the sum, over the life span of the project, of all discounted net benefits. Since the life span of a project may be long, it can be replaced by the planning horizon (t=h). In that case the remaining salvage or scrap value (SV) of the investment can be added as a benefit:

(9.2)    $NPV = \Sigma_{t=0}^{h} [(B_t - C_t)/(1 + i)^t] + SV/(1+i)^h$

where $B_t$ and $C_t$ are annual benefits and costs in year t, i is the discount (interest) rate, and t runs from zero to the planning horizon (h) of the project. In projects with a long service life, such as irrigation or infrastructure projects, it is usually not necessary to go beyond a fifteen or twenty year planning horizon because the discounted value of the final years is very small. In projects with shorter horizons, the investment may have a positive salvage value, which can be treated like a net benefit in the final year. The investment in the base year can be treated either like a one-time cost in year zero, or alternatively, annual depreciation charges can be included in the costs.

The decision criterion for adopting a project is that the NPV be positive. The method permits the planner to rank all alternative projects according to their net present value and to eliminate those with negative NPVs. The method is equivalent to the internal rate of return method, in which one computes the discount rate that reduces the NPV to zero. A positive NPV in the former method corresponds to an internal rate of return that exceeds the going interest rate.

## 9.3    Accounting for Resource Scarcities and Economic Objectives

The cash flow analysis presented above, which we also call commercial or financial cost-benefit analysis, uses market prices for the valuation of benefits and costs. The market prices may be distorted by various policy interventions or by market imperfections. In social or economic cost-benefit analysis such price distortions need to be eliminated so that the shadow prices reflect the true scarcities of resources. The terms 'economic' and 'social' are taken here to have the same meaning. To clarify the difference between the commercial and the economic perspectives of project analysis, let us take the case of a project that generates pollution.

While the commercial analysis does not typically take the cost of pollution into account, unless effluent charges are legally binding, the economic analysis must allow for such costs since they influence the net benefits of other activities. This raises the economic cost of projects above the commercial cost, so that a polluting project becomes a less desirable one, all other things being equal. Similarly, in a context of high unemployment and an existing wage distortion, for instance due to a minimum wage law, a labour-intensive project may not be profitable, that is, its NPV may be negative. However, using a shadow wage that is lower than the legal minimum wage, the same project may have a positive NPV and be considered beneficial from the economic point of view.

It is important then to assure that the social analysis captures all economic costs and benefits with the appropriate economic values. The analysis begins with an ordinary cash flow analysis as shown above. It is then transformed into social cost-benefit analysis by making the following changes. First, it must be decided whether the project involves any externalities, that is, economic costs or benefits that are not accounted for in the cash flow analysis. Additional economic benefits may arise from the provision of education or training, or a health programme may provide health benefits to others than the recipients, for instance in vaccination programmes. Economic costs beyond the commercial ones may arise from the emission of pollutants or environmental deterioration due, for instance, to deforestation.

Second, it must be examined whether all prices used in the commercial analysis do reflect the true scarcity of resources, and whether important socio-economic objectives dealing with externalities are borne out by these prices. In the presence of widespread unemployment, it would be inappropriate, as we have argued, to use the going wage rate as a true measure of the scarcity of unskilled labour. The going wage rate is likely to be influenced by, if not equal to, the minimum wage, which is known to be a source of unemployment. The appropriate scarcity price of unskilled labour should therefore be lower than the going wage rate. Similarly, the price of capital may also be distorted by various factors, such as interest rate ceilings, credit rationing, capital use subsidies and other investment incentives. Finally, benefits and costs may be distorted if they involve foreign exchange and the exchange rate is misaligned. Under currency over-valuation, export projects would typically appear less beneficial in a commercial appraisal than in an economic analysis using an exchange rate that reflects the true scarcity of foreign exchange.

For all factors whose scarcity value seems to differ from the market price used in the cash flow analysis, one must estimate shadow prices.

These are fictitious prices that reflect the true scarcities as well as the socio-economic objectives pursued by the policy maker. The accounting for such objectives in the computation of shadow prices is not difficult in theory, but it poses enormous problems in practice and often transcends the task of the project evaluator. In theory, shadow prices can be obtained as dual solution in the maximization of net social benefits under constraints. Linear programming is a technique that is used to compute shadow prices, when all resource constraints are adequately accounted for and the profit objective is replaced by socio-economic objectives. Problems arise in the identification, quantification and weighing of such objectives when the objective function is complex. In practice one proceeds often in a simpler fashion by making assumptions about the interrelationship of various objectives. For instance, the objectives of reducing unemployment and improving the income distribution can be both assumed to be served by choosing a lower shadow wage than the going wage, and a single objective function may then be used. Finally, all benefits and costs are then re-evaluated by replacing market prices by shadow prices, so that the commercial NPV becomes an economic (social) NPV.

**Table 9.1     From cash-flow to social cost-benefit analysis**

| Year (t) | $B_t$ | $C_t$ | SV | $B_t$ $-C_t$ $+SV$ | DF | DF $(B_t-C_t$ $+SV)$ | $B_t^s$ $+$ SV | $C_t^s$ | DF($B_t^s$ $-C_t^s$ $+SV$) |
|---|---|---|---|---|---|---|---|---|---|
| 0 | - | 120 | - | -120 | 1 | -120 | - | 120 | -120 |
| 1 | 50 | 20 | - | 30 | 0.91 | 27.3 | 60 | 10 | 45.5 |
| 2 | 50 | 20 | - | 30 | 0.83 | 24.9 | 60 | 10 | 41.5 |
| 3 | 50 | 20 | - | 30 | 0.75 | 22.5 | 60 | 10 | 37.5 |
| 4 | 50 | 20 | - | 30 | 0.68 | 20.4 | 60 | 10 | 34.0 |
| 5 | - | - | 20 | 20 | 0.62 | 12.4 | 20 | | +12.4 |
| NPV | | | | | | $\Sigma = -12.5$ | | | $\Sigma = 50.9$ |

The simple numerical example in Table 9.1 demonstrates the difference between commercial and economic evaluation of projects. In this five-year model it is assumed that an initial investment of $120 million generates a constant revenue flow of $50 million, with the recurrent cost limited to unskilled labour paid at the minimum wage. The shadow wage of unskilled labour is assumed to be at 50 percent of the minimum wage; therefore the economic cost of labour is half the amount that is actually paid. The revenue accrues from exports and the exchange rate is assumed to over-value the currency by 20 percent. This leads to an upward adjustment of the benefits by 20 percent, because in the absence of currency misalignment both imports and exports would be more expensive in terms of domestic currency. The investment, as well as the salvage, value are assumed to be free of any distortions. The discount factor is based on an interest rate of 10 percent.

The computation of the private NPV as -12.5, based on market prices, suggests that the project is not commercially profitable. The social NPV of 50.9 indicates that it is profitable from a socio-economic point of view. If it was a public sector project, the government should implement it in the interest of maximizing economic benefits. If it is a private sector project, the government has an interest to entice the private owner to realize the project. This can be done by a subsidy, in which case, however, the subsidy should not be larger than needed to turn the private NPV into a positive number, and certainly not larger than the economic NPV.

## 9.4     Estimating Shadow Prices

There are various ways of calculating shadow prices, including the already mentioned linear programming method. There are two principal 'schools of thought' regarding the calculation of shadow prices and the general approach to social cost-benefit analysis. One is the so-called OECD method (Little and Mirrlees, 1969), and the other is the one sponsored by UNIDO and proposed by Dasgupta, Marglin and Sen (1972). The two methods differ mainly in terms of their assumptions about the treatment of taxes. In praxis, however, both methods require a higher level of welfare theory and a large amount of information, additional assumptions and computations. In the present context, it would be difficult to deal with these methods adequately. There are, however, simpler methods that are often used in the practice of project analysis, which we discuss here briefly.

Starting with the shadow exchange rate, we have already seen how the purchasing power parity theory can be used to estimate the degree of misalignment. To recall, we compute the real exchange rate index (RERI) by choosing a past time period as base year, in which external equilibrium prevailed, setting the index equal to 100 in that base year. The RERI will then indicate whether the currency is over- or undervalued in any subsequent year, since it takes nominal rate changes as well as domestic and foreign price movements into account. Since the RERI measures the currency value in terms of a foreign currency, a value above unity indicates over-valuation, and below unity under-valuation. Once we know the degree of misalignment, we can then calculate the parity rate in any time period, adjusting the nominal rate by the degree of misalignment. In the absence of knowledge about misalignment in any preceding period, the researcher often resorts to the use of the parallel or black market rate as a proxy for the parity rate.

The shadow price of labour, which is the shadow wage rate, is estimated most easily by considering the alternative uses of each specific kind of labour. Shadow prices are also defined as social opportunity costs, so that this approach fits the definition of the concept. For skilled labour, it is common to assume that the market wage correctly reflects the social opportunity cost, since skilled labour is usually scarce. In special situations of widespread unemployment of skilled labour, this assumption may have to be modified. For unskilled labour, the social opportunity cost is the forgone earnings in alternative uses, such as agriculture or the informal sector. The practitioner therefore tries to obtain estimates of the marginal product in agriculture or the unskilled wage rate paid in the informal sector. The agricultural and informal sectors are chosen because their labour market characteristics are often as close as one can get to those of perfect competition. In the formal or modern sectors of the economy minimum wages and other wage distortions are frequent. The value of the shadow wage estimated in this fashion may be significantly lower than the market wage, and possibly close to zero. A project employing such kind of labour, without using much of other scarce factors, is therefore likely to provide positive net benefits to the economy.

For the price of capital, the shadow interest rate can be estimated in a pragmatic fashion by adjusting the international interest rate (LIBOR) for country-specific factors. The LIBOR,[1] is the interest rate commercial banks in London charge each other for loans. This approach is based on the assumption that capital is highly mobile and has a similar opportunity cost everywhere. It must be adjusted, however, since the cost of capital should also reflect the country-specific rate of inflation and higher risk of investing than in the major financial markets.

## 9.5    Competitiveness and Comparative Advantage

Competitiveness is a concept that is widely used in the literature, but that is rarely defined with some precision. Its interpretations range from macroeconomic to microeconomic ones, from positive to normative, and from static to dynamic ones. The economy-wide concepts, that is, indicators that identify and rank whole economies in terms of

---

[1]    The London Interbank Offer Rate (LIBOR) is published by the IMF in the International Financial Statistics for various important currencies.

competitiveness, are not further considered here, because they either cover only part of the essence of competitiveness, such as the real exchange rate index, or they cover many other aspects, such as education levels, the size and power of government, the structure of taxation and the openness of the economy. This is the case of the World Competitiveness Report (IMD/WEF, 1995) and index, which ranks the countries in terms of the quality of their business environments, using a large number of variables.

The most meaningful microeconomic concept of competitiveness, in our view, is that of cost competitiveness, because it is related to productivity and comparative advantage. To see the relationship and differences between competitive and comparative advantage, we derive here a measure of competitiveness from the fundamental principle of comparative advantage best known in its Ricardian form. The Ricardian model of comparative advantage is a model with two countries, two products and only one factor of production, as the reader will recall. Let us take the example of two products, wine and cloth, use Lw as the symbol of labour input per unit of wine and Lc as labour coefficient per unit of cloth. Also let the superscripts A and B indicate the countries A and B. Country A then has comparative advantage in wine production if:

$$(9.3) \quad Lw^A/Lc^A < Lw^B/Lc^B$$

because the left-hand side is A's opportunity cost of producing wine, and the right-hand side is B's opportunity cost of producing wine in terms of cloth. The inequality 9.3 can be re-written as:

$$(9.4) \quad Lw^A/Lw^B < Lc^A/Lc^B$$

where 1/Lw is the labour productivity in the production of wine. This means that B's relative labour productivity in the production of wine (relative to A's productivity) is lower than in the production of cloth; in other words, B is relatively more productive in the production of cloth, giving it comparative advantage in making cloth. This is the classical case of comparative advantage.

In order to extend the principle to n products, we can now establish similar comparisons between n-1 pairs of productivity ratios. But this would only allow us to conclude whether any one product has a comparative advantage *vis-à-vis* any other product. It would lead to a ranking in terms of productivity ratios from the highest to the lowest one. It would not allow us to decide which ones of all products have comparative advantage and which ones do not. In order to do this, we need to introduce the cost of labour by replacing the productivity ratio on the left-hand side of 9.4 by the relative wage, and the product indices w and c by the general index n for the nth product:

$$(9.5) \quad w^B/w^A < Ln^A/Ln^B$$

Since $1/Ln^B$ is B's labour productivity in producing the nth product, the inequality 9.5 means that B's relative wage rate (relative to A's) must be inferior to B's relative productivity in producing the product n. But is this inequality still a criterion of comparative advantage? Since (w Ln) is the cost of production of the nth product, the inequality 9.5 is a simple cost comparison, for any one of n products, between countries A and B. It states that B's relative productivity, relative to that of A, in the production of n must exceed its relative wage. This comparison, however, amounts to competitive, rather than comparative, advantage. This can be seen easily by assuming that one of the countries, say country B, raises its wage rate so substantially that for all products its relative wage exceeds its relative productivity. This would mean that the cost of production in B is higher for all products than in A, and that it would have lost comparative advantage in all activities. Such a conclusion would contradict the very principle of comparative advantage and shows that it is only a criterion of the ability to sell or of competitive advantage. In order to transform it into a criterion of comparative advantage, we must not use any kind of wage rate, but the equilibrium wage rate, which equates the demand and supply of labour. Only then can we restate the inequality 9.5 as a criterion of comparative advantage. In fact, we can now use the relative equilibrium wage as a cut-off mark to separate products with comparative advantage from products with comparative disadvantage. For country A relative to country B we get:

$$(9.6) \quad L_1^B/L_1^A < L_2^B/L_2^A \ldots < w^A/w^B < \ldots L_{n-1}^B/L_{n-1}^A < L_n^B/L_n^A.$$

This chain of inequalities states that A's relative productivity in activity 1 is inferior to that in activity 2, which is inferior to its relative wage and to A's productivity in activities n-1 and n. A has comparative advantage in activities (n-1) and n but not in activities 1 and 2. If, however, the wage rates used are not equilibrium or shadow wage rates, then the inequality 9.6 reduces to a simple cost comparison, implying that A cannot sell the goods 1 and 2 to country B, but that it can sell (n-1) and n. This criterion, based on non-equilibrium wages, is clearly one of competitive advantage or cost competitiveness for activities (n-1) and n.

The last step in deriving a general measure of comparative and competitive advantage is the introduction of other factors of production, in particular capital and intermediate inputs, and to use total costs of production for comparison. The indicator that can be used for the measurement of both, comparative and competitive advantage is the unit cost ratio (UC). Unit cost normally means cost per physical unit of output; but since the output differs substantially among firms, even within the same industry, it is useful to measure unit cost as the ratio of total cost of production (TC) to the value of output (VO). A firm or an industry can then be said to have a competitive advantage when its unit cost is inferior or equal to that of its competitor. The international competitor's unit cost, however, can be replaced by the world price value of output (Q Pw), assuming that the world price is determined by the cost of the foreign best-practice producer under competition. In international competition, a firm is then deemed to be competitive, if its unit cost is smaller or equal to one:

$$(9.7) \quad UCx = TC/VOw = TC/(Q\ Pw) \leq 1,$$

where UCx refers to international or export competitiveness, VOw is the value of output measured in terms of international prices (Q Pw), and where the unit cost of international competitors has been replaced by the international price (Pw). The division of TC by VOw in this derivation serves a double purpose: first, it helps to overcome differences in output mix and quality and, second, it makes the indicator independent of the availability of international cost data. The former effect is based on the assumption that quality differences are always reflected by the prices of output, and the second by the assumption that the international price (Pw) equals the unit costs of the best international competitors. Pw can be measured as cif border or free-trade price for import substitutes, or as fob price for exports.[2]

A second meaning of cost competitiveness is that a firm competes successfully against imports in the protected domestic market, that is, at tariff-ridden domestic prices, rather than international prices. The criterion for domestic competitive advantage is then that unit costs are inferior or equal to the domestic price (Pd), which differs from Pw by the nominal rate of protection. For domestic competitive advantage the domestic unit cost ratio (UCd) must then be smaller or equal to one:

$$(9.8) \quad UCd = TC/VOd = TC/(Q\ Pd) \leq 1$$

---

[2]   The terms cif and fob mean 'cost, insurance, freight' and 'free on board', respectively.

A third meaning of competitiveness is obtained when both costs and the value of output are expressed in shadow or equilibrium prices. It can be shown that this criterion corresponds to the one of comparative advantage. The principle of comparative advantage requires that the unit cost of a firm or industry must be lower than that of an international competitor and that unit costs and the output price are measured in terms of equilibrium prices.

$$(9.9) \quad UCs = TCs/VOs = TCs/(Q\ Ps) \le 1,$$

where TCs is total cost in terms of shadow prices and Ps is the shadow price of output. The shadow price of output is normally equal to the international price, except if the currency is misaligned. In the latter case it is obtained by using the shadow exchange rate rather than the official exchange rate to obtain the international price, that is, $Ps = Pw*Es/E$, where Es and E are the shadow and official exchange rates, respectively. If the coefficient Es/E is larger than one, the currency is over-valued, and smaller than one if it is under-valued. The degree of over- or under-valuation can be measured by the real exchange rate, based on the purchasing power parity theory, as seen in Chapter 6.

The criterion of comparative advantage derived above corresponds, in principle, to that of the Domestic Resource Cost ratio (DRC), well known in the development literature (cf. Bruno, 1972 and Krueger, 1972) and defined as:

$$(9.10) \quad DRC = (L\ ws + K\ rs)/VAw \le 1,$$

where L and K are input quantities of labour and capital, ws and rs are the shadow prices of labour and capital, and VAw is the international value added, obtained by deducting intermediate input costs from the value of output, all in terms of international prices. Here again, the VAw must be replaced by its shadow value if the currency is misaligned. The only difference between UCs and DRC is that UCs compares total costs with the value of output, whereas DRC compares only the cost of primary inputs (labour and capital) with value added. The indicator UCs of comparative advantage is, in our view, superior to the DRC ratio because it applies to total costs rather than value added. This is important because comparative advantage can result from the presence and low cost of natural resources, which would not appear in the DRC criterion.

The indicators of competitiveness and comparative advantage derived above lend themselves to an analysis of the sources of competitiveness. The main source of competitiveness is of course comparative advantage, which is the real component of competitiveness and is captured by the condition UCs $\leq$ 1. The remainder, that is, (UCd − UCs), is the sum of all price distortions of output and inputs. Each of these distortions can be measured in turn and expressed as a proportion of the output value. This procedure permits us to quantify the relative importance of policy-induced and other distortions in unit cost. In other words, the method allows us to measure how much of a measured competitive advantage, or disadvantage, is attributable to real determinants like productivity and low factor cost, and how much of it is based on subsidies and other price distortions.

The main price distortions that can be identified in this analysis are the nominal rates of protection (NRP) of outputs and inputs, exchange rate misalignment, interest rate subsidies or penalties, wage subsidies or penalties such as minimum wages, and capital goods price distortions. The measurement of these distortions requires the estimation of shadow prices, as discussed earlier.

The method of evaluating competitiveness and comparative advantage outlined above has a number of limitations. One of them is that it is extremely data-hungry. The analysis requires quite detailed cost data, which are rarely available from statistics offices and need to be collected from firms.[3] In the absence of detailed cost data, the nominal rate of protection is sometimes taken as an indicator of competitiveness at the industry level. This approach has its merit, provided that the implicit NRP based on price comparison, is being used. In the absence of quantitative restrictions, smuggling and important tariff exemptions, the tariff may also be used instead of the implicit NRP. The use of NRP as an indicator of competitiveness is based on the likelihood that the level of protection is highly correlated with unit costs, because high protection induces inefficiency. The approach becomes problematic, however, when the observed NRPs differ very much from the tariff, especially when they are negative.[4] In this case the NRPnet, that is, the NRP adjusted for currency misalignment, may give a more reliable answer.

---

[3]  The unit cost indicator was proposed first by Siggel and Cockburn (1995) and has been applied since by using aggregate data from India (Siggel, 2001), and firm-level data from Mali and Cote d'Ivoire (Cockburn et al., 1999), from Kenya (Siggel, Ikiara, Nganda, 2002) and Uganda (Siggel, Ssemogerere, 2004).

[4]  In the mid-1980s the NRP of Mexican manufacturing industries were estimated to be widely negative by Ten Kate at SECOFI, Government of Mexico. This phenomenon could be explained by the currency devaluation that had led to real depreciation and some degree of temporary under-valuation of the peso. Given the temporary nature of such under-valuation, the negative NRPs could not be interpreted as sign of strong export competitiveness (cf. Siggel, 1998).

A numerical example may be helpful in demonstrating the point. Suppose a tradable product sells internationally at the price of 1U.S.$. Let this product be produced in Mexico at a price of 3.9 pesos, which results from an exchange rate of 3 pesos/$, a 30 percent tariff. Now assume that the peso is known to be over-valued by 1/3, the shadow exchange rate being 4 pesos/$. While the tariff and the implicit NRP of 30 percent would suggest that the Mexican product is non-competitive, in comparison with the international price of $4 (using the shadow exchange rate of 4 pesos/$) the Mexican product is export-competitive as its price of $3.9 is inferior to the international price. This conclusion is, however, meaningful only if (a) the domestic price is a true reflection of the costs of production, and (b) if the Mexican exporter is confronted with the shadow exchange rate. As long as all trade transactions take place at the official rate the product remains non-competitive. One may argue, however, that at a Mexican cost of $3.9 and an international price of $4, the product has comparative advantage at a rate of –0.025. In that sense the NRPnet may be used as a proxy indicator of comparative advantage.

## 9.6    Conclusion

In conclusion of this chapter, both approaches of measurement, that of cost benefit analysis and that of competitiveness and comparative advantage, are useful tools of analysis for the policy maker. In most developed countries they may be of lesser importance because the respective governments can afford to limit their interventions to macro-type policies, as discussed under stabilization. In developing countries, on the other hand, which cope with smaller and less perfect markets, externalities and very limited means to enhance growth, industrial policies are more important in order to draw resources into those activities that have positive externalities or potential comparative advantage. The methods of analysis discussed in this chapter are tools, which can help governments in analysing such activities and in designing appropriate industrial strategies.

## References

Bruno, M. (1972), 'Domestic Resource Costs and Effective Protection: Clarification and Synthesis', *Journal of Political Economy*, vol.80, 1.

Cockburn, J. et al. (1999), 'Measuring Competitiveness and its Sources: The case of Mali's Manufacturing Sector', *Canadian Journal of Development Studies*, vol.XX, no.3, 491-519.

Dasgupta, P., S. Marglin and A. Sen (1972), *Guidelines for Project Evaluation*, United Nations Industrial Development Organization, Vienna and New York.

IMD/WEF (1995), *World Competitiveness Report 1995*, International Institute for Management Development/World Economic Forum, Lausanne and Geneva.

Krueger, A.O. (1972), 'Evaluating Restrictionist Trade Regimes: Theory and Measurement', *Journal of Political Economy*, vol.80, 1.

Little, I.M.D. and J.A. Mirrlees (1968), *Manual of Industrial Project Analysis in Developing Countries*, OECD Development Centre, Paris.

Siggel, E. (2001), 'India's Trade Policy Reforms and Industry Competitiveness', *The World Economy*, vol.24, 2, February, 159-83.

Siggel, E. and J. Cockburn (1995), 'International Competitiveness and its Sources: A Method of Development Policy Analysis', Discussion Paper 9517, Concordia University, Department of Economics.

Siggel, E., G. Ikiara and B. Nganda (2002), 'Policy Reforms, Competitiveness and Prospects of Kenya's Manufacturing Industries: 1984-1997', *Journal of African Finance and Economic Development*, vol.5, 1.

Siggel, E. and G. Ssemogerere (2004), 'Uganda's Policy Reforms, Industry Competitiveness and Regional Integration: A Comparison with Kenya', *Journal of International Trade and Economic Development*, forthcoming.

# Case Study 16
# Competitiveness and Comparative Advantage in Indian Manufacturing

## Objective

The objective of this case study is to apply the analysis of competitiveness and comparative advantage to the data of three Indian manufacturing industries This is accomplished by computing first the unit cost ratios UCd, UCx and UCs, and by interpreting their meaning, first theoretically and then in terms of the numerical results. The data also allow us to draw inferences about the main obstacles to competitiveness in comparison to comparative advantage. The differences between UCd and UCx on the one hand, and UCs on the other, reveal the main distortions in costs and the value of output, which impose either a subsidy or a penalty on the industries.

## Background

The study, on which the present case study is based (Siggel, 2001) attempts to analyze whether the competitiveness and comparative advantage of Indian manufacturing industries have changed in the expected way as a consequence of the early (1980s) reforms in Indian trade and industrial policies. Unfortunately, in the moment the study was undertaken, the required data were available only until 1991/92, the moment when major changes occurred. Therefore, the study observes only very modest changes in India's trade regime in the 1980s. The data used are from the Annual Survey of Industries of 1980/81, 1987/88 and 1991/92, but in the present context only those of the year 1987/88 are used. The reason is another data limitation. While the Survey of Industries provides us only with revenue and cost data, other sources have to be used for estimates of shadow prices and, in particular, for the implicit rates of protection per industry. The implicit NRP, it will be remembered, reflects, in addition to the tariff, also quantitative restrictions, exonerations and smuggling. Such rates of protection were available only for the year 1987/88 from two World Bank documents (1989 and 1990).

While the underlying study (referred to as base study, Siggel, 2001) summarizes the changes in the policy environment, the present case study focuses entirely on the method of analysis and deals with only three of India's manufacturing industries (defined at the two-digit level of industrial classification, of which there are 17). These industries are Cotton textiles, Basic metals and Transportation equipment. The reader will find in the base study a short description of these industries, together with an attempt to reconcile the numerical findings with the observations of other authors.

## Method of Analysis

The method of analysis to be used in this case study consists of the computation of the three unit cost ratios discussed in the present chapter, which are indicators of domestic competitiveness, export competitiveness and comparative advantage. While the derivation of these indicators is not repeated here, the analysis of the sources of competitiveness needs further elaboration. The following equation defines the unit cost ratio at domestic prices and its components. This indicator is then broken down into unit costs at shadow prices and various distortions of output value and costs.

(1)     $UCd = (\Sigma j Aj\ Pdj + \Sigma n An\ Pn + wu \cdot Lu + ws \cdot Ls + Kb \cdot rb + Ko\ r + d \cdot K)/\Sigma i QiPdi$

where the output consists of i products, Aj are tradable input quantities and Pj their prices, An and Pn are the quantities and prices of non-tradable inputs, wu and ws are the average wage rates of unskilled and skilled workers, Lu and Ls the corresponding labour input quantities, rb is the actually paid interest rate on borrowed capital, r the (market) opportunity cost of own capital, d the rate of depreciation, and Kb, Ko and K are borrowed, owned and total capital stock, respectively.

The indicator of export competitiveness (UCx) is defined in the same way as equation (1), except that the domestic product prices (Pdi) in the first term are replaced by free-trade or border prices (Pwi). Finally, for the indicator of comparative advantage all domestic prices, wages and interest rates are replaced by the corresponding shadow prices. The price distortions, which are the differences between domestic and shadow prices, are then expressed as fractions of the output value in shadow prices, so that the three indicators can be shown to be related in the following accounting framework:

| (2) | VITs/VOs | (Shadow unit cost of tradable inputs) |
| | +VINs/VOs | (Shadow unit cost of non-tradable inputs) |
| | +LCs/VOs | (Shadow unit cost of labour inputs) |
| | +KCs/VOs | (Shadow unit cost of capital inputs) |
| | = TCs/VOs = UCs | (Total unit cost at shadow prices) |
| | + dpe | (Exchange rate distortion of output) |
| | + dpj | (Tradable input price distortion of output) |
| | + dpje | (Exchange rate dist. of tradable inputs) |
| | + dw | (Wage rate distortion of unskilled labour) |
| | + dr | (Interest rate distortion) |
| | + ds | (direct subsidy, negative) |
| | = TCd/VOx = UCx | (Total unit cost at international prices) |
| | = dpp | (Output price distortion). |
| | = TCd/VOd = UCd | (Total unit cost in domestic prices) |

the distortion elements are computed as follows:

$$dpp = (TCd/VOw)(-ti/(1+ti))$$
$$dpj = (VIs/VOs)(tj/CCM)$$
$$dpe = (TCd/VOs)(CCM-1)$$
$$dpje = ((1-CCM)/CCM)(VIs/VOs)$$
$$dw = 0.8 \ Wu)/VOs$$
$$dr = (rb-rs)Kb/VOs + (r-rs)Ko/VOS$$

Two simplifications have been made here, relative to the original method. First, capital stock distortions are being ignored due to lack of information about the capital structure and the price of capital goods included in the investments of the past. Second, the non-traded inputs are also assumed to be non-distorted. This assumption is made because it would be extremely difficult to estimate the potential distortions of utility prices due to monopoly or regulation.

The exchange rate (E), which links the domestic prices of tradable products and inputs to their international prices, was found to have been over-valued substantially (by 56 percent) in 1987/88. Its shadow value (Es) is taken to be an equilibrium rate, which, in the long run, also reflects the real purchasing power of the currency. For traded goods the shadow price differs from the domestic price only by the nominal rate of protection (NRP) and the coefficient of currency misalignment (CCM = Es/E), that is, Ps = Pd*CCM/(1+ti).

The shadow price of labour is determined here in a pragmatic and simplified fashion. While the actually paid salaries of white-collar workers are treated here as shadow rates, assuming that skilled labour is in scarce supply, the wage rates of blue-collar workers are adjusted by 20 percent downwards to account for unemployment among the unskilled labour force. The distinction between white and blue-collar workers only is, of course, very crude, and so is the hypothesis of zero unemployment among the skilled. The discount for unskilled unemployment of 20 percent is based on comparisons between the actually paid average wage rate and the going informal sector wage. The imputed salary of working owners is assumed to be non-distorted.

The financial cost of capital (excluding depreciation) at market prices is computed as the product of owned capital stock and the average lending rate, which was 16.5 percent in 1987/88, (IMF, IFS Yearbook 1999), plus the actually paid interest. For shadow costs, the total capital stock is multiplied by the shadow interest rate, which is computed as median value (17 percent) of two estimates and approaches. The first one simply adjusts the international rate (LIBOR)[5] by the inflation differential between India and the industrial country average as reported by the IMF (IFS Yearbook, 1993 and 1999, CPI, line 110). The second estimate is computed as LIBOR plus the expected rate of currency depreciation, which, in addition to the inflation differential, also accounts for expected real depreciation. This procedure implies that the lending rate of 16.5 percent was slightly inferior to the shadow rate and that capital use was therefore implicitly subsidized, at a rate of 0.5 percent.

The unit cost analysis provides a breakdown of unit costs at market prices into shadow costs and various distortion differentials, all expressed as proportions of the output value. It allows us to conclude whether various distortions are unit cost-lowering, (UCd > UCs), or increasing, (UCd < UCs), that is, whether competitive advantage exceeds or falls short of comparative advantage. The major distortions are obviously the rates of protection of tradable outputs and inputs. While the nominal rates of protection (NRPs) on output are cost-reducing, as they increase the output value in the denominator, NRPs on inputs are cost-increasing and thereby lowering competitive advantage. The exchange rate overvaluation acts inversely to the NRPs. The wage distortion also increases unit costs, while capital cost distortions may go in either direction, depending on the interest rates of the period and the ones actually paid by the firms. It is cost-increasing when the interest rate paid and the opportunity cost of capital exceeds the shadow interest rate, reflecting non-competitiveness of the financial sector, or cost-decreasing when the interest rates imply a subsidy on capital use.

## Assigned Questions

1) Compute the total cost or production (TCd) and the unit cost ratio at domestic prices (UCd), using the EXCEL spreadsheet, which contains the data on diskette. To check all your results, compare them with the values reported in the article (Siggel, 2001).

2) Interpret the meaning of UCd. What do you infer from your computations about the competitiveness of the three industries?

3) Compute the indicator of export competitiveness (UCx) by dividing TCd by the international value of output (VOw), which is obtained as VOd/(1+ti).

4) How competitive are the three industries on export markets?

---

[5]  The one-year London Interbank Offer Rate for U.S. dollar deposits in 1987/88 was 8 percent (IMF, IFS, 1999).

5) Compute UCs after transforming TCd and VOd into their shadow price equivalents (TCs and VOs).
6) What do you conclude about comparative advantage in the three industries?
7) What are the main distortions in terms of their impact on unit costs? Consider the price distortions contained in the output values as well as in input costs. You may answer this question either by computing the distortion elements as shown above, or by simply estimating their approximate size given the magnitudes of the distortions.

250        *Development Economics: A Policy Analysis Approach*

**Table CS16    Revenues and costs in three Indian manufacturing industries**

| (all values in million Rupees) | | Cotton textiles | Basic metals | Transport equipment |
|---|---|---|---|---|
| Domest.value of output | VOd | 81,905.50 | 177723.7 | 85415 |
| NRP output | ti | 0.15 | 0.54 | 0.25 |
| Internat. value of output | VOw | | | |
| Coeff. of currency misalignment | Es/E | 1.5625 | 1.5625 | 1.5625 |
| Shadow value of output | VOs | | | |
| Dom. value of traded inputs | VITd | 57,814.50 | 131384.1 | 56426.8 |
| NRP inputs | tj | 0.15 | 0.22 | 0.3 |
| Internat. value of traded inputs | VITw | | | |
| Shadow value of traded inputs | VITs | | | |
| Dom. value of non-traded inputs | VINd | 5,350.20 | 12792.3 | 6929.1 |
| Shadow value of non-traded inputs | VINs | 5,350.20 | 12792.3 | 6929.1 |
| Domestic value added | VAd | | | |
| Shadow value added | VAs | | | |
| Gross wages (unskilled) | Wud | 11,879.59 | 11316.86 | 9054.65 |
| Shadow value of gross wages | Wus | 9,503.67 | 9053.49 | 7243.72 |
| Gross salaries (skilled) | Wsd | 2,729.61 | 5382.9 | 4790.55 |
| Shadow value of gross salaries | Wss | 2,729.61 | 5382.9 | 4790.55 |
| Imputed salaries of working owners | Wwo | 284.79 | 283.2 | 150.23 |
| Total invested capital stock | K | 42,128.10 | 150198.6 | 53702.6 |
| Depreciation | D | 3,564.20 | 8103.8 | 3474.8 |
| Interest paid | Int | 4,580.60 | 7831.8 | 3854.8 |
| Borrowed capital | Kb | 42,402.90 | 60338.2 | 29689.7 |
| Own capital | Ko | -274.80 | 89,860.40 | 24,012.90 |
| Market interest rate | r | 0.165 | 0.165 | 0.165 |
| Shadow interest rate | rs | 0.170 | 0.170 | 0.170 |
| Total capital cost (domestic) | CKd | | | |
| Total capital cost (shadow) | CKs | | | |
| Total cost (domestic) | TCd | | | |
| Total cost (shadow) | TCs | | | |
| Domestic unit cost ratio | UCd | | | |
| Export unit cost ratio | UCx | | | |
| Shadow unit cost ratio | UCs | | | |

*Source*: Siggel (2001).

Chapter 10

# Privatization and
# Public Sector Reform

The privatization of state-owned enterprises (SOEs) can be seen as one of
the important initiatives destined to improve the functioning and efficiency
of economies. It is not limited to the sale or liquidation of SOEs but
includes also a variety of measures that reduce the role of government in
business, such as deregulation, de-monopolization, subcontracting with
private-sector firms, and other initiatives. Obviously, the topic is wide-
ranging and can only be sketched in the present context. Some of the
initiatives mentioned above may also apply to the intrinsic part of the
public sector, that is, the government as a supplier of public services, as
opposed to those SOEs that supply private goods and services. State-owned
enterprises are business ventures that primarily produce and sell goods and
services to the public and are owned and controlled by governments. The
present chapter places most emphasis on the reform of the SOEs, but some
reform measures also apply to public services, such as health care and
education, and even to the administration of government itself. In the first
section we examine the role of government in business, as well as the main
problems with state ownership that require either privatization or other
reform measures. The second section reviews the success and failure of
SOE reforms in developing countries during the last two decades, and the
third section discusses the cost-benefit approach to analyzing the
divestiture of SOEs. The chapter draws heavily on a comprehensive study
by the World Bank (1995), as well as two more recent surveys (Sheshinski,
Lopez-Calva, 2003; Prizzia, 2003).

## 10.1    Rationale and Problems of Government Ownership

The prime reasons for governments to own business enterprises are (a)
various forms of market failure, such as external benefits or costs for which
markets do not provide the appropriate signals, (b) the underdevelopment
of financial markets and (c) the minimum efficient size of some
investments, especially in infrastructure such as airports, harbors or

railroads, relative to the economies. All or most of these conditions are usually met in developing countries, and it is therefore not surprising that state-owned enterprises account for a substantial proportion, typically above 10 percent, of the GDP in these countries. Their share of domestic investment is known to be even higher, somewhere around 20 percent, due to their privileged access to domestic credit. These numbers hide the very wide variation among different countries and regions of the world. The SOEs account for the highest proportions of GDP in Africa, followed by Latin America, Asia and Europe, if one excludes the transition economies of Eastern Europe and China. The latter regions deserve special attention because of the fundamental change in Eastern Europe and because of the substantial role of SOEs in China.

The problems created by state ownership of business can be summarized as inefficiency and financial burden to the state. It is useful to examine the causes and economic consequences of such inefficiency. First, the causes of SOE inefficiency are quite complex and are related to the lack of appropriate incentives and to the multitude of objectives and constraints. Decision makers in SOEs include politicians, bureaucrats and technocrats. Their objectives are imposed by political agendas, by management and technical considerations, and by private interests. Goals of employment, output and profit maximization may coexist with social objectives such as the supply of water or electricity at low cost. This ambiguity in the priority of objectives leads to distorted incentives, reduces managerial effort and increases transaction costs.

In a recent survey of the theory and evidence of privatization Sheshinski and Lopéz-Calva (2003) discuss the microeconomic problems of state ownership from two perspectives, the political and the managerial. In the political view, managers of SOE pursue objectives that differ from those of private firm managers. Public managers pursue political careers and incorporate into the objective function of the firm aspects related to maximization of their political prestige. They can do so because they face a soft-budget constraint, implying the possibility of bailout by the state. Under public ownership, the threat of bankruptcy is non-credible. In situations, in which the firms have engaged in unwise investments, it will be in the interest of the government to bail the firm out using the public purse. Indeed, bankruptcy of the firm would have a high political cost, whose burden would be distributed within a well-defined political group. The cost of bailout, on the other hand, can be spread over the taxpayers. The political loss involved in closing a publicly owned company is larger than the political cost of using taxpayer money to bail it out. Consequently, distorted objectives of public managers and the soft-budget constraint they face lead to lower efficiency of the firm.

The management view refers to the weaker monitoring that public managers face. The reason why the managers of SOEs are poorly monitored has to do with the fact that the firms are not traded in the market, as is the case of private firms. This fact eliminates the threat of take-over when the firm performs poorly. In addition, shareholders cannot observe and influence the performance of the enterprises. The fact that bankruptcy is a non-credible threat under public ownership makes the mangers increase the scale of production, whereas a private manager would face a real threat of failure that induces productive efficiency. These arguments imply that under competitive conditions privatization is likely to lead to efficiency gains.

The consequences of inefficiency are financial losses that are a burden to the public purse. They are manifest in the SOE's share of government deficits, which in turn can lead to indebtedness, external imbalance and inflation. Government borrowing in the domestic market, which requires a certain level of development of the domestic financial market, tends to crowd out private investments and to slow down economic growth. If governments borrow in international markets, they aggravate the problem of servicing external debt. The finance of SOE-generated deficits by printing money fuels inflation. All of these consequences are well documented in the literature on public enterprises (cf. Jones, 1975; Vickers and Yarrow, 1988).

The solution to these problems is usually not simple privatization in the sense of selling SOEs to private interests. It requires, instead, careful identification of the problems and their causes, and tailoring reform measures to the diagnosis. For instance, privatization may not help an industry that faces multiple regulatory constraints. Privatization may also be unfeasible if the financial sector is not sufficiently developed. Reforms of SOEs typically include revision of the regulatory framework in which industries function, structural changes within industries (e.g. de-monopolization) and within firms (e.g. re-definition of firm objectives and managerial roles), in addition to divestiture (selling, giving away or liquidating enterprises).

From a macroeconomic viewpoint privatization allows the government to raise funds in the short term and eliminates the need for permanent subsidies to publicly owned enterprises. If firms go from deficit to surplus in their operation, the government will not only eleiminate subsidies, but actually start collecting taxes from them. The actual change in the financial position of the government is determined by the difference between foregone dividends and taxes collected from companies.

If the revenue from asset sales is used to reduce public debt, lower interest payments would be observed and, consequently, a stronger cash-flow position of the public sector. Moreover, lower interest rates foster investment, growth and lower inflation.

Privatization, especially when it is done through public offerings and mixed sales, leads to the increase in the level of stock market capitalization and, in general, the development of the financial sector. It mobilizes resources in the financial sector, reallocating credit to more productive uses.

Finally, the sale of public sector enterprises tends to reduce the aggregate level of employment in the short run, due to the elimination of the redundant labour. Unemployment should decrease, however, in the medium and long run as the rate of growth of the economy increases, due to efficiency gains at the micro level and increased macroeconomic stability.

## 10.2    The Experience of SOE Reforms in Developing Countries

The economic analysis of public enterprise reform is a complex matter. A particular difficulty is the fact that the changes that are observed following the reforms are not necessarily the consequences of reform. If the observations by case study are limited to the affected enterprise, changes are more easily linked to the causes, but not all of the effects are captured. The sector perspective has its own problems. When SOEs are privatized the remainder of the SOE sector may be positively or negatively affected by the privatization, depending on whether the divested units were relatively good or bad performers before the reform. When good performers are shifted into the private sector, the remaining SOEs will appear to perform worse, on simple statistical grounds, while they may stay the same or even do better. Sector-specific data, therefore, must be treated with much caution, and case studies of individual firms are often more revealing than aggregate data.

Another problem is the complete identification of all benefits and costs to the economy and their measurement. A reduction of SOE deficits, and thereby of government budget deficits, may be achieved at the cost of reduction of welfare benefits to consumers. A full-fledged social cost-benefit analysis including all interested parties, government, other producers and consumers, is therefore required.

In the absence of such comprehensive approaches, studies have focused on three aspects, financial performance, productivity and the saving-investment deficit. Financial performance is usually evaluated by measuring the operating surplus or profits as a proportion of sales or the value of production. The return to capital may be a better indicator, but often it cannot be calculated due to lacking data on capital stocks. For similar reasons productivity is often evaluated by measuring the labour productivity only, although total factor productivity should be observed. Another way of evaluating productivity is to measure unit costs while holding factor costs constant.

The saving-investment deficit, although widely used by World Bank studies, is one of the more problematic indicators. An excess of investment over saving (defined as revenue net of all current expenses) may indicate poor performance and low saving, or it may indicate strong investment relative to normal saving. The measure focuses on the transfer of funds from the government to the SOEs, whenever investment exceeds saving. The World Bank study (1995) demonstrates that such government transfers to SOEs are very substantial in both absolute and relative terms. In Mexico they accounted for about 50 percent of the Central Government education budget and for 450 percent of the Central Government health budget. In India they accounted for a staggering 550 percent of the Central Government education budget and close to 600 percent of the health budget.

Based on a survey of SOE reforms in 12 countries (9 developing and 3 transition economies including China), the Wold Bank (1995) reports that in most countries (7 out of 9) the financial performance of SOEs improved through various reforms. Productivity gains were achieved only in about half of the sample countries, and the S-I deficit/surplus also improved only in half of the countries. Three countries excelled in SOE performance on account of all three criteria and also showed improvements in already good performance: Mexico, Chile and Korea. SOEs performed worse in India, Senegal and Turkey. The performance of SOEs in Ghana, the Philippines and Egypt was more of a mixed kind, with improvements in some measures offset by deteriorations in others. Ghana, Egypt and India seemed to have improved their financial performance in the late 1980s in comparison to the early 1980s.

The reform measures considered by the study (ibid.) are divestiture, increased competition, hard budgets, financial sector reform and changes in the relationship between SOEs and government. While divestiture clearly reduces the governments' ownership and control, increased competition can also be achieved without a change in ownership. For instance, a state monopoly can be broken up by creating two or more units that compete with each other. Hard budgets refer to the financial restraint exercised by the state budget. Unlimited financing of deficits by the state corresponds to a soft budget, and budgets are hardened when this way of financing deficits is less available. Financial sector reform is often necessary in order to guarantee the success of divestiture and increased competition. Finally, the relationship between governments and SOE managers is changed through the introduction of new oversight bodies, increasing managerial autonomy and signing explicit performance agreements.

When governments wish to avoid divestiture, but are committed to SOE reform, they may introduce or change existing contracts with these enterprises. Three types of contract can be distinguished: performance, management and regulatory contracts. Performance contracts define the relationship between government and public managers with respect to the performance of the enterprise. Management contracts define the relationship between government and private managers exercising the management function in SOEs. Regulatory contracts define the relationship between government and a regulated monopoly or its private successor. The World Bank study found that the latter two contract types 'do a better job of improving company performance than contracts with public managers'.

In a more recent survey of the evidence concerning privatization benefits Sheshsinski and Lopez-Calva (2003), based on several multi-firm, multi-sector and multi-country studies, the authors conclude that the realization of efficiency gains depends on the competitive environment, that full privatization is generally more effective than partial divestiture, and that privatization improves the public sector's financial health through lower deficits and debt.

On a more critical note, the survey by Prizzia (2003) concludes that the effectiveness of most privatization activities is based primarily on economic measures of success. In order to assure that privatization is successful from a socio-economic point of view, economic and social measures need to be applied in a balanced fashion.

## 10.3    The Cost-Benefit Approach to Analyzing SOE Divestiture

Applying the principles of welfare analysis to the case of SOE divestiture means comparing the social value of an enterprise after divestiture with what it would have been without divestiture, in order to examine whether the total social value has increased or decreased as a consequence of divestiture. The social value of an enterprise can be defined as the sum of its net welfare benefits to all economic agents involved. The main agents involved are the owners, the workers, the consumers or customers of the enterprise, and the government. Secondary agents are suppliers and creditors, who may also be affected by the divestiture. The government plays two roles in this context, as former owner and as fiscal agent. The main problem to be overcome in this comparison is the fact that an ex-post analysis typically uses the data before and after divestiture, where the latter data are influenced by all kinds of other changes in the economy. In order to isolate the impact of divestiture, one needs to construct a counterfactual scenario, in other words generate data reflecting the performance of all agents assuming that the divestiture has not occurred. Marking all social values with an 'a' for actual performance (SVa) and with a 'c' for the counterfactual (SVc), the total change in welfare is then stated as:

$$(10.1) \quad \Delta W = (SVOa - SVOc) + (SVWa - SVWc) + (SVCa - SVCc) + (SVGa - SVGc)$$

where SVO, SVW, SVC and SVG refer to the social value to owners, workers, consumers and government, respectively. The actual social value to the new owners (SVOa) is the present value of the stream of expected net profits, which needs to be forecast on the basis of the observed performance in the years following divestiture. The SVOc, on the other hand, is the net present value to the old owners (government), assuming that the public ownership of the firm had continued. This forecast is problematic because it is difficult to separate fundamental causes of poor performance from transitory and accidental causes in the last years before the divestiture. In order to facilitate this exercise somewhat, one often does not isolate the impact of divestiture in its narrow meaning from other changes that occurred together with divestiture, such as deregulation of the enterprise's industry, especially its prices, as well as changes in taxation. In this case, the analysis of privatization becomes one of public sector reform.

Similar considerations pertain to the social value to workers, consumers and the government. Workers are most strongly affected by attrition and wage cuts (or increases). Their remuneration appears as a cost in the calculation of profits (SVO), as a gross benefit in SVW, where it is balanced against consumption. It is therefore necessary to deal only with the distortions of the wage rates. Workers who lose their jobs in the public-to-private transition of an enterprise are assumed to find new jobs elsewhere. The presence of unemployment, however, is dealt with by computing shadow wages, as explained in Chapter 9. If the privatization is accompanied by a change in the minimum wage, this would appear as an increase or decrease of SVW. Similarly, for consumers only the changes in consumers' surplus are recorded as $\Delta SVC$. For the government as fiscal agent, the ΔSVG is usually positive because the tax revenue from privatized enterprises typically rises from zero to some positive value, except if the divestiture is accompanied by the creation of incentives to new investors in the form of tax holidays.

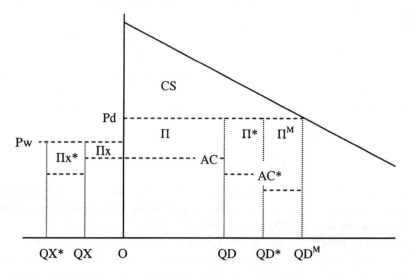

**Figure 10.1 Welfare analysis of a privatized corporation**

   The approach can be described graphically by assuming that the main economic activity of the divested enterprise is reflected by a standard market diagram. Total demand consists of domestic demand to the right of the vertical (price) axis and international demand to the left. The SOE's supply is shown by the distance QD and that of other domestic producers by (QD*-QD). The quantity imported is shown as (QD$^M$-QD*). The export supply of the firm is shown as QX and the exports of domestic competitors as (QX*-QX). Average costs of the firm are AC and those of domestic competitors AC*. Total profits (net benefits) of the enterprise are (Π + Πx), from domestic and export sales, and the profits of domestic and foreign competitors are (Π* + Πx*), and those of importers Π$^M$, respectively. The total welfare benefits of the activity to domestic agents are then the sum of consumer surplus (CS) and profits (Π + Πx + Π* + Πx*). Not shown are the revenues of the government, which come out of profits, as well as benefits to workers and suppliers, both of which are included in average costs. Changes in total welfare following divestiture would occur through changes in average costs and appear as changes in the size of the relevant surfaces. The domestic price (Pd) may be a regulated one, in which case deregulation accompanying the divestiture would also lead to changes of the price, consumer surplus and profits.

The approach proposed here is based on the assumption that profits to private owners, consumer surplus and government revenue have the same per-dollar value to the society. One may argue, however, that this is not a valid assumption because of concerns for the distribution of income or for externalities associated with government spending. Galal et al. (1994) propose to use multipliers attributing different weights to the components of total welfare benefits. Since the computation of such multipliers would require further welfare theory and assumptions, we propose in the present context to proceed with equal weights.

The computation of profits is based on the revenue and cost data provided by the privatized firm and it can also be done in various ways, depending on specific assumptions concerning the depreciation, interest payments and working capital. At the most general level, profit is obtained by deducting from the value of output (VO) the cost of intermediate inputs (CII), labour payments (W), depreciation (D), rentals (R) and interest payments (Int), so that the residual is the return to all invested capital, fixed and working capital. Galal et al. (1994) use the concept of public profit, which differs from the above concept in that it includes depreciation and interest, but excludes the opportunity cost of working capital. Since the authors do not provide a convincing rationale for this concept of public profit, we adhere to the general concept of private profit. It postulates that depreciation must be included in costs so that the capital substance is preserved, and that interest is also a true cost since the financing decision is part of the investment decision.

Finally, all welfare benefits and their changes must be defined as those of the total life time of the enterprise. In other words, they must be the net present values of the stream of net benefits over the economic life of the enterprise. Since that life span is not a well-defined period, it is practical to assume that all annual net benefits occur as perpetual annuities, in which case their net present value equals the net benefit divided by the discount rate. For the divesting owners (government) the actual value is of course the net sales value of the enterprise, whereas for the new owners the purchase value enters as the invested capital. The purchase value should normally exceed the net present value of the benefits to the new owners, otherwise the latter would face perpetual losses. The net sales value may, however, be much less, even zero or negative, depending on the accumulated debt of the firm. To minimize such debt payments, the old owners sometimes declare bankruptcy. In this case there are losses to suppliers and other creditors, which should also enter the computation of the total change in social welfare.

An application of this framework of analysis is provided in Case Study 17 at the end of this chapter. It is based on the case study of Aeroméxico by Galal et al. (1994), but, due to lack of important information, not allowing us to reconstruct the case with the authors' method of analysis, it is fictitious in detail and referred to as that of a Mexican airline. Before reverting to this case study, however, we discuss the special problems of privatization in the context of former communist countries.

## 10.4     Privatization in Central and Eastern Europe (CEE)

In the late 1980s successive political revolutions caused the communist systems in the CEE countries to collapse one after another. After an experience with soviet-type socialism that had lasted more than half a century, the countries of this region began to transform into market economies with dominant private ownership. At that time, there was a common conviction that the creation of markets was the most important step the countries had to take in order to dismantle their inefficient and inflexible centrally-planned economies.

To increase economic efficiency and to reach similar living standards as in the capitalist countries of the West were the main reasons for the decision of the CEE countries to transform into market economies. But they were not the only reasons. To understand these decisions, we have to remember that under the communist rule politics and economy were very closely intertwined. The political and economic power was almost exclusively in the hands of communist party officials. Private ownership had been nearly absent and state-owned property accounted for 85 to over 90 percent of the national assets. The communist party ruled the state, and the state controlled most of the resources and productive assets. The primacy of the state over private ownership had been one of the central pillars of the soviet-type socialism. It also led to poor performance of the economies and ultimately caused their fatal decline.

After they had successfully rid themselves from communism, the CEE countries' primary concern was to establish and develop political democracy. There was a widely shared belief that without a sound market economy and extensive private ownership there was a great danger that this process could be undermined or even reversed. Some experts also warned that without swift and comprehensive privatization initiated by the state, some shady forms of 'wild' privatization might occur during the transition period, very likely to the benefit of the members of the former communist party cadres. Viewed from this angle, the privatization and emergence of market economies in Central and Eastern Europe was based on reasons as much political as economic.

Given the limited scope of this chapter, it is impossible to cover privatization in all the CEE countries and with sufficient detail. We shall therefore examine only the privatization strategies used by four of them: former Czechoslovakia, Poland, Hungary and former East Germany. Although different in many aspects, these countries had similar starting conditions after the collapse of their communist regimes and faced similar problems at that time. However, they differed in the ways they approached them. For the CEE countries privatization was not only a process of transferring ownership rights of productive assets. The governments also had to address issues like social justice, speed and timing, technical arrangements and potential long-run effects.

One of the most important issues, which dominated economic debate among East European politicians and experts, was the speed of the privatization process. There was a general understanding that privatization had to be pursued as fast as possible. It was, however, rather unclear precisely how fast this process should be and how the speed of it could affect other ongoing economic and political processes. There were basically two competing opinions. The first one perceived privatization as a gradual, step-by-step process, which should not be undertaken with too much haste. This approach assumed that institutional reforms aimed at providing a guarantee for legal security of the private sector and at the creation of a liberal and competitive environment, would take a considerable amount of time and should not be sacrificed for faster privatization.

Unlike the potentially time-consuming gradualist approach, the alternative opinion favored the idea of rapid privatization as the fastest way of establishing the 'rules of the game' of an economy and creating a large private sector in a very short period of time. The advocates of this approach emphasized that the reallocation of property rights to the majority of national assets from the state to private owners was so essential to the process of transition, that it could not wait for the framework to be completed.[1]

At the time when the CEE governments were deciding upon privatization, it was not obvious to what consequences the choice of one concept over the other would lead and, therefore, there was no easy answer to the question of which one should be preferred. Despite the fact that the privatization effort in the countries we consider here had its peak in the

---

[1]   For more details see, Major (1993).

early 1990s, the privatization process is by no means finished. Thus, passing any final judgment on the basis of existing results would be premature. However, after more than a decade of transformation in the post-communist countries of Central and Eastern Europe, we notice some patterns emerging from applying distinct privatization programs.

In our sample of four CEE countries, former Czechoslovakia and East Germany privatized more rapidly compared to Hungary and Poland, which preferred the slower way. The difference can be seen in the following facts:[2] In 1990, at the outset of the reforms, the share of private sector in GDP was the lowest, about only five percent, in former Czechoslovakia. The state control over the economy was less significant in Hungary, where the private sector accounted for 20 percent, and in Poland, where it contributed 25 percent to the GDP. The situation changed profoundly by 1995. In the Czech Republic and Slovakia,[3] the private sector's share of GDP had climbed to 70 percent, which left Hungary and Poland behind with 65 percent, despite their more favorable position at the start. The situation of East Germany was somewhat special, due to the unification with West Germany in October 1990. Nevertheless, the privatization process was by all means fast. Stark (1993) mentions, for example, that by May 1991, 1,670 enterprises of the approximately 7,000 that had been operating in former East Germany had already been privatized.

There were more differences among the strategies the CEE countries used than just the speed at which they privatized. David Stark suggested a typology based on differences in coping with three basic problems of privatization: (1) How should the state-owned assets be evaluated? (2) Who can acquire these assets? and (3) With what resources are ownership rights acquired? This typology attempts to identify distinct traits of privatization programs rather than provide an exhaustive description of them. It is mainly concerned with the privatization schemes for large enterprises and it does not include those for retail trade and agriculture cooperatives. The following Figure 10.2 provides a cross-country summary of privatization processes in three dimensions, which correspond to Stark's classification.

*Dimension 1: The Valuation of Assets*

There are two extreme cases of how the assets of public enterprises selected for privatization can be priced: evaluation by administrative means and

---

[2]   Source: EBRD (1997).
[3]   In 1992, after the privatization process had already been launched, Czechoslovakia split
      into two independent sovereign states: the Czech Republic and the Slovak Republic.

evaluation directly through a market mechanism. In the former case, a single state agency is responsible for every aspect of the privatization process. It selects enterprises for privatization, evaluates their assets and seeks private buyers. The latter case could be imagined as some form of public auctions where auctioneers announce an initial price at which bidding starts, and the final selling price is determined by competitive bidding. Indeed, there is a wide range of other mechanisms of asset evaluation and price formation. Stark mentions two of such mechanisms: contracting and bargaining. Contracting means that a government contracts consulting firms to organize privatization. As to bargaining, the selling price of enterprises may be established on the basis of political connections and considerations. In Figure 10.2 bargaining denotes all the cases that do not fall into the extremes of administrative or market evaluation.

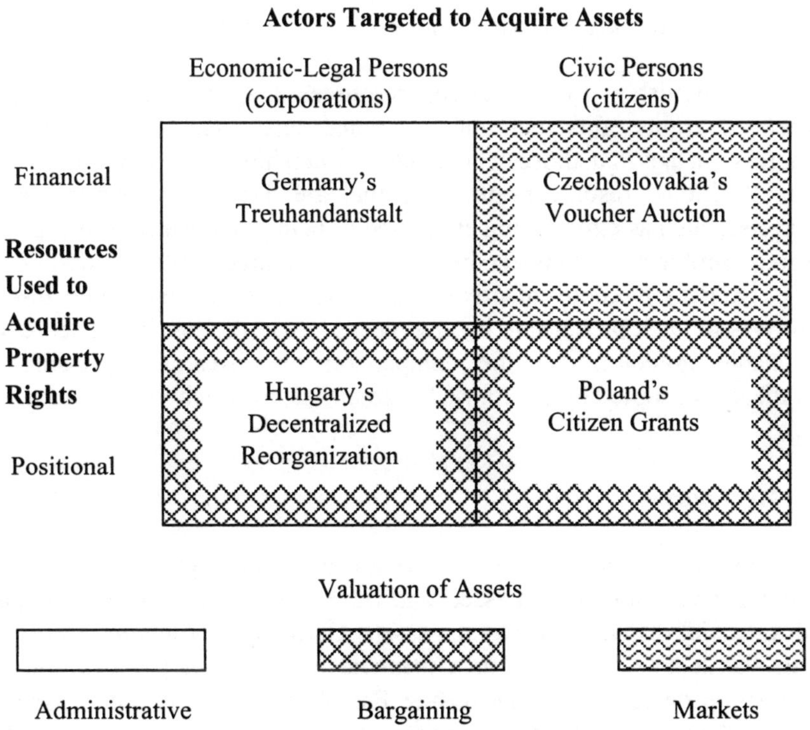

**Actors Targeted to Acquire Assets**

**Figure 10.2  A typology of privatization strategies in CEE countries**

*Source*: Stark and Bruszt (1998).

*Dimension 2: Actors Targeted to Acquire Assets*

The predominance of the state over private ownership in the CEE countries at the outset of reforms raised an important question for the governments involved: How to divest themselves of such a vast portion of national assets and, at the same time, achieve the economic objectives of privatization (increase the wealth of the nation) with principles of democratic societies they were trying to build (problem of distributional justice). Two approaches can be identified: (1) governments emphasizing civic principles would want to involve their citizens as participants in privatization and as recipients of the privatized assets, and (2) governments emphasizing economic principles would target corporations (legal-economic persons) with no regard to citizenship.

*Dimension 3: Resources Used to Acquire Ownership Rights*

Stark distinguishes two types of resources that are used to acquire ownership rights: financial and positional ones. The use of financial resources means that those who obtain ownership rights have to pay for them. Positional resources are those that are based on positions in the enterprise, such as either being employed or being in a managerial capacity. Various combinations between both types of resources are also possible.

Stark's typology of privatization strategies in Central and Eastern Europe is not comprehensive by any means. Nevertheless, it can serve as a reasonable guideline for the comparison of different approaches to privatization adopted by the four CEE countries, to which we now turn.

## East Germany

East Germany implemented a privatization strategy based on the administrative evaluation of assets and was aimed at corporations equipped with financial resources to buy the assets. Germany's *Treuhandanstalt* was created as a state agency with a mandate to carry out privatization and monitor the operations of the former East German public enterprises. As mentioned earlier, the East German privatization was rather swift. By 1991, the *Treuhandanstalt* had managed to privatize a substantial portion of the firms in its portfolio. A proportion of about ninety percent, was sold to West Germans, five percent to non-German foreign capital, and five percent to their former managers.

## Czechoslovakia

The former Czechoslovakia, like Germany, opted for a rapid privatization. However, its strategy differed significantly. First of all, unlike the German administrative method, Czechoslovakia decided to use a market mechanism of price formation, the public auctions of citizen vouchers for shares of public enterprises. The whole voucher scheme involved the distribution of over fifty percent of the equity of more than one thousand large state-owned companies. Furthermore, the Czechoslovakian voucher privatization targeted citizens as participants and recipients of ownership rights to the privatized assets. All Czechoslovak citizens over the age of eighteen were authorized to purchase vouchers for the registration fee of 1000 Czechoslovak crowns.[4] These vouchers entitled each holder to 1000 so-called investment points. These could then be exchanged for shares in the enterprises designated for privatization. Thus, the voucher scheme represented an interesting combination of citizens' financial participation and their right to benefit from privatization. The actual process of exchanging vouchers for shares was fairly complicated, and we can only outline the basics here.

There were two waves of voucher privatization. For each of them the Ministry of Privatization designated the enterprises whose equity would be offered in auction, and posted an initial asking price in terms of investment points. In other words, the Ministry announced how many investment points required for a share of a given enterprise. The 'opening price' of a share for each privatized firm was set according to a rough evaluation of their performance and future prospects, so some were more 'expensive' than others. The citizens then made their bidding iteratively in a computerized auction market and the final price of a share in investment points was determined by the supply and demand. After that, the citizens received the number of shares according to the final price and number of points they 'invested'. Unlike the vouchers, whose trading was not allowed, the shares were tradable in a standard way[5] shortly after the privatization waves were over.

---

[4] About 35 U.S.D.
[5] On the Prague Stock Exchange or the RM System, another secondary market of a computerized stock-exchange type.

## Poland

In 1990 Poland established the legal framework for privatization and created the Ministry of Ownership Transformation to coordinate it. For small enterprises (in retail trade, road transportation, etc.) the process was quite successful and fast. The privatization of industry was, however, much less successful. Jeffrey Sachs (1993) mentions that, of the estimated 2,890 industrial enterprises, only between 100 and 150 had been privatized. The most popular privatization method at that time, especially for medium-sized firms, was a leveraged buyout by workers. A few firms were privatized through traditional methods of initial public offering, a sale to a foreign buyer or a management buyout, but most of the large industrial enterprises remained state-owned.

In 1991, in order to accelerate privatization, the Polish government announced the program of mass privatization. The most important component of it was a universal citizen's grant in the form of vouchers issued to every Polish citizen. At first glance, this method may resemble the Czechoslovak voucher privatization. However, the Polish voucher scheme differed in some key features. Firstly, unlike Czechs and Slovaks, Polish citizens received vouchers for free. Secondly, vouchers were not supposed to be exchanged for shares in a privatized enterprise directly, but through an 'asset manager'. Moreover, citizens could not withdraw their shares and change asset managers for some time. They were entitled only to collect dividends. Obviously, this method made citizens' role in privatization rather passive. On the other hand, it gave an unrestricted access to shares to Polish citizens, who provided the Polish government with the political support needed in the years of transformation.

## Hungary

Hungary represents the fourth type of privatization process, characterized by the combination of bargaining as the method of asset pricing, targeting corporations as recipients of ownership rights, and positional resources. The country established a bureaucratic institution called the State Property Agency endowed with a strong legislative mandate to supervise privatization. However, the evaluation of assets was not primarily conducted in an administrative fashion and neither was it done by market mechanisms. Hungary contracted this task to external, non-governmental consulting firms, especially for privatization of large firms. In the first round of privatization, the State Property Agency enlisted the enterprises to be sold and announced an open invitation to investment banks and consulting firms to place their proposals on how they would evaluate assets, find a buyer for a given enterprise, and arrange credit. The consultant's reward, provided that it succeeded in the process, was a percentage of the final selling price.

Another form of restructuring the ownership rights of the large state-owned enterprises was the decentralized reorganization of property. In a typical case, management of a state-owned enterprise divided the organization into a number of corporations, joint-stock or limited-liability companies, usually along divisional, factory or departmental units. Since the property shares in these new companies were not restricted to the founding state enterprise, more diversified ownership patterns developed (banks, managers, workers, etc.). Nevertheless, in most cases controlling shares of these satellite companies were held by the founding state enterprises themselves.

## 10.5  Conclusion

Privatization and its analysis remain complex matters. Not only is its financial success uncertain because of the weakness of financial markets in developing countries, but economic and social success are even more uncertain. While an improved financial position of governments ridding themselves of state-owned enterprises is the most likely success, efficiency gains are often obtained at the cost of reduced consumer benefits or employment losses. The conclusion of some studies that partial privatization is likely to be less effective than full privatization, is of some concern because private-public partnerships are increasingly recommended in public sector reforms (cf. Stryker, 2004). The integration of financial, economic and social objectives in policy making and in policy analysis deserves more attention.

## References

European Bank for Reconstruction and Development (EBRD, 1997), *Transition Report*.

Galal, A., L. Jones, P. Tandon and I. Vogelsang, (1994), *The Welfare Consequences of Selling Public Sector Enterprises,* Oxford University Press, Oxford.

Jones, Leroy (1975), *Public Enterprise and Economic Development: The Korean Case*, Seoul, Korea Development Institute.

Major, Ivan (1993), *Privatization in Eastern Europe: A Critical Approach*, Aldershot, Elgar Publishers.

Prizzia, Ross (2003), 'An international perspective of privatization: The need to balance economic and social performance', *American Review of Public Administration*, vol.33, No.3.

Sachs, J. (1993), 'The Economic Transformation of Eastern Europe: The Case of Poland', in: K. Poznanski (ed.), *Stabilization and Privatization in Poland*, International Studies in Economics and Econometrics, vol.29, Kluwer Academic Publishers.

Sheshinski, E. and L.F. Lopez-Calva (2003), 'Privatization and its Benefits: Theory and Evidence', *CESifo Economic Studies*, vol.49, 3.

Stark, David (1998), 'Path Dependence and Privatization Strategies', in: D. Stark abd L. Bruszt, *Postsocialist Pathways: Transforming Politics and Property in East Central Europe*, Cambridge University Press.

Stryker, D. (2004), *Public-Private Partnerships for Integrating Small, Poor Countries into the Global Trading System*, Research Report to USAID, Nathan Associates Inc. and Associates for International Resources and Development.

Vickers, J. and G. Yarrow (1988), *Privatization: An Economic Analysis*, MIT Press, Cambridge, Mass.

World Bank (1995), *Bureaucrats in Business: The Economics and Politics of Government Ownership*, Oxford University Press.

# Case Study 17
## Privatization of a Mexican Airline

**Objectives**

In this case study, you will make use of the cost-benefit approach described in the present chapter and evaluate the welfare effect of the privatization of a fictitious company called Mexican Airlines. Although Mexican Airlines does not exist, the case itself is based on the analysis of a real-world case of privatization, the one of Aeromexico undertaken by the Mexican government in 1988. Using the data provided by Galal et al. (1994), you will tackle specific cost-benefit calculations and, ultimately, conclude what are the consequences of the privatization for the welfare of the country, and how the welfare gains and losses are distributed among different members of the society.

For further reading see: Gallal, A. et al., *Welfare Consequences of Selling Public Enterprises*, Oxford University Press, 1994, Chapter 20.

The company's performance in the five years preceding and in the three years following its privatization are shown below. Mexican Airlines was privatized in 1988. The year of privatization is taken as base year for the purpose of present value calculations ('the present'), but the data of 1988 are not being used, due to abnormal circumstances in that year. For the calculations use 10 percent as discount rate.

**Table CS17a   Revenues and costs of the Mexican airline**

(billions of pesos, in 1986 prices)

|          | 1983   | 1984   | 1985   | 1986   | 1987   | 1988   | 1989   | 1990   | 1991   |
|----------|--------|--------|--------|--------|--------|--------|--------|--------|--------|
| Revenue  | 233.60 | 220.40 | 223.50 | 246.00 | 276.10 | 99.10  | 164.70 | 215.30 | 251.00 |
| Costs    | 257.60 | 255.40 | 264.50 | 281.00 | 316.10 | 145.10 | 163.85 | 215.17 | 247.20 |

**Assigned Questions**

1)   Using the data on costs and revenues, calculate the net benefits generated by Mexican Airlines from 1983 to 1991.

2)   Compute the total net present value of the stream of net benefits generated under the actual scenario. For that, assume that after the first two years of private operation, which were non-representative of the future, the firm expects a perpetual stream of net benefits corresponding to the ones in 1991.

3)   Use the net benefit of 1987 as the basis of the counterfactual scenario, that is, assume that without divestiture the firm would have continued to generate losses of the 1987 magnitude. Calculate the total NPV of the stream of net benefits under the counterfactual scenario.

4)   Calculate the welfare change for the new (private) owner of the company as well as for the old one (i.e. the government) as:

$$\Delta W_N = -P_P + \sum_{t=1989}^{\infty} NPV_t^{A}$$

$$\Delta W_O = P_P - \sum_{t=1989}^{\infty} NPV_t^{C}$$

where $\Delta W$ stands for the welfare increment, the subscript N for new owner, O for the old owner, A for the actual, and C for the counterfactual scenario, and $P_P = 31.6$ billion pesos (in real terms) represents the price at which the airline was sold. Although the government received this price from the new owner, it did not gain any revenue since the sales price was fully used to pay back outstanding debt.

5)      The tax payments from the airline are shown in the following table:

**Table CS17b    Taxes paid by the Mexican airline**

| | | | | (billions of pesos, in 1986 prices) | | | | | |
|---|---|---|---|---|---|---|---|---|---|
| | 1983 | 1984 | 1985 | 1986 | 1987 | 1988 | 1989 | 1990 | 1991 |
| Tax | 0 | 0 | 0 | 0 | 0 | 0 | 0.7 | 1.5 | 0.7 |

Since the company was generating losses over the whole period from 1983 until the privatization, it did not pay any taxes. Positive tax payments occur only after the privatization.

Calculate the NPV of the stream of tax payments from 1989 to infinity by assuming again that the performance of 1991 is representative of future tax revenues.

6)      We now turn to the change in consumer surplus. We assume that in the first year after the privatization there was a one-time 10 percent increase in the real price of flights due to deregulation of airfare. As a result of this price increase, the demand (measured as the number of passengers) fell by 15 percent the same year. Additionally, we know that in 1988 the real unit price $P_{1988} = 43,000$ pesos, and the demand $Q_{1988} = 5$ million.

Calculate $P_{1989}$ and $Q_{1989}$ from the information given above, as well as the change in consumer surplus from 1988 to 1989, assuming a linear demand curve, and that this change in consumer surplus per year takes the form of a perpetual annuity of this amount.

7)      Summarize your findings and determine who benefits and who loses from the privatization of the airline and how much. Was the privatization a success?

**Case Study 17: Solution**

1)      Net benefits are computed as revenue minus costs. They are given in billions of pesos in prices of 1986.

**Table CS17c    Net benefits of the Mexican airline**

| 1983 | 1984 | 1985 | 1986 | 1987 | 1988 | 1989 | 1990 | 1991 |
|------|------|------|------|------|------|------|------|------|
| -24.0 | -35.0 | -41.0 | -35.0 | -40.0 | -46.0 | +0.85 | +0.13 | +3.8 |

2)      The net present value (NPV) of a perpetual stream of annual net benefits (NB) equals NB/r, where r is the discount rate, taken to be the interest rate. Taking the year 1991 as representative for the future under the actual scenario, and using a discount rate of ten percent, we obtain as NPVact.

NPVact. = 3.8/0.1 = 38.0 (billion pesos)

3)      Under the counterfactual scenario, taking 1987 as typical for the operation without privatization, we obtain as net present value.

NPVcount. = -40.1/0.1 = -400.0.

4)      The welfare change incurred by the new and previous owners of the company is computed as the sum of the net present value of the company computed under (3) and the purchase or sales price of the company. The asymmetry of treatment for new and old owners is due to the fact that the old owners (government) sold the company without debt burden and used the sales price to pay off the existing debt.

$\Delta$Wn = -31.6 + 38.0 = 6.4
$\Delta$Wo = 0 – (-400.0) = +400.0

5)      The tax paid by the company after its privatization is already taken into consideration in the computation of net benefits. Therefore, it appears here only as a benefit accruing to the government. Its net present value is:

NPVtax = 0.7/0.1 = 7.0 (billion pesos)

6)     To compute the change in consumer surplus we assume that the demand curve for air travel is linear and downward sloping.

P1989 = 43,000*1.1 = 47,300 pesos/passenger
Q1989 = 5 million*0.85 = 4.25 million passengers

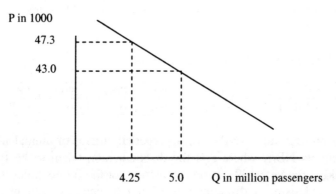

**Figure CS17    Consumers' surplus change in Mexican air travel**

Loss of consumer surplus: ΔCS    = (47.3 – 43.0)*4.25
                                 +0.5(5.0 – 4.25)(47.3-43.0)
                                 = 19.89 billion pesos
NPV of ΔCS = 19.89/0.1 = 198.9 billion pesos

7)     Total welfare gain/loss:    = ΔWn + ΔWo + NPVtax + ΔCS
                                   = 6.4 +400.0 + 7.0 -198.9
                                   = 214.5

The welfare gain accrues mainly to the government, by turning future losses into tax revenue. About half of it comes from consumers paying higher prices and the rest is a gain of efficiency. The new owners' gain is relatively small.

# Index